**Methods of Treatment
of Unstable Ground**

# Methods of Treatment of Unstable Ground

Edited by

**F. G. BELL,** B.Sc., M.Sc., Ph.D., C.Eng., M.I.M.M., M.I. Min.E., F.G.S.

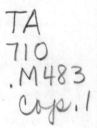

LONDON

**NEWNES – BUTTERWORTHS**

## THE BUTTERWORTH GROUP

ENGLAND

Butterworth & Co (Publishers) Ltd
London: 88 Kingsway, WC2B 6AB

AUSTRALIA

Butterworths Pty Ltd
Sydney: 586 Pacific Highway, NSW 2067
Melbourne: 343 Little Collins Street, 3000
Brisbane: 240 Queen Street, 4000

CANADA

Butterworth & Co (Canada) Ltd
Scarborough: 2265 Midland Avenue, Ontario M1P 4S1

NEW ZEALAND

Butterworths of New Zealand Ltd
Wellington: 26–28 Waring Taylor Street, 1

SOUTH AFRICA

Butterworth & Co (South Africa) (Pty) Ltd
Durban: 152–154 Gale Street

First published in 1975 by
Newnes-Butterworths, an imprint
of the Butterworth Group

ISBN 0 408 00166 6

Text set in 11 pt. Photon Times, printed by photolithography,
and bound in Great Britain at The Pitman Press, Bath

# Preface

Since World War II the construction industry has placed a heavy demand on land, particularly as far as urban development and redevelopment are concerned. This has, in certain cases, meant that land which was formerly considered unsuitable has now been built over. However, before this can be done, the problems which made the land unsuitable in the first instance have to be overcome by the engineer, either by special design or ground treatment.

This text is concerned with the latter aspect, that is, how to make unsuitable ground usable. It reviews most of the methods of treatment which have been adopted by engineers in their attempts to stabilise ground, either temporarily such as in ground-water lowering or freezing techniques, or permanently as in grouting. The individual chapters have been written by specialists, many of whom are leading authorities. Consequently, the text should prove useful to all those engineers engaged in ground engineering.

F. G. Bell

# Contents

# Contents

**Chapter 1**

# The Problems of Unstable Ground: A Review of Modern Techniques of Ground Treatment

In recent years there has been an increase in the extent to which the various ground-treatment processes have been applied to below-ground construction work. These techniques in themselves are not new and most of them were developed in either the late nineteenth century or the early years of this century. However, in the past they were used more as desperate remedies for dealing with unforeseen problems connected with unstable ground, than their use today when they are recognised as part of the normally planned construction process. The reasons for this change of attitude are two-fold. The first is due to the greatly increased speed of construction work as a result of mechanisation. Nowadays construction programmes tend to be tight and inflexible. Delays in the below-ground work (usually the first stage of a project after site clearance) could affect the numerous complex and interlocking follow-on stages, and in the case of industrial process plant or high-rental buildings the delays could have costly consequences. Experience has shown that it is preferable to anticipate the problems posed by difficult ground conditions and to plan in advance the construction methods to overcome them in a manner which will ensure complete success. The alternative is to provide for conventional methods of construction and to adopt whichever particular process appears to be appropriate to the severity of the conditions which are met as construction proceeds. The latter procedure may save money, particularly where conditions are less severe than might be anticipated from borehole investigations. However, time will not be saved if prices for specialist work have to be obtained during the course of construction, and time then has to be allowed for the sub-contractor to mobilise his men and equipment and then to carry out the work.

A further factor which influences decisions to plan at the outset to use specialist geotechnical processes is the scarcity of operatives with the necessary manual skills for dealing with bad ground. Many years ago any experienced contractor could, at short notice, supply men experienced in close timbering, clay pugging and other traditional means of dealing with localised areas of soft soil or flowing water. Nowadays such men are hard to find, and while the designer may have the knowledge and experience to anticipate trouble and solve problems by traditional methods, he would be unwise to assume that the successful tenderer will have labour available at short notice to do the work in such a way.

The second reason for the increased adoption of geotechnical processes is the

1

increasing scarcity of suitable sites for industrial or housing projects. Sites which were previously regarded as unsuitable because of steep topography, mining subsidence or difficult excavation conditions, are now, of necessity, being developed. These sites may require one or more of the various specialist techniques to deal with excavation or stability problems presented by the ground conditions.

The problems due to unstable ground which will be dealt with in this paper include those caused by water in excavations, instability of natural or excavated slopes, the settlement of structures on soft or loose soils and the subsidence caused by extracting minerals from the ground.

## Excavation for structural foundations

### GROUND-WATER LOWERING

The great majority of problems in foundation excavations are concerned with ground water. Surface water or shallow subsoil water can be dealt with by diversionary ditches or drains, but where water-bearing layers are met at depth in excavations it is necessary either to adopt a ground-water lowering system or else to exclude the inflow by means of an impermeable barrier.

The simplest method of ground-water lowering is to pump from a sump within the excavation, and it is feasible in most rock excavations and in gravels where the rate of inflow is not sufficient to cause instability of the sides or base of the excavation. However, in silts and sand the rate of inflow may be such as to cause erosion and slumping of the sides and 'boiling' of the base of an excavation. In these conditions a ground-water lowering system with wellpoints or bored wells installed outside the excavated face becomes necessary.

Wellpointing is normally cheaper than bored wells for foundation excavation work. This is because the equipment is available on hire at short notice and virtually the whole of it can be recovered for use elsewhere. The installation of wellpoints is rapid and the flexibility of the system allows for closing up their spacing in areas of heavy inflow, or widening the spacing as may be required. Except for the introduction of horizontal wellpointing as described in Chapter 2 there have been no recent developments of any note in the basic principles of the system, but there have been a number of improvements in the equipment. The use of plastic piping for header-main and swing connections, and of nylon mesh for filters, have improved the lightness, flexibility and freedom from corrosion of these components.

Bored wells are preferable to wellpointing for deep excavations where the area of the excavation is small in relation to the depth, e.g. for shafts, because the installation can comprise a single stage of lowering, whereas the wellpoint system is limited by the suction lift of the pump to a 4·5–5·0 m stage. This necessitates sloping and stepping back the face of the excavation (Fig. 1.1) and the volume of additional excavation required for this purpose may represent a large proportion of the total volume. Bored wells are also preferable in ground containing cobbles and boulders where the boreholes can be drilled rapidly by large and powerful grabbing or reverse-circulation rotary-drilling machines, whereas wellpoints are normally jetted down, and it may be impossible to do this if the obstructions are large and numerous.

Bored wells are also the appropriate method of dewatering an aquifer at depth

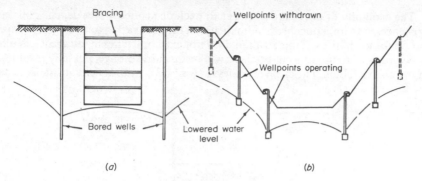

Fig. 1.1. Ground-water lowering for shaft excavation: (*a*) bored wells and timbered-shaft excavation and (*b*) wellpointing and open-shaft excavation

beneath an impermeable stratum to prevent a 'blow' in an excavation terminating within the impermeable material (Fig. 1.2).

## EXCLUDING GROUND WATER BY AN IMPERMEABLE BARRIER

The ground-water lowering methods described earlier, while achieving stability in the excavation, may be unsuitable for adoption because of the effect on surrounding property of a general lowering of the water table. In a properly designed and installed system there will be no appreciable loss of ground, but the effect of lowering the water table is to increase the effective density of the dewatered soil. If the latter has a high compressibility, as for example where the water pressure is reduced beneath a soft clay layer, then a soft clay will undergo appreciable consolidation settlement. Therefore where surrounding property has to be safeguarded it may be preferable to provide a barrier around the excavation which will prevent inflow and at the same time maintain the surrounding water table at its normal level. Methods of forming the barrier in a rough order of relative cost (cheapest first) are as follows: steel-sheet piling, concrete diaphragm wall, contiguous bored pile wall, bentonite cut-off wall, cement or clay-cement grout curtain and frozen-soil barrier.

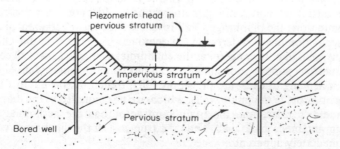

Fig. 1.2. Bored wells used to reduce piezometric head beneath an excavation in an impervious stratum

The economy of providing a barrier to exclude ground water depends on the existence of an impermeable stratum beneath the excavation to form an effective cut-off for the barrier. If this stratum does not exist or if it lies at too great a depth to be practical to use as a cut-off there will be upward seepage, possibly resulting in instability (boiling) at excavation level (Fig. 1.3). In these circumstances the

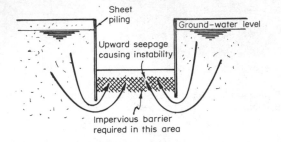

Fig. 1.3. Instability in a sheeted excavation due to upward flow at base

barrier will not be effective unless it can be extended horizontally beneath the excavation. The only methods of forming a horizontal barrier are by grouting or freezing. Grouting will be effective only if there is a stratum below excavation level having a porosity suitable for accepting grout. The horizontal barrier will be very costly if chemical grouts are required to permeate a fine-grained granular soil. A grouted barrier also requires a close-spaced grid of injection holes beneath the excavated area. Ground freezing will be effective in forming a barrier in most types of soil and rock, but the time and cost of installing a grid of freezing wells over the whole foundation area could be prohibitive for all but special cases.

A vertical barrier can be used effectively in conjunction with a bored-well ground-water lowering system if an impermeable stratum lies at or beneath excavation level. The water level is maintained beneath property surrounding the excavation and the piezometric head is lowered only in the deeper aquifers, thus preventing catastrophic uplift due to artesian pressure below excavation level (Fig. 1.4).

Steel-sheet piling is still the cheapest method of forming an impermeable barrier. Provided that it can be extracted for several re-uses it is cheaper than the *in-situ* concrete diaphragm wall or the contiguous bored pile wall whether or not these walls are incorporated in the permanent construction. Steel-sheet piling cannot be used in ground containing numerous boulders or other obstructions. In these conditions the diaphragm wall is usually the most economical form of construction since the boulders can be removed by grabbing and chiselling. However, a point to note concerning the economics of diaphragm-wall construction is the need to provide substantial reinforced-concrete guide walls (Fig. 1.5), before commencing to excavate the slurry-filled trench. It is usual for the main contractor to provide the guide walls, which are not included in the diaphragm-wall-contractor's price, and the main contractor has the additional task of demolishing the inner guide wall. Thus the true cost of the diaphragm wall may not be immediately apparent.

The contiguous bored pile wall can be economical in clays where mechanical augers can be used for drilling. However, in waterbearing granular soils or silts

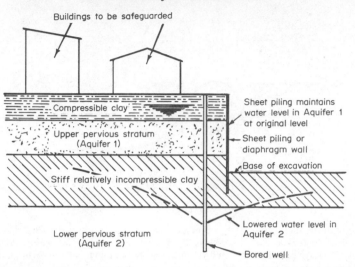

Fig. 1.4. Preventing settlement of buildings close to an excavation by maintaining existing ground-water level

the required impermeability of a bored pile wall can be obtained only by keying alternate 'secant' piles after casting by a special grooving chisel, and then concreting the intervening drilled-out space (Fig. 1.6). If this is not done the water-bearing soil will bleed through gaps between abutting piles since it is impractical to drill the holes in a truly vertical direction, or at a precise spacing. In coarse granular soils it may be possible to seal the gaps by cement or chemical grouting.

The filling with concrete of a trench excavated with support by a bentonite slurry is not necessary if only an impermeable barrier is required. The bentonite itself will act as the barrier. However, the slurry has no structural strength to act as a support to the sides of an excavation, and space around an excavation may

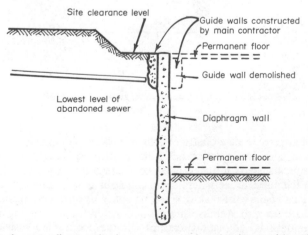

Fig. 1.5. Diaphragm wall supporting basement excavation, showing provision of guide walls

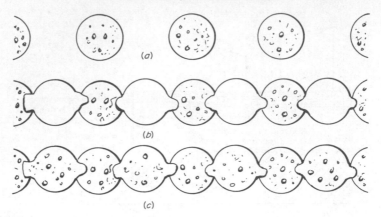

Fig. 1.6. Construction of secant bored pile retaining wall. (*a*) Alternate pile holes drilled and filled with concrete (including reinforcement), (*b*) intermediate pile holes drilled and keys cut in sides of first stage piles by chisel and (*c*) intermediate piles concreted to form continuous interlocking wall

not be available in which to provide stable slopes (Fig. 1.7). The bentonite barrier or 'slurry' trench used in the manner described by Boyes[1] can be economical for surrounding large areas where a number of individual excavations are to be made, e.g. on the site of a sewage-disposal works.

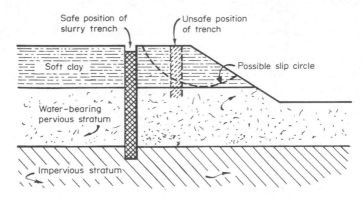

Fig. 1.7. Location of slurry trench beyond zone of possible slope instability

A grout barrier can be a costly expedient because of the need to drill a large number of close-spaced injection holes and to provide the large quantities of cement or chemicals used for injection. In soils, grouting is used mainly to stabilise fairly small localised areas where sheet piling or diaphragm-wall construction cannot be used because of lack of working space or obstructions in the ground. The use of grouting to stabilise the ground around underpinning pits beneath existing foundations is a good example of the economical use of grouting. Grouting or freezing are the only methods of forming an impermeable barrier in a water-bearing rock formation where inflow can be heavy through wide joints or fissures.

## Excavation for shafts and tunnels

### DEALING WITH GROUND WATER IN SHAFT EXCAVATIONS

A simple and effective method of dealing with ground water for shaft sinking is to pump from a sump within the shaft using a compressed air or electrically-driven sump pump. Problems arise when the quantity pumped is so large that the rate of inflow under high head causes instability of the shaft sides, or prevents the fixing and back-grouting of the shaft lining.

Although the concept of surrounding the shaft by a ring of bored wells is at first sight attractive, there are practical difficulties in achieving effective lowering of the water table. In fissured rocks or variable water-bearing soils there is a tendency for the water flow to by-pass the wells and take preferential paths directly into the excavation. These difficulties were experienced when sinking the access shaft at Tilbury for the Tilbury–Gravesend cable tunnel as described by Haswell[2]. The nine bored wells within and around the 6 m diameter shaft were barely able to cope with the inflow of water through fissured chalk. It is probable that the water flow to the shaft travelled along fissures which were not intercepted by the wells.

Grouting can be an economical method of eliminating or reducing inflow to shafts if the soil or rock conditions are suitable for accepting cement or chemical grouts, since the perimeter of the grouted zone is relatively small in relation to the depth of the excavation. For the same reason, ground freezing can also be economical, particularly when complete assurance of eliminating inflow can be obtained by the freezing method. Because of this assurance, freezing was adopted for six shafts up to 60 m deep on the Ely–Ouse water tunnel as described by Collins and Deacon[3].

### DEALING WITH GROUND WATER IN TUNNEL EXCAVATIONS

It is rarely possible to use a ground-water lowering system to facilitate tunnel excavations. The cost of installing a row of close-spaced bored wells on both sides of a deep tunnel is prohibitive, and in any case deep wells (or a wellpoint installation for shallow tunnels) cannot be installed where the tunnel is driven beneath a waterway or a main highway. Horizontal drainage can be provided in the form of bored wells drilled radially from a deep shaft (Fig. 1.8), but this system is costly and depends for its effectiveness on favourable inclination of the strata. Where the tunnel invert level is not more than about 15 m below ground water level, shield driving in compressed air is the most effective and economical method of achieving stable conditions at the tunnel face when driving through water-bearing soils or soft rocks. The advantages of compressed-air work for shallow tunnels have been described by Smith and Bevan[4].

Where tunnels are driven at depths greater than 15 m the physiological effects on the men working in compressed air become an increasingly severe problem with increasing depth, and eventually the method becomes unsafe to use.

Generally, the only feasible alternative to compressed-air work is grouting the soil or rock ahead of the advancing face. This method made possible the driving of the Tilbury–Gravesend[2] and Severn–Wye cable tunnels[5], at depths much greater than would have been possible with compressed-air driving. Tunnels can be driven through the harder water-bearing rocks without pregrouting, but working conditions are most uncomfortable and in heavily fissured or broken rocks instability of the face and sides of the tunnel can occur due to the velocity of the inflowing water.

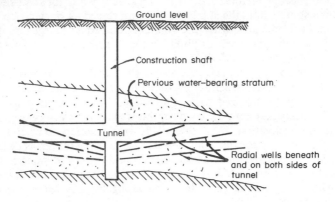

Fig. 1.8. Radial drainage wells installed from shaft for ground-water lowering in advance of tunnel construction

Chemical and clay-cement grouting in the form of a blanket on the tunnel alignment have been used as a means of reducing the quantity of compressed air.

An interesting development is the use of bentonite in a chamber at the front of a tunnel shield. A rotary cutter operates within the chamber where the bentonite serves the dual function of supporting the face and as a fluid to carry away the excavated material in the form of a suspension which is pumped to the surface.

Tunnel driving within a barrier of frozen ground is not normally feasible except for short lengths, e.g. in escalator tunnels. This is because of difficulties in access for drilling the freezing wells and the high installation costs for the relatively short time that the ground is required to be frozen as the tunnel is driven and lined. Freezing by the injection of liquid nitrogen through probes driven into the tunnel face is an economical method of dealing with an occasional pocket of water-bearing silt or fine sand in otherwise stable ground, but the method is too costly for adoption for continuous operation along the tunnel line.

## The stability of slopes

### NATURAL SLOPES

It is sometimes necessary to construct engineering or building works in areas which have a history of landslides. Because of the extensive areas of unstable ground any specialist treatment to stabilise the ground is likely to be costly. A general lowering of the ground-water table is often effective and this can be achieved by deep drainage trenches, or by a system of horizontal drainage wells or tunnels linked to shafts from which the water is removed by gravity discharge or by pumping.

Grouting alone is not generally effective in stabilising rock slopes, since the instability is usually associated with ground-water flow. The injected material merely forms a barrier behind which the head of water builds up until either the barrier breaks down or a major slip occurs.

Ground anchors require a system of interconnected waling beams, steel-mesh fabric or reinforced-concrete cribwork to stabilise a rock or soil slope. Because of the cost involved, the method can be used only for localised areas of instability. Anchorage systems can also disfigure a natural slope, although with care and some elaboration of techniques, the stabilisation work can be made to blend into the natural surroundings. The use of grouted anchors in conjunction with resin spraying of decomposed rock to support the rock cliffs beneath the walls of the Edinburgh and Stirling castles has been described by Price and Plaisted[6]. On these sites great care was required to preserve the natural appearance of the treated areas.

## EXCAVATED SLOPES

In the case of permanent slopes for road or railway cuttings the long term stability can be calculated by soil mechanics or rock mechanics methods with reasonable certainty, and provided that sufficient land is available the required stable slope angles can be provided without the need for recourse to any specialist system of stabilisation. However, in restricted site conditions where there is no space available for cutting back to a stable slope, the use of a rock or soil anchor system may be more economical than the conventional gravity-type retaining wall.

Problems arise in slopes excavated in granular soils which may be subjected to erosion by wind or water before a stable growth of vegetation can be achieved. Spraying with bitumen emulsion or resins can be used to give temporary stability while the grass-root system develops, but these methods are ineffective if there is water seepage from the slope. In the latter case, porous nylon or Terylene sheeting can be used for slope protection, but some of these materials are subject to degradation by ultra-violet light and will burn or char if accidentally ignited. The use of rock blanketing, interlocking concrete blocks or pervious sand asphalt, are more costly expedients but provide better assurance of stability where water seepage occurs.

The most difficult problems arise where slopes must be stable only for short periods, i.e. for foundation excavation. The short-term stability of soft-clay slopes can be calculated with reasonable certainty, but safe slope angles for stiff-fissured clays or laminated clays and silts, cannot be predicted in the short-term by analyses based on conventional laboratory tests. For these soils, ground-treatment processes are generally ineffective. Experience is the only guide for designing slopes, and for economical construction calculated risks must be taken having due regard to the safety of operatives and the effects of a slip on the permanent construction.

Electro-osmosis has been used to stabilise slopes in soft silts, but the method is too slow in operation and too costly in terms of electric-power consumption to be considered for general use.

**The foundation of structures**

*Foundations on soft cohesive soils*

Instability of foundations on soft clays or silts can occur as a result either of general shear failure of the soil or of excessive consolidation settlement. No ground-treatment system is effective in these soil conditions and the only solution is to adopt piled foundations or to place the structure on a buoyant raft.

*Foundations on loose granular soils*

Shear failure is unlikely to occur with normal foundation loadings on loose granular soils, but the consolidation settlement may be excessive for certain types of structure, particularly if vibrating loads are transmitted to the soil, e.g. for machinery foundations. In the latter case the use of cement injections for loose gravels or gravelly sands, or chemical injections for loose sands, can be effective and economical.

The use of deep-vibration techniques for consolidating loose granular soils is described in Chapter 11.

*Foundations on fill*

Loose granular fills can be dealt with in a similar manner to loose granular soils, as just described, by grouting or by deep vibration techniques. Where urban renewal schemes are undertaken it is frequently necessary to construct buildings on areas covered by demolition rubble. In most cases the fill has not been compacted to any worthwhile extent and where the rubble has been allowed to collapse into old cellars there can be very large voids in the fill due to arching of lintels, ceiling joists and masses of brickwork.

The demolition rubble fill is usually comparatively shallow and the most economical methods of constructing foundations are to cut a trench through the fill, and to backfill it with lean concrete or to uplift all the fill beneath the structure and replace it with compacted layers. Deep-vibration techniques are only economical in areas of old cellars where it may be difficult to operate a backacter excavator to cut a trench through the fill. Economies can be achieved by recording the positions of cellars before commencing demolition, and then as far as possible siting the new building clear of the cellars.

Injections and deep-vibration treatments are ineffective in fills consisting of domestic refuse. The only possible foundation methods, if heavy settlement is to be avoided, are to construct buildings on piled foundations, or to preload the foundation area by embankments of sand or rock. The preload fills must remain in position until settlement of the ground surface has ceased or slowed down to an acceptable degree.

*Foundations in areas of mining subsidence*

The most frequent problems in the UK due to mining subsidence are those concerned with coal mining, but subsidence can also occur in areas of ironstone mining, salt extraction and prehistoric or later flint workings in the chalk.

The foundation treatments in areas of longwall mining, or abandoned 'pillar and stall' workings are described in Chapter 7. In addition to the grouting treatments described it may be possible to use piled foundations in areas of very shallow workings near the coal outcrop. Where there is a thin cover of weak rock over the cavities, driven piles can be used to break through the roof of the cavity, and the piles are then seated in the rock beneath the coal seam. For a greater thickness of rock cover, bored piles can be used, but the concrete must be placed in a sleeve constructed from coated p.v.c. or light corrugated-steel sections. The sleeving serves the purpose of preventing concrete from flowing into the cavities.

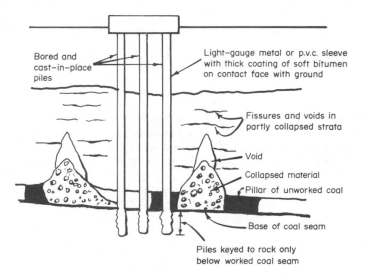

Fig. 1.9. Use of piled foundations in areas of mining subsidence

Also the coating, which may consist of a thick layer of soft bitumen, greatly minimises the dragdown on the pile shaft due to collapse of the overburden above the coal seal at some period of time after installing the piles (Fig. 1.9).

REFERENCES

1. Boyes, R. G. H., 'Uses of Bentonite in Civil Engineering', *Proc. Inst. Civ. Eng.,* **52** No. 1, 25–37, May (1972)
2. Haswell, C. K., 'Thames Cable Tunnel', *Proc. Inst. Civ. Eng.,* **44**, 323–340, Dec. (1969)
3. Collins, S. P. and Deacon, W. G., 'Shaft Sinking by Ground Freezing: Ely Ouse-Essex Scheme', *Inst. Civ. Eng. Suppl.,* Paper 7506S (1972)
4. Smith, W. and Bevan, O. M., 'Municipal Tunnelling—A Contractor's Viewpoint', *Tunnels and Tunnelling,* **4** No. 3, 237–247, May–June (1972)
5. Haswell, C. K., 'Tunnel under the Severn and Wye Estuaries', *Proc. Inst. Civ. Eng.,* **54** No. 1., 451–486, Aug. (1973).
6. Price, D. G. and Plaisted, A. C., 'Epoxy Resins in Rock Slopes Stabilisation Works', *Proc. Symp. Int. Soc. of Rock Mech.,* Nancy (1971)

## Chapter 2

# Control of Ground-water by Ground-water Lowering

Excavation in water-bearing ground has always been a difficult operation, and even with the sophisticated techniques available to the engineer today, it is still possible to get into serious trouble unless detailed thought has been given to the nature of the problems to be overcome and, in particular, the properties of the ground through which work is to be carried out before such work is commenced. This implies that adequate prior knowledge of the soil conditions at the site is available (i.e. for all jobs the site investigation should be realistically related to both the costs and the difficulties likely to be involved).

### History

In general, until the early nineteenth century civil engineers endeavoured to avoid pumping wherever possible. However, where there was no alternative, pumping was usually undertaken by the rag and chain pump known in France as *le chapelet* (rosary). Often the magnitude of the pumping duty was considerable and the work most exhausting.

In 1811 Telford, when working on the construction of a lock on the Caledonian canal, at first used a rag and chain pump driven by horses, but replaced them by a 7 kW (9 h.p.) steam engine. After that, steam-driven pumps were used during the construction of the remaining principal locks on that canal.

Fourteen years later in 1825, Brunel used a 10·5 kW (14 h.p.) steam engine when sinking the shafts for the Thames tunnel to carry the Metropolitan Railway between Wapping and Rotherhithe. By this date steam pumping seems to have become the common practice.

The first major ground-water lowering project undertaken in this country was carried out under the supervision of that great railway engineer, Robert Stephenson, during the construction of the Kilsby tunnel on the London to Birmingham Railway. He may be said to have invented ground-water lowering by means of deep wells.The following description of this work is taken from the 1898 James Forrest Lecture to the Institution of Civil Engineers by Professor Boyd Dawkins, FRS, "The Kilsby tunnel on the London to Birmingham Railway, near Rugby, completed in the year 1838, presented extreme difficulty because it had to be carried through the water-logged sands of the Inferior Oolites, so highly charged with water as to be a veritable quicksand. The difficulty was overcome in the following manner. Shafts were sunk and steam pumps erected near the line of the tunnel. 'As pumping progressed', writes Stephenson, 'the most careful measurements were taken at the level at which water stood in the various shafts and boreholes; and I was, incidentally, soon much surprised to find how slightly the depression of the water level in the one shaft influenced that of the other, notwithstanding a free communication existed between them through the medium of the sand, which was very open and coarse. It then occurred to me that the resistance which the water encountered in its passage through the sands to the pumps would be accurately measured by the angle or inclination which the surface of the water assumed towards the pumps, and that it would be unnecessary to draw the whole of the water off from the quicksands, but to persevere in pumping only in the precise level of the tunnel, allowing the surface of the water flowing through the sand to assume that inclination which was due to its resistance.' The simple result, therefore, of all the pumping was merely to establish and maintain a channel of comparatively dry sand in the immediate line of the intended tunnel, leaving water heaped up on each side by the resistance which the sand offered to its descent to that line on which the pumps and shafts were situated. The results of observations, carried on for two years, led to the conclusion that no extent of pumping would completely drain the sands, and that the cone of depression did not extend much beyond 200 yards away from the line of pumps."

In his account, buried in a report to the London and Westminster Company, dated 1841, it is difficult to decide which is the more admirable, the scientific perception which enabled Stephenson to arrive at the conclusion that the size of the cone of depression was small in range, or the practical application of the phenomenon of making a dry pathway for the railway between the waters heaped up on either side. It is surprising that having made an exceedingly interesting and useful discovery, namely, that deep-well pumping could be used to achieve temporary lowering of the ground water in the region where construction is to be undertaken and also how to control the same, there were no further uses of, or advances in, this technique of deep-well ground-water lowering in Britain for over three quarters of a century.

Shortly after World War I the firm of Siemens developed a reliable electrically driven submersible borehole pump. These were used for ground-water lowering on the construction of the Berlin underground railway. About the same time, the wellpoint was introduced into the USA. This was based on a simple form of driven wellpoint similar to that first developed and used by Sir Robert Napier in his 1868 Abyssinian Campaign, and which subsequently had become a standard piece of equipment in the Royal Engineers. The principal advance in America was the use of water jetting instead of driving techniques to install these in the ground.

## Ground-water control

Open excavations may be straightforward or difficult, depending on the soil and ground-water conditions. It was Terzaghi (1939) the 'father' of soil mechanics who first postulated that with no water in soils there would be no soil mechanics[1].

There are two cases to be considered here, (*a*) the case of an excavation into a sandy soil penetrating below the level of the ground water, and (*b*) the case of a sheeted excavation through an impermeable bed into sand charged with water under pressure.

Considering case (*a*); unless precautions are taken, the sides of a hole dug in a fine sand below water level will begin to slump soon after excavation penetrates below water level. As digging continues, the slumping becomes progressively worse as seepage carries fines from the ground into the excavation, and the sides of the excavation become unstable and collapse.

Now consider case (*b*); if, without taking any precautions, a cofferdam is sunk through clay into an underlying aquifer of sand containing water under pressure, then there will be a sudden inrush of water and sand at the point when the upward pressure of water at the level of the toe of the piles exceeds the downward weight of the remaining soil within the cofferdam. This can be prevented either by having a sufficient penetration of the piles or by reducing the pressure head in the aquifer beneath the cofferdam.

It follows, therefore, that in order to avoid unstable ground conditions it is necessary to control the ground water in the neighbourhood of a proposed excavation. Ground-water control may be achieved by:

1. Some geotechnical process which more or less permanently excludes ground water from a proposed foundation area by forming a relatively impermeable barrier around the area, e.g. sheet piling, grouting or a diaphragm wall.
2. Some geotechnical process which lowers the water levels or water pressures either temporarily or permanently in the region of a proposed foundation area.

This particular paper deals specifically with ground-water lowering, but in the interests of completeness, and for easy reference, the main methods of ground-water control (both 1 and 2) are summarised in Table 2.1. Certain aspects of some of these methods will be dealt with in some detail in other chapters.

## Theory of ground-water lowering

The theory of the flow of water through permeable ground originated with the researches of Darcy (1846)[2] and Dupuit (1863)[3]. Since the beginning of the second quarter of this century a vast amount of theoretical work has been published. To this day, most writers are agreed that for many practical purposes the discharge $Q$ necessary to achieve a stated requisite amount of lowering can be assessed with sufficient accuracy by using Dupuit's formula. Dupuit is more nearly valid for the confined aquifer condition than for the water table condition. The Dupuit equation for the water-table or gravity-well condition is:

$$Q = \frac{\pi k(H^2 - h_0^2)}{\log_e(R/r_0)} \tag{2.1}$$

where $H$ = elevation of the original piezometric surface above the impermeable base,

$h_0$ = elevation of the operating level of the pumping well above the base,

**Table 2.1**   APPLICATIONS OF METHODS FOR GROUNDWATER CONTROL

| Method | Soils suitable for treatment | Uses | Advantages | Disadvantages |
|---|---|---|---|---|
| PERMANENT EXCLUSION OF GROUND-WATER | | | | |
| 1. Sheet piling | All types of soil (except boulder beds) | Practically unrestricted | Well-understood method using readily available plant. Rapid installation. Steel can be incorporated in permanent works or recovered | Difficult to drive and maintain seal in boulders. Vibration and noise of driving may not be acceptable Capital investment in piles can be high if re-usage is restricted. Seal may not be perfect |
| 2. Diaphragm walls (structural concrete) | All soil types including those containing boulders (rotary percussion drilling suitable for penetrating rocks and boulders by reverse circulation using bentonite slurry) | Deep basements. Underground car parks. Underground pumping stations. Shafts. Dry docks, etc. | Can be designed to form part of a permanent foundation. Particularly efficient for circular excavations. Can be keyed into rock. Minimum vibration and noise. Treatment is permanent. Can be used in restricted space. Can be put down very close to existing foundation | High cost may make it un-economical unless it can be incorporated into permanent structure. There is an upper limit to the density of steel reinforcement that can be accepted |
| 3. Slurry trench cut-off (Wanapum method or paroi mince) | Silts, sands, gravels and cobbles | Practically unrestricted. Extensive curtain walls round open excavation | A rapidly installed, cheaper form of diaphragm wall. Can be keyed into impermeable strata such as clays or soft shales | Must be adequately supported. Cost increases greatly with depth. Costly to attempt to key into hard or irregular bedrock surfaces |
| 4. Thin, grouted membrane | Silts and sands | As for 3 | As for 3 | The driving and extracting of the sheet pile element used to form the membrane limits the depth achievable and the type of soil. Also as for 3 |

**Table 2.1** (Contd.)

| Method | Soils suitable for treatment | Uses | Advantages | Disadvantages |
|---|---|---|---|---|
| 5. Contiguous-bored pile walls | All soil types, but penetration through boulders may be difficult and costly | As for 2. Underpasses in stiff clay soils | Can be used on small and confined sites. Can be put down very close to existing foundations. Minimum noise and vibration. Treatment is permanent | Ensuring complete contact of all piles over their full length may be difficult in practice. Joints may be sealed by grouting externally. Efficiency of reinforcing steel not as high as for 2 |
| 6. Cement grouts | Fissured and jointed rocks | Filling fissures to stop water flow (filler added for major voids) | Equipment is simple and can be used in confined spaces. Treatment is permanent | Treatment needs to be extensive to be effective |
| GROUTED CUT-OFFS | | | | |
| 7. Clay/cement grouts | Sands and gravels | Filling voids to exclude water. To form relatively impermeable barriers (vertical or horizontal). Suitable for conditions where long-term flexibility is desirable, e.g. cores of dams | Equipment is simple and can be used in confined spaces. Treatment is permanent. Grout is introduced by means of a sleeved grout pipe which limits its spread. Can be sealed to an irregular or hard stratum | A comparatively thick barrier is needed to ensure continuity. At least 4 m of natural cover needed (or equivalent) |
| 8. Silicates, Joosten, Guttman and other processes | Medium and coarse sands and gravels | As for 7 but non-flexible | Comparatively high mechanical strength. High degree of control of grout spread. Simple means of injection by lances. Indefinite life. Favoured for underpinning works below water level | Comparatively high cost of chemicals. Requires at least 2 m of natural cover or equivalent. Treatment can be incomplete in silty material or in presence of silt or clay lenses |
| 9. Resin grouts | Silty fine sands | As for 7 but only some flexibility | Can be used in conjunction with clay/cement grouts for treating finer strata | High cost so usually economical only on larger civil-engineering works. Requires strict site control |

| Method | Soils suitable for treatment | Uses | Economics and other advantages | Disadvantages and limitations |
|---|---|---|---|---|
| 10. Ammonium/brine refrigeration | All types of saturated soils and rock | Formation of ... voids stops water | Imparts temporary mechanical strength to soils. Treatment effective from working surface outwards. Better for large applications of long duration | ...develop. Initial installation costs are high and refrigeration plant is expensive. Requires strict site control. Some ground heave |
| 11. Liquid nitrogen refrigerant | As for 10 | As for 10 | As for 10, but better for small applications of short duration or where quick freezing is required | Liquid nitrogen is expensive. Requires strict site control. Some ground heave |

TEMPORARY EXCLUSION OF GROUND-WATER BY GROUND-WATER LOWERING

| Method | Soils suitable for treatment | Uses | Economics and other advantages | Disadvantages and limitations |
|---|---|---|---|---|
| 12. Sump pumping | Clean gravels and coarse sands | Open, shallow excavations | Simplest pumping equipment | Fines easily removed from ground. Encourages instability of formation |
| 13. Wellpoint systems with suction pumps (including the machine-laid horizontal system) | Sandy gravels down to fine sands (with proper control can also be used in silty sands) | Open excavations including rolling-pipe trench excavations. Horizontal system particularly pertinent for pipe trench excavations outside urban areas | Quick and easy to install in suitable soils. Economical for short pumping periods of a few weeks | Difficult to install in open gravels or ground containing cobbles and boulders. Pumping must be continuous and noise of pump may be a problem in a built-up area. Suction lift is limited to about 4·0–5·5 m, depending on soils. If greater lowering is needed, multi-stage installation is necessary |
| 14. Bored, shallow wells with suction pumps | Sandy gravels to silty fine sands and water-bearing rocks | Similar to wellpoint pumping. More appropriate for installations to be pumped for several months or for use in silty soils where correct filtering is important | Generally costs less to run than a comparable wellpoint installation, so if pumping is required for several months costs should be compared. Correct filtering can be controlled better than with points to prevent removal of fines from silty soils | Initial installation is fairly costly. Pumping must be continuous and noise of pump may be a problem in a built-up area. Suction is limited to about 4·0–5·5 m, depending on soils. If greater lowering is needed, multi-stage installation is necessary |

**Table 2.1** (Contd.)

| Method | Soils suitable for treatment | Uses | Advantages | Disadvantages |
|---|---|---|---|---|
| 15. Deep-bored filter wells with electric submersible pumps (long-shaft pumps with motor mounted at well head used in some countries) | Gravels to silty fine sands and water-bearing rocks | Deep excavations in, through or above water-bearing formations | No limitation on amount of drawdown as there is for suction pumping. A well can be constructed to draw water from several layers throughout its depth. Vacuum can be applied to assist drainage of fine soils. Wells can be sited clear of working area. No noise problem if mains electricity supply is available | High installation cost |
| 16. Electro-osmosis | Silts, silty clays and some peats | Open excavations in appropriate soils or to speed dissipation of construction pore pressures | In appropriate soils can be used when no other water-lowering method is applicable | Installation and running costs are usually high |
| 17. Electrochemical consolidation | Soft clays | Improve shear strength of soft clay without causing settlement | See Uses | Installation and running costs are usually high |
| 18. Drainage galleries | Any water-bearing strata underlain by low permeability strata suitable for tunnelling | Removal of large quantities of water for dam abutment, cut-offs, etc. | Very large quantities of water can be drained into gallery and disposed of by conventional large-scale pumps | Very expensive. Galleries may need to be concreted and grouted later |
| 19. Jet eductor system using high-pressure water to create vacuum as well as to lift the water | Sands (with proper control can also be used in silty sands and sandy silts) | Deep excavations in space so confined that multi-stage wellpointing can-not be used. Usually more appropriate to low-permeability soils | No limitation on amount of drawdown. Raking holes are possible | Initial installation is fairly costly. Risk of flooding excavation if high-pressure watermain is ruptured. Optimum operation difficult to control |

   $R$ = radius of the Dupuit island,
   $r_0$ = radius of the well and
   $k$ = coefficient of permeability (see Fig. 2.1$a$).

His equation for the confined aquifer or artesian-well condition is:

$$Q = \frac{2\pi k b (H - h_0)}{\log_e (R/r_0)} \qquad (2.2)$$

where $b$ = thickness of the confined pervious stratum, and the other symbols are as in equation 2.1 (see Fig. 2.1$b$).

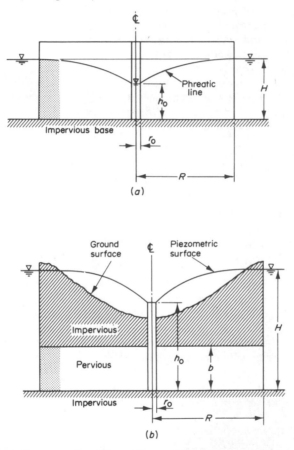

Fig. 2.1. (*a*) Water-table or gravity-well condition and (*b*) confined-aquifer or artesian-well condition

   Dupuit made two simplifying assumptions: (*a*) the gradient is the same at all points in a vertical section and (*b*) the gradient at the phreatic surface (or at the piezometric surface in the case of artesian flow) is equal to the slope of the surface at that point.

Readers who wish to make more detailed studies with particular reference to the non-steady-state flow regimens should study Forchheimer[4], Weber[5], Bolton[6] and the considerable number of American authors led by Theis[7], Muskat[8], and Jacob[9].

## Methods of ground-water lowering

The actual form of usage of ground-water lowering systems varies from one country to another depending mainly upon the predominant geology encountered, but there are also other factors. For instance, there is a considerable amount of usage of multi-stage wellpointing systems in the USA for projects which, in the UK, would more usually be dealt with by means of a deep-well installation. This difference in approach is symptomatic of the considerable volume of routine wellpointing experience that is available in the USA. It is probably true to say that there is a greater range of varying geological conditions in the UK than in any other comparable land area in the world. Therefore the philosophy of the British soils engineer will tend to be more varied than that of others, who may expect large areas where the soil conditions remain similar, as, for instance, the relative sameness of the soil conditions encountered in the Netherlands.

The various ground-water lowering processes most commonly used in construction will now be considered.

### Conventional sump pumping

This is the economic and recommended method for dealing with surface water. Also, if properly carried out, it may be entirely satisfactory for the sinking of excavations in clean gravels and coarse sands to limited depths below ground-water level. However, whenever fines are being removed in noticeable proportions sump pumping should cease.

This method causes flow towards the bottom of the excavation and in so doing may encourage instability of the formation. The remaining methods listed below seek to lower the water to below excavation level (in the water-table condition) so that the formation will be both dry and stable.

### Wellpoint (vertical and horizontal) pumping

This method uses suction pumps fitted with air take-off facilities, and is most useful where the required lowering is not more than about 4–5.5 m, depending on the soils to be de-watered. The amount of lowering that can be achieved by this method is limited by the physical bounds of suction lift and greatly influenced by the efficiency of the total pumping system (Fig. 2.2).

A wellpoint is a small well screen, usually 40 mm diameter and 0.5 or 1.0 m long, secured to the bottom end of a length of riser pipe (see Fig. 2.3). The whole is generally installed using a high-pressure-water jetting pump. On completion of installation including any necessary 'sanding in', the individual wellpoints are connected via a common suction-header main to a high-vacuum suction pump.

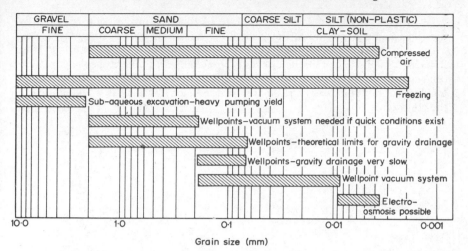

Fig. 2.2. Relationship of wellpointing and some other methods of ground stabilisation to soil type

In silty soils the mesh screen of the wellpoint may not prevent extraction of fines and so extra measures may be required.

In suitable soils the installation of wellpoints is speedy, e.g. in some cases it may be a matter of minutes, and it is therefore economical. In order to achieve lowering greater than about 5 m, another stage of wellpoints, header main and pumps must be installed when excavation reaches the limit of lowering that can be achieved with the upper stage pumping system.

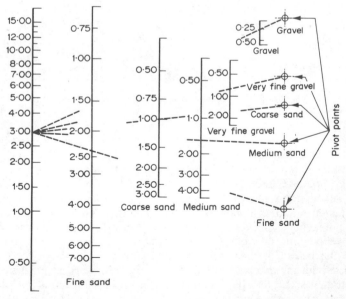

Fig. 2.3. Nomogram for wellpoint spacing (m) in clean, uniform sand and gravel

In order to accommodate the fast rate of forward progression required by pipe-lining, the Sykes B500/B600 machine has been developed to lay a continuous horizontal wellpoint at 6 m depth in lengths of up to 100 m or so (Fig. 2.4). In certain site conditions, for both pipe-lining and other types of construction works, this technique may be preferred because of its fast rate of installation, and lack of multiple risers and suction headers, leaving a clear working area to the contractor.

Fig. 2.4. Typical wellpoint layout (courtesy Henry Sykes, Ltd.)

These specially adapted trenching machines have a continuous-chain bucket system which cuts a trench approximately 225 mm wide. At the same time a perforated plastic pipe is laid in the bottom of the trench at a depth of up to 6 m below ground level and the soil excavated is immediately returned to the trench on top of the perforated pipe. Thus the 225 mm wide trench in water-bearing ground is open and unsupported only momentarily. This mechanised process is capable of laying a considerable length of pipe per day and gets over the conventional wellpointing difficulty of jetting water. In addition, due to the speed of laying, the period of time from the initial arrival on site of the dewatering specialist until the main contractor can commence work, is measured in days rather than weeks. These big machines are ideally suitable for large pipe-line contracts but can, with imagination and foresight, be used on relatively small ground-water lowering installations which might previously have been considered as conventional wellpointing contracts and land drainage needs.

### Bored filter wells

One well consists of a perforated tube surrounded by an annulus of filter media and the depth may, in theory, be unlimited (Fig. 2.5). The grading of this filter media must be correlated with the base material in the ground so that only clean filtered water is transported into the pump well.

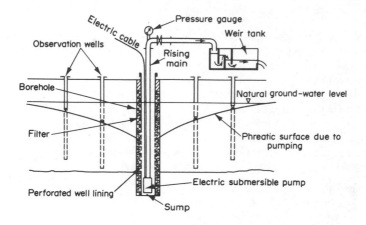

Fig. 2.5. Typical deep well with observation wells, etc., for pumping test in either soil or rock

Generally wells are bored in, say, a 600 mm diameter hole size. The type of rig may be either percussive or reverse circulation, depending on the type of ground, availability and the skill of the well-boring contractor. The hole having been bored to a sufficient penetration into the aquifer (in the case of a thin aquifer the well bore is often taken some 1–2 m into the impervious stratum beneath the aquifer), the perforated tube (well screen) is lowered into place centrally in the borehole. The appropriate filter media is then placed in the annulus. In certain circumstances a double-stage filter may be placed.

The current practice in the USA is to use a well-graded filter and to advocate 'swabbing' of the well, but in the UK it is generally the practice to use single-sized filter or filters and so minimise the 'swabbing' requirements. An electric submersible pump is lowered into each well on its own riser pipe, connected to a common discharge main and its electrical supply.

The successful operation of a deep-well system depends to a large extent on the selection of optimum filter grading and a proper initial stabilisation of the filters.

### Bored shallow wells

These are a synthesis of the deep-well installation and the wellpoint pumping technique. The installation of the wells is basically identical to that for deep-bored filter wells with its inherent facility to ensure satisfactory filtering. The individual riser pipes to each well are connected via a common suction-header main to a high-vacuum suction pump.

The cost of the well installation may be significant. Usually the shallow-well system is more appropriate to a static installation on a high-permeability site where pumping is required for several months. In particular it may be favoured where the wellpoint alternative would require risers at close centres which could hinder construction operations.

## Settlement due to water lowering

Whenever the phreatic or piezometric surface is lowered (whether it be by water lowering or by installation of a new land-drainage system), the effective load on the soil is increased. The increase in the effective overburden pressure causes additional compression which in turn affects settlement. Abstraction of water from clean sands will increase the effective pressure, but any resulting settlement is unlikely to be significant unless the soil was initially very loose.

Pumping from an aquifer containing layers of soft clay, peat or other compressible soils or from a confined aquifer overlain by compressible soils may cause significant settlements due to the increase in effective pressures.

The amount of settlement will depend on several factors:

(a) The thickness of the compressible layers.
(b) The compressibility of the layers.
(c) The amount of lowering.

Rate of settlement will depend on the permeability of the soil and also on the length of the pumping period.

It may be feasible to limit the radius of influence (i.e. the amount of lowering at a given point) by the use of ground-water recharge methods[10]. However, it should be remembered that whereas a pumping well tends to be self-cleansing, a recharge well tends to be self-clogging. It is prudent therefore to construct an infiltration well in a similar manner to a pump-out well so that, if desired, it may be pumped occasionally to clear its filters.

## Electro-osmosis and electrochemical consolidation

There are two further methods of ground-water lowering which are occasionally referred to, but not often used in practice, namely, electro-osmosis and electrochemical consolidation[11,12]. Both of these processes have a common facet in that, by passing a d.c. current through a soil, water in the soil voids is made to travel in the same sense as the electrical current. Thus, if the cathode is so constructed that it is also a water abstraction point, in time the moisture content of the soil is decreased.

The relevant physical laws were established by L. Casagrande (1947)[13] and tended to indicate that its predominant usage should be in silts. In practice this may not be necessarily so, because conditions during the deposition of silts tend to change, giving rise to alternating layers of greater and lesser permeability. Under these conditions the layers of greater permeability tend to act as preferential drainage paths, and therefore enable acceptable ground-water lowering to be successfully achieved by conventional pumping. Hence it is probable that electro-osmosis is more viable when dealing with low-strength alluvial-clay deposits[14].

The application of electro-osmosis to these soils can usually effect sufficient reduction in their moisture content and accordingly increase their shear strength to enable open excavation to be undertaken without exceedingly flat slopes. Electrochemical consolidation is a variant of electro-osmosis in that if a salt solution is introduced at the positive electrode, it is possible to cause the solution to migrate through the ground. If the solution is suitably chosen, this migration will ensure consolidation by ionic permeation. This consolidation, unlike that due to electro-osmosis, is obtainable without settlement.

A fuller account of these two processes is given in Chapter 3.

REFERENCES

1. Terzaghi, K., 'Soil Mechanics—a New Chapter in Engineering Science', *Proc. Instn. Civ. Engrs.*, **12**, 106–142 (1939)
2. Darcy, H., *Les Fontaines Publiques de la Ville de Dijon*, Paris (1856)
3. Dupuit, J., *Etudes Théoretiques et Practiques sur le Mouvement des Eaux*, Paris (1863)
4. Forchheimer, P., *Hydraulik*, Teubner, Leipzig and Berlin (1930)
5. Weber, H., *Die Reichweite von Grundwasserabsenkungen Mittels Rohrbrunnen*, Springer, Berlin (1928)
6. Bolton, N. S., 'The Flow Pattern Near a Gravity Well in a Uniform Water Bearing Medium', *J. Inst. Civ. Eng.*, **36**, 534–550 (1951)
7. Theis, C. V., 'The Relation Between the Lowering of the Piezometric Surface and the Rate and Duration of Discharge of a Well Using Groundwater Storage', *Trans. Am. Geophys. Union Reports and Papers, Hydrology* (1935)
8. Muskat, M., *The Flow of Homogenous Fluids Through Porous Media*, McGraw-Hill, New York and London (1937)
9. Jacob, C. E., 'On the Flow in an Elastic Artesian Aquifer', *Trans Am. Geophys. Union*, **21** (1940)
10. Parson, J. D., 'Foundation Installation Requiring Recharging of Groundwater', *J. Cons. Div.*, Proc. Am. Soc. Civ. Eng., **85**, 1–21, Sept. (1959)
11. Camberfort, H. and Caron, C., 'Electro-osmose et Consolidation Electrochimique des Argiles', *Géotechnique*, **11**, Sept. (1961)
12. Belluigi, A., 'Elettroconsolidamento di un Pendio Argilloso Franante', *Mentano*, No. 1 (1959)
13. Casagrande, L., 'The Application of Electro-osmosis to Practical Problems in Foundations and Earthworks', D.S.I.R. Building Research Technical Paper No. 30, H.M.S.O., London (1947)
14. Bjerrum, L., Moum, L. and Eide, O., 'Application of Electro-osmosis to a Foundation Problem in a Norwegian Quick Clay', *Géotechnique*, **17**, London, 214–235 (1967)

# Chapter 3

# Electro-osmosis and Electrochemical Stabilisation

Electro-osmosis was originally developed by Casagrande[1] as a method for de-watering low-permeability active clay soils. It has since been used on a fairly wide scale with varying success; the fundamental drawback being that used solely for de-watering electro-osmosis is a decelerating process, becoming progressively less efficient as the soil water content is reduced. This means that the soil water content is rarely reduced by a large enough amount to significantly affect the soil stability, and where it is, subsequent re-hydration may often rapidly reverse the process.

Where electro-osmosis has been successful, it has usually been as a result of using the process to introduce a chemical into the soil, either through anode solution or direct electrolyte replacement. This improves soil stability either by chemical change (ion replacement) in the clay mineral, or by partial cementation of the pore space. Used initially accidentally and latterly deliberately, this adaption of electro-osmosis is known as *electrochemical stabilisation* and forms a possible method of treatment for small quantities of clay soils.

In this chapter some of the factors affecting the use of electrochemical stabilisation in ground engineering are considered and the potential of the process is discussed.

### Electro-osmotic flow

If an electric potential is applied to a saturated porous material, electrolyte will flow from the anode to the cathode. This is known as *electro-osmosis* and may be explained most simply in terms of the double-layer theory of Helmholtz, which postulates that in a capillary filled with electrolyte there exist two liquid layers adsorbed at the capillary surface. Of these the surface layer, which is extremely thin compared with the total layer thickness, is negatively charged and rigidly attached to the surface. The outer layer, comprising soluble ions and associated water molecules attached to the surface layer, is positively charged and mobile. Thus when an electric potential is applied to the capillary, the positively charged layer moves towards the cathode, carrying with it the rest of the electrolyte in the capillary. A mathematical treatment of this concept variously ascribed to Helmholtz, Smoluchowski[2], and Schmid[3], may be based on the analogy between the double-layer structure and a condenser, the potential across the double layer being termed the *electrokinetic* or *zeta* potential $Z$. The solution may be expressed in the form:

$$q_0 = \frac{ZDr^2}{8\eta} \times \frac{\Delta E}{\Delta L} \qquad (3.1)$$

where $q_0$ = rate of flow through the capillary,

      $D$ = dielectric constant of the electrolyte,

      $r$ = capillary radius,

      $\eta$ = viscosity of the liquid,

      $\Delta E$ = electric potential and

      $\Delta L$ = distance between electrodes.

In Schmid's[3] form the factors $A_0$ (the volume pore charge density) and $F$ (the Faraday constant) are substituted for $Z$ and $D$ respectively for the case of a fine-grained structure where the double-layer theory is unrealistic. The zeta potential, which is related to the thickness of the adsorbed layer, will depend on the concentration and valency of soluble ions in the electrolyte. In a dilute solution, the zeta potential will be high and the adsorbed layer thick (up to $10^{-6}$ m). In a concentrated solution the zeta potential may be reduced to zero or reversed due to collapse and reformation of the double layer.

In extending this analysis to soils it is reasonable to assume that in the normal range of natural electrolyte concentrations found in soils, variations in the zeta potential are unlikely to affect flow rates. However, if, as may be the case in unsaturated soils, the thickness of adsorbed layers is reduced due to absence of water, the subsequent increase in concentration of ions will reduce the zeta potential to a magnitude where electro-osmotic flow rates are minimal.

There is an obvious analogy between electro-osmotic flow as represented by equation 3.1 and hydraulic flow. An expression for electro-osmotic flow through soils can be obtained by considering the soil structure as a bundle of capillaries whose openings as a fraction of total area are represented by the soil porosity $n$. Thus discharge flow $q$ will be given by

$$q = nq_0 = K_e E_i A \qquad (3.2)$$

where $K_e = ZDn/8\pi\eta$ and can be designated the *electro-osmotic coefficient of permeability* with equivalent units of mm/s per V/mm of potential gradient, $E_i = \Delta E/\Delta L$ is the potential gradient, and $A$ is the area of discharge.

This can be compared with the D'arcy form of Poisseuille's law for laminar flow through a similar series of capillaries:

$$q = kiA \qquad (3.3)$$

where $k$ is the *hydraulic coefficient of permeability and* $i$ is the hydraulic gradient. By comparing equation 3.3 with the Kozeny-Carman equation for flow through porous media, it can be shown that $k$ is proportional to the square of the hydraulic radius, and hence the equivalent capillary area. Since $K_e$ is obviously independent of capillary area, it follows that it must be independent of soil pore size and will remain essentially the same magnitude in either sand, silt or clays, provided $Z$ and $D$ or $A_0$ and $F$ remain constant.

Casagrande[4,5] has shown that for the majority of *saturated* soils in a natural state this is the case (see Table 3.1). His data suggest an average value for the electro-osmotic coefficient of permeability in the region of $5 \times 10^{-4}$ mm/s, at a potential gradient of $0.1$ V/mm or $5 \times 10^{-3}$ mm²/Vs. Zhinkin suggests a rather wider range of $K_e$ values between $0.5 \times 10^{-3}$ and $13 \times 10^{-3}$ mm²/Vs at a potential gradient of $0.1$ V/mm, with the majority of values in the $3 \times 10^{-3}$ mm²/Vs to $5 \times 10^{-3}$ mm²/Vs range.

**Table 3.1**   VALUES OF $K_e$ (AFTER CASAGRANDE[5])

| *Material* | *Moisture content* (%) | $K_e$ (mm²/Vs $\times 10^{-3}$) |
|---|---|---|
| London clay | 52·3 | 5·8 |
| Boston blue clay | 50·8 | 5·1 |
| Commercial kaolin | 67·7 | 5·7 |
| Clayey silt (England) | 31·7 | 5·0 |
| Rock flour (Hartwick, N.Y.) | 27·2 | 4·5 |
| Red marl (Scotland) | 18·4–29·1 | 0·7–2·6 |
| Na-bentonite | 170·0 | 2·0 |
| Na-bentonite | 2 000·0 | 12·0 |
| Mica powder | 49·7 | 6·9 |
| Fine sand | 26·0 | 4·1 |
| Quartz powder | 23·5 | 4·3 |

Accepting an average value of $5 \times 10^{-3}$ mm²/Vs for $K_e$ in most saturated soils, it is evident that in many fine-grained soils having hydraulic coefficients of permeability less than $10^{-4}$ mm/s, notional advantages in de-watering operations may be obtained by using electro-osmotic techniques. The relative advantage may be expressed in terms of the ratio between $K_e$ and $k$, sometimes known as the *coefficient of electro-osmotic effectiveness*, which increases with increasing clay fraction in the soil.

An estimate of the power requirements for electro-osmosis may be obtained from equation 3.2 by substituting for $A$ in terms of the electrical resistance $R$ and resistivity $\rho$ of the soil, whence:

$$q = K_e E_i \rho \frac{\Delta L}{R} \qquad (3.4)$$

and

$$q = K_e \rho \frac{\Delta E}{R} \quad \text{or} \quad q = K_e \rho \Delta I \qquad (3.5)$$

Thus the rate of water removal is directly proportional to the current $I$ and resistivity in a saturated soil.

Although from a ground treatment point of view this is an extremely attractive concept, two factors mitigate against its application on a large scale. Firstly, few clay soils have uniformly low permeability. In practice their permeability is determined by their fabric and the presence of silt or sand layers or fissures may significantly reduce the mass permeability, making the use of other, cheaper, drainage methods more attractive. Secondly, $K_e$ is only constant in some saturated soils.

Gray and Mitchell[6], in a study of fundamental aspects of electro-osmosis, show a specific increasing near-linear relationship between $K_e$ and water content, $K_e$ increasing from zero, at zero water content, to $5 \times 10^{-3}$ mm²/Vs at an average water content of about 60%. They also show that $K_e$ is inversely proportional to ion exchange capacity and also to pore-water electrolyte concentration, although the latter effect is not significant in soils with high exchange capacities. None of these observations are surprising since individually or collectively they will tend to reduce $Z$ and $D$, $A_0$ and $F$. they are, however, significant in that the practical effect of electro-osmosis in a saturated soil will be to reduce water content and increase electrolyte concentration. They are also significant in that the low-ion-exchange-capacity soils which are most amenable to electro-osmotic flow are in any case likely to be the most stable.

Electro-osmosis is therefore a decelerating process in all soils, as pore-water content decreases and electrolyte concentration increases, with flow being further retarded by gas generation at the electrodes. In active and potentially unstable clays, flow rates will also be reduced by the high exchangeable cation content, and stabilisation by de-watering will be limited and reversible.

To obtain more permanent stability it is therefore essential that the techniques of electro-osmosis be extended to permit some form of soil stabilisation in a wet state, utilising the ability of the process to create fluid flow in a relatively impermeable medium. This is the basis of electrochemical stabilisation, which will now be considered.

## Electrochemical stabilisation

The mechanical properties of a clay vary with the type of cations associated with it. If the clay contains a significant proportion of weakly bonded cations with high exchange capacity such as sodium or lithium, it will have a tendency to adsorb and retain large quantities of water between the surfaces of its particles, and have a low shearing strength. On the other hand, if the clay comprises cations of stronger bonding strength and lower exchange capacity such as calcium and magnesium, or particularly iron or aluminium, it will adsorb less water and its structure will be more stable. The difference between these two conditions is very marked for montmorillonites, less so for other types of clay such as kaolinites.

Cations associated with clays are exchangeable and therefore the introduction of solutions containing an excess of cations with stronger bonding strength into a clay rich in high-exchange-capacity weakly-bonded cations will lead to ion exchange and improvement of soil properties. This is the main basis for surface stabilisation of montmorillonite clays by addition of excess lime, cement or other compounds. The low permeability of clays, however, will prevent dispersion by conventional methods of dissolved additives in bulk clays. This can be achieved in association with electro-osmosis in high-ion-exchange-capacity soils where electro-osmotic flow rates (although initially low) will not be affected by increases in pore-water electrolyte concentration.

There are two basic methods of introducing stabilising electrolytes into a clay soil, i.e. by solution and dispersion of the anode material through electrolysis, and by direct introduction of additives at the anode.

Electrolysis normally comprises two chemical reactions, i.e. decomposition of the electrolyte, accompanied by solution of the anode material. The rate of solution is related through Faraday's laws of electrolysis to the rate of decomposition of the electrolyte. Electrochemical stabilisation achieved by anode solution relies on two main processes, i.e. initial base-exchange reactions on the surface-active area of the clay mineral particles, replacing weak by strong cations, and the formation of soil-cementing compounds by reaction between the electrolyte and the dissolved anode.

In the simplest cases these reactions can be obtained by hydrolysis and oxidisation of the anode material, where this is readily oxidisable (i.e. iron, aluminium). In the case of iron, ions released from the anode will react with water to form ferrous hydroxide, at the same time increasing the hydrogen ions and hence the acidity of the electrolyte:

$$Fe^{2+} + 2H_2O = Fe(OH)_2 + 2H^+$$

The ferrous hydroxide will in turn be readily oxidised to form ferric hydroxide:

$$4Fe(OH)_2 + O_2 + 2H_2O = 4Fe(OH)_3$$

Both ferrous and ferric hydroxides are amorphous colloids acting as cementing compounds and binding the soil particles together. Release of hydrogen ions in the anode zone will tend to retard the reactions, encouraging movement of divalent iron ions towards the cathode and enabling an even spread of the cementing material over the stabilisation zone. A similar reaction occurs where aluminium electrodes are used.

This type of process can be utilised to give permanent stability in relatively wet clays, giving a high increase in strength for a relatively low reduction in water content. This has been (mistakenly) attributed in many cases to electro-osmotic de-watering, when in fact stability has been due to base exchange and formation of ferric hydroxide following solution of cast-iron anodes.

An example of increases in strength after electrical treatment involving solution of anodes alone is illustrated in Fig. 3.1. The average increase in shear strength of a bed of clay, electrically treated, was about $15 \, kN/m^2$ or about 60% above the original shear strength of the clay, with a decrease of water content of only 2·5%.

Addition of additives to the anode (in addition to the dissolved electrode material) may be designed to increase the base-exchange reaction, and to act as a catalyst to the formation of cementitious material or to improve the quality and quantity of the cementitious material. To increase the base-exchange reaction, most of the additives used are organic and inorganic compounds of aluminium or calcium, iron being normally present as the electrode material. Of these the most commonly used is calcium chloride. This intensifies dissolution of the iron anode by formation of ferrous chlorides, at the same time producing calcium hydroxide which acts as a cementing agent.

Since virtually any electrolyte can be distributed into relatively impermeable soils by electro-osmotic flow, there is obviously a wide choice of additives based on the specific physical and chemical properties of the clay minerals present in a particular clay soil. One useful group may be polyelectrolytes which are primarily organic additives combining electrolytic properties and the ability to gel. Phosphoric acid has also been used to a limited extent (probably in combination with aluminium electrodes). The mechanism of stabilisation in this instance, according to Gillot[7], involves release of aluminium hydroxide and aluminium phosphates which act as cementing compounds.

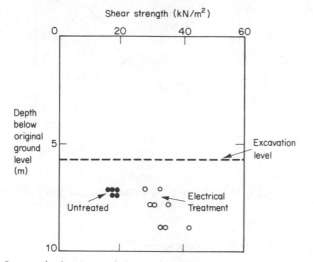

Fig. 3.1. Increase in shear strength due to electrical treatment (after Casagrande[4])

Laboratory experiments conducted by Adamson, *et al.*[8,9] on clay (Fig. 3.2) and on clayey sand (Fig. 3.3) indicated that such soils could be stabilised by electrical treatment using an electrolyte containing aluminium sulphate and calcium chloride. X-ray analyses of the treated soils revealed a change in clay particle structure and the formation of cementing compounds.

An important disadvantage in the use of additives is the tendency to reduced flow with increase in electrolyte concentration, which may effectively limit stabilisation beyond a certain level.

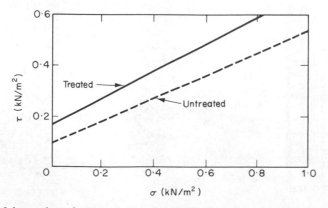

Fig. 3.2. Mohr envelopes for bentonite clay electrically treated with saturated solutions of calcium chloride and aluminium sulphate (after Adamson, *et al.*[8])

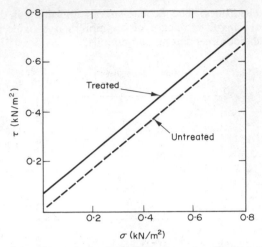

Fig. 3.3. Mohr envelopes for sand plus 1·5% sodium montmorillonite treated with saturated solutions of calcium chloride and aluminium sulphate (after Adamson, *et al.*[9])

## Application of electrochemical processes

The site equipment for electrochemical stabilisation is relatively simple, comprising solid or perforated steel (or aluminium) pipes, 13–100 mm diameter at the anode, and standard or adapted well points (Fig. 3.4)[10] at the cathode, which will be recovered undamaged. Protruding and near-surface parts of anodes and cables must be insulated.

The layout of electrodes is primarily dependent on the subsurface water conditions, on the electrical potential available and on the optimum potential

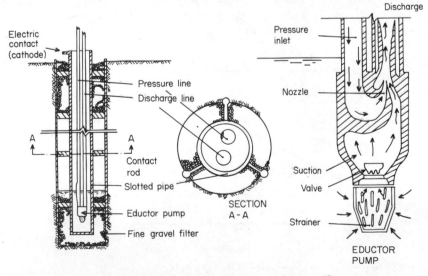

Fig. 3.4. Typical cathode well system (after Perry[10])

gradient required for a particular soil. As a rough guide, Zhinkin[11] suggests a potential gradient of 90 V/m for sandy loams, 70 V/m for loams, 60 V/m for clays and 40 V/m for silts. For an available d.c. potential of 100 V, this would mean electrode separation ranging from just over 1 m to 2·5 m.

For maximum effectiveness, it is essential that the potential gradient follows the same direction as the hydraulic gradient, and that the water table is below the surface. For this reason the most commonly quoted examples of electrochemical stabilisation are embankments in clay (Fig. 3.5) where well-defined internal water creates conditions of failure due to inadequate drainage[4].

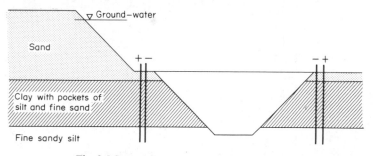

Fig. 3.5 Successful test layout (after Casagrande[4])

Since the water flow rate is related to the charge, it is obviously desirable to have as high a current as is feasible. However, this will normally be limited by site generating equipment to currents in the region of 150 A.

A summary of field applications of electrochemical stabilisation where technical data is available is given in Table 3.2. The materials treated include silt, loess, loam and clays, and mixtures of clays, silts, sands and gravels. In the latter case, treatment of the clay component would be sufficient to stabilise the whole deposit. The applications normally concern embankments, particularly those associated with river and harbour works, and side-walls of excavations. This confirms the supposition that electro-osmotic flow is most successful where the potential gradient is used to reinforce a pre-existing well-defined hydraulic gradient.

Information on the water content of the soil (where available) confirms that electro-osmotic flow is not primarily a method of de-watering (water reduction is often negligible), but essentially a method of promoting chemical stabilisation. The most common stabilising agents are iron from the anode or calcium chloride fed through an anode opening. It could be said therefore, that the process is similar in many ways to chemical grouting techniques, except that the chemical grout is introduced into the soil by electro-osmotic flow instead of by pumping, and that the stabilisation process involves base exchange as well as depositing cementitious materials.

Electrochemical stabilisation has also been successfully used to increase the load-bearing capacity of pile foundations. Increase in soil strength is expressed in lower compressibility and higher load-bearing capacity of the soil[16,17]. Zhinkin[11], in particular, describes construction of bridge piles of 0·2–0·4 m diameter and 30 m long, driven into silty sand having 1% clay content. Observations on piles in treated ground showed that penetration under test loads of 1000 kN could be reduced from 17 mm to 1 or 2 mm.

**Table 3.2** EXAMPLES OF FIELD APPLICATION OF ELECTRO-OSMOTIC STABILISATION SOIL AND SITE DATA

| Case no. | Source | Site location | Job description | Material causing problem | Moisture content Before % | After % | Additional comments on soil and moisture conditions |
|---|---|---|---|---|---|---|---|
| 1. | Casagrande[12] | Halle, Germany | Embankment slopes unstable | Soft loess-gravel mixture | 23·8-25·8 | 14·5-17·4 | Instability over a 30 m length |
| 2. | Casagrande[5,12] | Ayton, Scotland, Scottish Railways | Improve embankment stability prior to tunnelling | Red Marl, clayey material containing sand, gravel and boulders | 19 | 14-17 | 40 000 litre of water removed |
| 3. | Fetzer[13] | Warren, Ohio, USA | West Branch Dam, foundation unstable | 18 m clay layer | 21-40 | | 24 m embankment; dry density 1·3-1·8 Mg/m³ |
| 4. | Casagrande[1,5,12] | Salzgitter, Germany | Improve stability to deepen railway cut | Loess-loam, clayey silt | | | Flow rate 17 litre/h before, 250 litre/h after stabilisation |
| 5. | Casagrande[1,5,12] | Trondhjem, Norway | Improve stability for excavation of 'U'-boat pen | Thick stratum of silty clay | 37 | 36·5 | Saline soil. Flow rate 2 litre/h before, 20 litre/h after treatment |
| 6. | Casagrande[1,12] | Lerkendal, nr. Trondhjem | Improve stability, railway tunnel approach | Deep deposit of soft clayey silt | 18-37 | | Area disturbed by old slides. Flow rate zero before, 5 litre/h per well after treatment |
| 7. | Zenczykowski quoted by Casagrande[12] | Warsaw, Poland | Improve stability in cut for street-car | Glacial till overlain by fine sand and fill | | | Retaining walls blocked natural drainage |
| 8. | Zhinkin[11] | USSR | Combat deformation of subgrades and increase embankment strength | Embankment and sand base | | | No information |
| 9. | Zhinkin[11] | Kiev, USSR | Collapse of walls of driven shaft | Water-filled loams | | | Loam in fluid state, $k = 6 \times 10^{-6}$ mm/s |
| 10. | Zaretti, quoted by Casagrande[12] | Italy | Unstable canal bank | Highly plastic clay; high Na content ($\phi = 15°$ max.) | | | Flow rate 7 litre/day per well |
| 11. | Soletanche in Casagrande[12] | Bordeaux, France | Excavation for treatment plant | Clayey silt | | | Ground-water level close to surface. Flow rate 300 litre/h before, 300 litre/h after treatment |
| 12. | Casagrande[4,12] | Essexville, Michigan, USA | Test section for excavation stabilisation | Soft clayey strata | | | Water content decreased by 2·5% after treatment |
| 13. | Perry[10] | Mexico City, Mexico | Stabilising prior to excavation | No information | | | Excavation 6 m deep. Water table lowered 5 m by treatment |
| 14. | Loughney in Zeiler[14] | Ontario, Canada | Excavation for bridge piers and abutment, Trans Canada highway | Silt | 26 | 22·5 | Loose saturated silt 20-40 m thick |
| 15. | Bjerrum[15] | Ås, Norway | Increase stability prior to excavation | Quick clay | 31 | 27·2 | Sensitivity reduced from 100 to 4; $k = 2 \times 10^{-7}$ mm/s |

**Table 3.2** (CONTINUED): STABILISATION DETAILS

| Case no. | Volume of material treated or excavated (m³) | Electrode material (No.) and depth (m) Anode | Cathode | Anode–cathode distance (m) | Potential (V) | Potential gradient (V/m) | Current (A) | Treatment period | Comments on treatment |
|---|---|---|---|---|---|---|---|---|---|
| 1. | 2 800 | Gas pipe | Gas pipe | 4·5 | 110 | 24 | | Several weeks | Treatment successful |
| 2. | | Scrap sheet piles (4), 12–15 m | 88 mm wellpoint bronze mesh (5), 10–15 m | 3·3–3·6 | 90–110 | 25–27 | | 6 months | Treatment successful |
| 3. | 580 000 | 64 mm steel pipe (660), 40 m | 50 mm steel pipe (990), 40 m | 6 | 100–150 | 8–25 | 40 per cathode | 10–12 months | Insufficient power to treat all areas simultaneously |
| 4. | 90 m test section | 12 m gas pipe (20), 7 m | 100 mm wellpoints (20), 7 m | 4·5 | 180, reduced 90 | 17–25<br>39<br>20 | 19 per cathode | 8 weeks test section | Excavation resumed 1 day after start of treatment. Entire cut constructed in similar manner |
| 5. | | 38 mm gas pipe (—), 18 m | 200 mm pipe (—), 18 m | 4·5 | 90, reduced 40 | 9 | 20–30 per cathode | 6 months | Potential gradient low because of high soil conductivity. Treatment successful, flowrates increased ten-fold |
| 6. | | 38 mm gas pipe | 300 mm wellpoints | 4·5 | 30 | 7 | 15 per cathode | | Low voltage because of salt-bearing soil |
| 7. | 30 000 | Steel pipe 18–23 m | | 9–36 | 50–80 | 2–6 | 1·5–45 per cathode | 7 weeks | Treatment at two locations on slope |
| 8. | | 38–50 mm gas pipe, 1·5–2·5 m deep | 38–50 mm gas pipe, 1·5–2·5 m long, 0·6–0·9 m | 1·5–3 | 100–200 | 50–70 | | | 4–8% solution of CaCl₂ fed through anodes. Soil strength increased 2–4 times |
| 9. | | Material not specified, (21), 1·5–2 m | Material not specified, (21), 1·5–2 m | 1–2 | 120 | 60–120 | 145 | 60 h | 17% solution of CaCl₂ fed through anodes, zones of strengthened soil formed around anodes, water content dropped by 8–10% |
| 10. | 210 | 89 mm aluminium pipe (—), 2·4 m | 89 mm aluminium pipe (—), 2·4 m | 2·4 | 40 | 16 | 0·2 per cathode | 1 month | |
| 11. | | 25 mm rebars in 178 mm holes (130) | 50 mm rebars in 178 mm holes (130) | 2·4 | 40–60 | 16–25 | 600 dropped to 100. 3–20 per cathode | 3 months | Anodes replaced every 3 months due to heavy corrosion |
| 12. | 130 | 12 mm rebars (11), 4·2 m | Common wellpoints (11), 4·2 m | 2·2 | 100 | 44 | 300 | | Treatment caused increase in shear strength by 60% |
| 13. | 11 000 | 25 mm corrugated steel bars | 100 mm wellpoint in 300 mm hole | 4 | 70 | 18 | 27 per cathode 1 500 | 12 days prior to excavating, until end of foundation phase | Site divided into four sections each section de-watered separately |
| 14. | 3 rows, 12 m deep | 3 rows, 24–36 m deep | 3 rows, 12 m deep | 2–3 | 100–150 | 33–82 | Low | 3 months | As a result of treatment, density of silt increased |
| 15. | 2 700 | 19 mm dia. rebars (93 pairs), 9·6 m | | 0·2 | 40 | 61–66 | 250 | 120 days | Potential and current varied during treatment period. Average shear strength increased from 9 to 38 kN/m² |

In general, case histories show that electro-osmosis and electrochemical stabilisation are acceptable methods of soil stabilisation from a technical point of view. They have, however, the fundamental limitation that they are decelerating processes, their effectiveness reducing with time due to reduced soil-exchange capacity with electrolyte build-up. This means that any application tends to be lengthy and expensive with costs exceeding conventional well-point de-watering by at least £20/$m^3$ of stabilised soil. Because of this, electrochemical stabilisation methods would be expected to be limited to applications where they are the only feasible method of stabilisation and where the results obtained could justify high operational costs. Such applications would concern, in the main, homogeneous low-permeability saturated active clays, subject to a significant hydraulic gradient.

## Acknowledgements

This chapter is based on a report prepared by the author and Mr. M. Goldberger for the Cementation Company Ltd., to whom due acknowledgement is given.

REFERENCES

1. Casagrande, L., 'The Application of Electro-osmosis to Practical Problems in Foundations and Earthworks', Build. Res. Tech. paper No. 30, Dept. of Scientific and Industrial Res. (1947)
2. Smoluchowski, M., *Handbuch der Elektrisitat und des Magnetismus*, Vol. 2, ed. L. Graetz, Barth, Leipzig (1914).
3. Schmid, G., 'Zur Elektrochemie Feinporiger Kapillarsystems', *Zh. Elektrochemie*, **54**, 424 and **55**, 684 (1950 and 1951)
4. Casagrande, L. 'Electrical Stabilisation in Earthwork and Foundation Engineering', Proc. M.I.T. Conf. on Soil Stabilisation, 84–106 (1952)
5. Casagrande, L., 'Electro-osmotic Stabilisation of Soils', *J. Boston Soc. Civ. Eng.*, **39**, 51–83 (1952)
6. Gray, D. H. and Mitchell, J. K., 'Fundamental Aspects of Electro-osmosis in Soils', *J. Soil Mechs. Found. Eng. Div.*, Amer. Soc. Civ. Engs., **93** No. SM6, 209–236 (1967)
7. Gillot, J. E., *Clay in Engineering Geology*, Elsevier, Amsterdam (1968)
8. Adamson, L. G., Chilingar, G. V., Beeson, C. M. and Armstrong, R. A., 'Electrokinetic Dewatering, Consolidation and Stabilisation of Soils', *Eng. Geol.*, **1**, 291–304 (1966)
9. Adamson, L. G., Quigley, D. W., Ainsworth, H. R. and Chilingar, G. V., 'Electrochemical Strengthening of Clayey Sandy Soils', *Eng. Geol.*, **1**, 451–499 (1966)
10. Perry, W., 'Electro-osmosis Dewaters Large Foundation Excavation', *Construction Methods*, **45** No. 9, 116–119 (1963)
11. Zhinkin, G. N., *Electrochemical Stabilisation of Soils*, Stroiizdet, Moscow, abridged C.E.R.E. translation No. 21 (1966)
12. Casagrande, L., 'Review of Past and Current Work on Electro-osmotic Stabilisation of Soils', Harvard Soil Mechanics Series, No. 45, part 1 (1953)
13. Fetzer, C. A., 'Electro-osmotic Stabilisation of West Branch Dam', *J. Soil Mechs. Found. Eng. Div.*, Amer. Soc. Civ. Engs., **93** No. SM4, 85–106 (1967)
14. Zeiler, B., 'Investigation of the Electro-osmotic Method of Fill Foundation Stabilisation', California State Division of Highways, Materials and Research Dept., PB 177346 (1967)
15. Bjerrum, L., Moum, J. and Eide, O., 'Application of Electro-osmosis to a Foundation Problem in Norwegian Quick Clay', *Geotechnique*, **17**, 214–235 (1967)
16. Spangler, M. G. and King, L. H., 'Electrical Hardening of Clays Adjacent to Aluminium Friction Piles', Proc. 29th Ann. Meeting Highways Res. Bd., 589–599 (1949)
17. Murayama, S. and Mise, T., 'On the Electrochemical Consolidation of Soil Using Aluminium Electrodes', *Proc. 3rd Int. Conf. S.M.F.E.*, **1**, 156–159 (1953)

# Chapter 4

# Ground-water Control by Exclusion

Control of ground water may be achieved by removing it with drainage or by excluding it, wholly or partially; removal has been dealt with in Chapter 2. Methods of exclusion may be classified under the following five headings:

1. Grouting.
2. Sheet piling which may consist of driven, preformed timber, concrete or steel.
3. Membranes formed *in situ* by casting contiguous piles or by grouting in preformed holes (membrane or screen grouting).
4. Membranes formed *in situ* by panels of impermeable materials in slurry trenches.
5. Freezing.

Each of these merits extended treatment, but this chapter is devoted largely to grouting, with brief references to a few of the other methods.

The term *grouting* means the injection, under pressure through a tube or hose, of various materials intended to fill voids, either pre-existing or created by the grouting process. For water stopping, grouting may be either preplanned or an emergency expedient. By preplanning grouting, not only does the engineer avoid the panic and expense of an emergency operation but he has the opportunity to include the grouting as part of the permanent works. This is common practice, e.g. beneath dams of both concrete and embankment types. An emergency grouting operation may be unavoidable if an unforeseen condition is met, but modern techniques of site investigation are reducing the number of occasions on which this happens.

When grouting, the object of the operation should be borne in mind. Estimating in advance the cost of a grouting operation is a chancy business and there is, consequently, a temptation to engineers to restrict the grouting if they see any chance of their estimate being exceeded. However, the object of grouting is to achieve a certain technical result, not to economise on materials. Therefore the engineer should exercise strict control and, if his judgement requires it, continue with grouting until he is satisfied that the desired result has been achieved. Too many cases are on record where financial stringency has caused the termination of grouting followed by a subsequent return for expensive remedial operations. A substantial contingency item should always be added to any grouting estimate and the client should be warned in advance of the uncertain nature of the estimated costs.

## Development of grouting

Glossop[1], who has made a close study of the subject, says that Charles Bérigny invented and used the grouting process at Dieppe in 1802. Bérigny first made injections of clay; subsequently he used pozzolanic cement, although he does not appear ever to have mixed clay and cement together. His technique was frequently used in France but the knowledge spread slowly and it was not until 38 years later, in 1840, that the first paper in English on the subject was published. From 1851, grouting was more and more widely practised by British engineers. W. R. Kinipple experimented from 1856 to 1858 on cementing gravel in foundations; he used grouted concrete for the foundations of a breakwater in Jersey and remained throughout his life an advocate of injections of either cement or clay. Initially, injections had been made mainly in coarse alluvium but, in 1876, Thomas Hawksley injected cement into rock fissures beneath the Tunstall dam. From that date, rock grouting was widely practiced and grouting gradually came to mean cement grouting exclusively. In 1896, British engineers grouted dams on the Nile using Portland cement under gravity head, although Brown[2] says Kinipple tried to use clay. A Belgian engineer, Albert François, developed cement injections for shaft sinking before World War I mainly by careful attention to positioning drill holes and by the use of high pressures. He also injected fine fissures in sandstone with sodium silicate and aluminium sulphate, increasing the subsequent acceptance of cement grout*. In 1915, grouting beneath dams was still sufficient of a novelty, at least in the USA, for the injection at Mathis dam of 2 300 sacks of cement with added sand through grout holes sunk with steam-driven drills, to be described by Lauchli[3] as an unusual feature of the construction. The use of a grouted cutoff for Estacada dam about the same time also created much interest. In 1925, Hugo Joosten invented a hard gel injection using the *two-shot* method, but it became known as 'chemical consolidation' rather than grouting, and the latter term was still reserved for cement injection, a usage which persisted until about 30 years ago.

'Grouting' is now taken to include the injection of any material with the purposes of water stopping, filling cavities, strengthening rock slopes or preventing settlement and subsidence. More familiar injected materials are cement, clay, resins, silicates, bitumens and proprietaries like *AM9* or *TDM* with fillers like sand, rock dust or ashes. More exotic materials have been used, e.g. dried beet pulp, wood shavings, zacato grass, chopped corn cobs, chopped corn stalks, cotton flock, bran, diesel oil, rags, old carpets and burlap. Even foamed plastics like polystyrene have been suggested by Vinson and Mitchell[4] for grouting on the Moon. The Soletanche Co.[5] have successfully used foam-grout at May-sur-Orne, near Caen in Normandy, France, where sealing without penetration was required.

## Techniques of grouting

Grout is introduced into the ground by a pipe or hose in one of the following ways:

---

* It is now known that this treatment retarded water bleeding off from the cement/water suspension, but at the time, François believed the treatment to provide some form of lubrication for the cement grout.

1. Into an open hole (in rock for instance) through pipes caulked at the surface.
2. Through an injection pipe held in place in the hole or casing with a packer.
3. From a pipe driven into the ground and withdrawn as injection proceeds.
4. Through a pipe left in place in the ground (as with a *tube-à-manchette*).

One of the greatest difficulties in grouting is controlling the flow of grout. Grout injected into an open hole may travel long distances, especially when under high pressure, and may turn up at unexpected or even embarrassing places. In rock grouting, some degree of control is achieved by using packers. As the grout hole is drilled, a packer may be placed a metre or so above the bottom of the hole and grout injected through a pipe passing through the packer, the drilling then continuing on through the grouted zone with more grouting subsequently (Fig. 4.1). This is known as *stage-and-packer* grouting. Even so, a fissure may connect the space below and above the packer and nullify its effect.

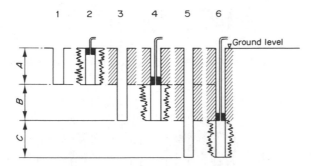

Fig. 4.1. Stage-and-packer grouting

The two-shot Joosten or Guttman processes also give some measure of control over grout injection. A steel pipe is driven into the ground to the required depth and a solution of sodium silicate injected through perforations in the end of the pipe; the pipe is then withdrawn, and at the same time calcium chloride is injected (Fig. 4.2). This solution reacts with the silicate already injected forming a strong, impermeable gel of calcium silicate. As modified by Guttman, who added sodium carbonate to the silicate thereby reducing its viscosity, the penetrating power of the grout was increased and it is thus possible to grout finer sands with the process. Single-shot chemical grouts contain an inhibitor which slows down the gel setting time permitting mixing at the surface, but injection must be within a short time of the mixing. In uncemented deposits like alluvium, the *tube-à-manchette* method can be used. This device allows injection and subsequent reinjection at any given level within the deposit. Although injection at one level does not guarantee that the grout will not travel to other levels, at least the zones of greatest grout-take can be determined and more attention given to them. An important feature in grouting control is measurement of quantities and pressures. The sophisticated instrumentation used in grouting at Portage Mountain dam is described by Benko[6].

Where there is a large flow of water underground, it may sometimes prove impossible to grout with cement or clay. Under these conditions, bitumen grouting has been successful. It has probably been used more by the T.V.A. and its predecessors than anyone else. They have a number of dams on cavernous limestone and several have been bitumen grouted. Hot bitumen injections are made through heated pipes. Although the outer skin of the injected material sets where it comes in contact with cooler rock or water, the interior of the injected material remains warm and plastic, permitting considerable penetration through large cavities.

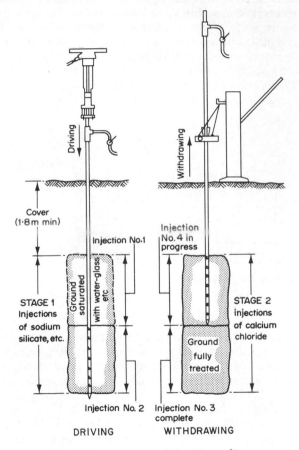

Fig. 4.2. Joosten process (after Glossop[1])

As well as their use under dams, bitumen injections are sometimes made in tunnels. Van Asbeck[7] describes an example from Marseilles where an average of 4 kg/m² was injected at 180°C through 40 mm diameter holes at metre spacings. Maximum injection pressure was 6 kg/cm²; injection times ranged from 4 to 50 min. By a curious inversion of the usual order, cement was injected into large cavities to save bitumen. For penetrating finer voids, e.g. in fine sands, cold bitumen emulsions with a suitable coagulant have been used.

Recent developments in down-hole grouting include Halliburton's Groutjet and Groutbullet. In the former, a shaped charge, electrically detonated, pierces the casing and formation leaving a passage for the injection of grout, whilst in the latter, a bullet, fired horizontally into the formation, performs the same function.

Control of pressure during grouting is of the utmost importance. Too high pressures can do more harm than good in rock grouting. It has been shown more than once (e.g. by Little, *et al.*[8]) that the use of high pressure has actually increased the permeability of the ground by cracking and breaking it up. In rock, the fissures so formed are frequently too fine to accept cement grout and can then be sealed, if at all, only with expensive chemical grouts.

This principle of breaking-up the ground by high pressure is well known and widely used in the oil industry where injections of water under pressure are used to increase the yield of oil wells. The principle is also the basis of much alluvial grouting. Cambefort[9] refers to the process as forming 'claquages' or 'sword cuts' and says that the fissures may extend as much as 10 m, sometimes more, from the injection point. From a study of rupture in gelatin models, it has been concluded that the plane of rupture is perpendicular to the minor principal stress. The ground is deliberately broken up along lines of weakness and a three-dimensional network of grout-filled fissures created which renders the ground more or less impermeable. For this reason an appreciable heave must always accompany such alluvial grouting, unlike rock grouting where it is necessary to limit injection pressures to avoid damaging the rock. It should be remembered that the column of grout in the grout hole is liquid and its pressure should be included in the calculation of pressure at the point of injection. Pressure gauges should be near the entry of the grout pipe into the hole so that the hydraulic losses from the pump to the point of injection are not recorded on the gauge, otherwise there may be an unnecessary restriction on the injection pressures.

Jet grouting in sands is a technique which does not seem to have been widely applied. A horizontal water jet from the bottom of the grouting tube is used to sink the injection pipe to the required depth. Cement in suspension is injected as the pipe is withdrawn. The cement suspension mixes with the sand, forming a column of mortar. By suitably arranging the injections, Nicholson[10] has described how a barrier of injected columns can be formed.

## Grout curtains

A grout curtain is frequently used in water-stopping operations. The ideal is to form a continuous, impermeable diaphragm through rock or ground by filling all fissures and voids with grout[11]. A moment's consideration will show that the complete success of such an operation is impossible; there is bound to be water or air trapped in some fissures that will, in consequence, remain ungrouted and form zones of higher permeability. In his Rankine Lecture in 1961, Casagrande[12] spoke out forthrightly against grout curtains saying, "an objective review of all available observations cannot but lead to the conclusion that a single line grout curtain constructed before the filling of a reservoir is frequently inadequate. In a few cases, extensive additional grouting with the reservoir in operation, thus permitting continuous evaluation of the effect of new grout holes, has eventually been successful". It must be remembered that Casagrande was referring to USA practice in attempting to reduce uplift under dams. Casagrande's views were challenged by Mayer[13] who gave examples of successful grouting applications.

Nevertheless, the grout curtain idea remains popular and is frequently used in attempts to reduce water losses and flows to acceptable proportions. Beneath dams, in particular, two or three rows of grout holes may be used to form the grout curtain; sometimes, holes in different rows are staggered.

In a study of piezometer readings for Las Pirquitas dam in Argentina, Bolognesi, *et al.*[14] concluded that the single line of grouting used there was completely ineffective. However, a single row of grout holes may sometimes be sufficient. At Camarasa dam, Spain, Fergusson and Lancaster-Jones[15] describe how a leakage of 11 m³/s (220 Mgd) was reduced to 2·5 m³/s (50 Mgd) by a single-row grouting operation in 1926–1931. Although acceptable to the owners, permitting full-power generation, a leakage of 2·5 m³/s (50 Mgd) might still be considered excessive by some engineers.

## Grouts and grout mixes*

The simplest grout mix is cement and water. It is customary when grouting rock to start off with a thin mix, say 10 of water to one of cement (or even 20 of water to one of cement), to penetrate as far as possible. When it becomes necessary to fill larger voids, thicker mixtures are used. When grout acceptances become very large, fillers, of which sand is the most popular, are used to economise cement. However, care should be taken that the finer fissures are sufficiently grouted before thickening up the mix. Once the coarser voids have been filled, it may be impossible, without using undesirably high pressures, to get grout again into the fine fissures, which if insufficiently grouted can still form a serious source of leakage.

Some engineers believe that cement and water alone cannot be an efficient grout. It is claimed that subsequent examination of voids grouted with cement and water shows only the bottom part of the void to be filled with grout, the cement presumably having settled out of suspension before hardening. Sherard[16] recommends the use of about 3% of bentonite in the grout to keep the cement in suspension.

Additions to cement grouts may be inert fillers like sand or rock dust, or they may profoundly affect the final properties of the grout. Pulverised fuel ash (PFA) has important pozzolanic properties and may be used with Portland cement to resist attack of acid waters. For the contact grouting between the rock and the concrete lining of the Manshead tunnel near Halifax, Yorkshire, O'Brien[17] says that a grout was used consisting of 300 parts of water, 350 parts of PFA, 25 parts of Portland cement and 5 parts of deflocculant.

A large group of grouts has been developed which contain cement and clay, sometimes with a small quantity of some other additive such as aluminium powder or sodium silicate. A grout used for the very coarse alluvium at Mangla was 100 of water, 52 of local clay and 17 of cement; this had a Marsh cone viscosity of 40 seconds and a 7-day compression strength of 11 kN/m². Another, stronger grout for the upper part of the alluvium, designed to resist scour which was expected to be considerable, was 100 of water, 47 of local clay and 19 of cement. The Marsh cone viscosity was 35 seconds and the 7-day strength 17·3 kN/m². Sleeve grout requires to be much stronger and more brittle. The Mangla sleeve grout was 1 of cement to 1·5 of clay and 0·25 of bentonite; water was

---

* All quantities are given in terms of weight.

added to give a Marsh cone viscosity of 60 seconds; the compression strength at 28 days was $1\cdot5$–$2\cdot0$ $MN/m^2$.

Clays can be used as grouts with a deflocculant such as monosodium phosphate and a hardener like sodium silicate. At Mangla, to inject the sand lenses within the alluvium, Skempton and Cattin[18] say a mix of 100 water, $1\cdot85$ of phosphate, 42 of clay and 42 of silicate was used.

For filling large voids a fly ash mix has been used (*see* 'Balderhead', page 63).

A large group of proprietary grouts, although expensive and with other disadvantages (some are extremely poisonous or corrosive before reacting) nevertheless have such special properties that their disadvantages are outweighed in particular applications. The exact constitution of these proprietary grouts is not always fully disclosed and the following account is necessarily oversimplified.

Lignosulphite is a waste product of the paper industry; mixed with sodium dichromate, it forms an impermeable gel. This is the basis of several proprietary grouts such as TDM and Terranier. The setting time depends on the concentration and the strength depends on the proportions of the two chemicals.

Another group of chemical grouts is based on the polymerisation (i.e. the formation of long chains of identical molecules) of vinyls. *AM9* belongs to this group. The polymerisation of acrylamide is assisted by the addition of two catalysts, dimethylaminopropionitrile (DMAPN) and ammonium persulphate, Depending on the amount of catalyst, Fern[19] says that the reaction time can be controlled between 6 s and 20 min.

Typical of the one-shot injection based on the silicate reaction is the Monosol process of Gebhardt and Koenig. Sodium silicate is mixed with sodium aluminate and sodium hydroxide. By varying the dilutions, the gel setting time can be altered from 10 min to 1 h. A variant of the method, the Monodur process, using an organic acid reagent, produces a harder acetate gel of up to 80 $kg/cm^2$. A French variant is known as Carongel.

Other types of grout may be of the polyphenolic/formaldehyde type. Resin grouting at the Blackwall tunnel used a patented process based on a resorcinol/formaldehyde reaction. The grout is characterised by good penetration and high strength. At Blackwall, treated sand had a compression strength exceeding 410 $MN/m^2$.

## Limitations and failures of grouting

Like all other civil-engineering operations, grouting has its limitations and sometimes its failures as well. The most obvious limitation is the inability to inject the grout into the ground. Injected particles will enter fissures or void spaces only when the fissure dimensions are appreciably larger than the particle sizes.

The so called 'effective' size of a material is the particle size of the finest 10%; in other words, 90% of the sample is coarser than this size. This does not tell us anything about the maximum size which could be, and sometimes is, many hundreds of times larger than the effective size, but it has been found from experience that suspension grouts will not enter spaces in soils whose effective size is much less than ten times the effective size of the grout particles. According to Terzaghi[20], ordinary coarse ground Portland cement, for example, will not penetrate fine sand, nor will cement grout enter a fissure smaller than about $0\cdot1$ mm.

Figure 4.3 shows the result of trying to inject cement into a fine-to-medium sand at Hayle in Cornwall.

In terms of permeability, clay–cement mixes will not enter soils having a permeability less than about $10^{-3}$ cm/s; deflocculated clay will penetrate soils with a permeability down to $10^{-5}$ cm/s. For permeabilities below this, silicates or

Fig. 4.3. Hayle cement injection (courtesy Glossop and Skempton[21])

*TDM* must be used and, for the finest grained soils, resins or one of the proprietary grouts like *AM9* (Fig. 4.4).

By using the claquage technique greater penetrations can be achieved, but this method has its limitations where heave cannot be permitted.

Failures of completed grouting work are not unknown. Upland waters with low pHs from peat-derived organic acids, attack cement and in course of time may leach it out. It is known that some types of silicate grout are also susceptible to leaching. A series of tests by Cambefort and Caron[22] established that silicate–aluminate and silicate–phosphate grouts are most resistant, and this is confirmed by experience.

Whilst experience of cement grouts now extends over almost a century, the newer chemical grouts and the alluvial-type grouts are perhaps too recent for any confident pronouncements to be made about their durability, but indications so

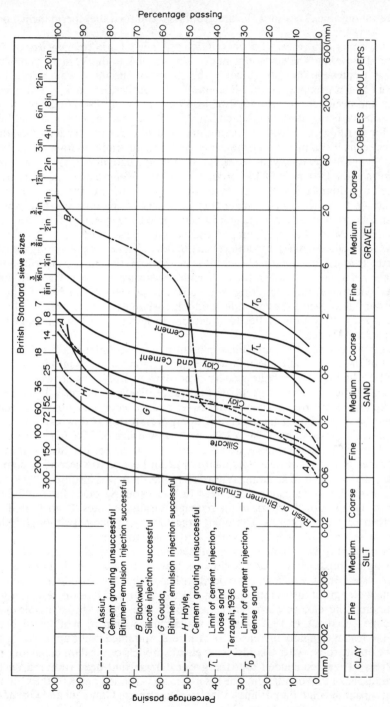

Fig. 4.4. Limits of injection processes (after Glossop and Skempton,[21] and Soletanche)

far are favourable. Two-shot silicate grouts have shown their permanence over about 40 years.

Unknown or unforeseen chemical effects may affect the permanence or performance of grouting. The development of a serious leak in the 39 m high embankment at Fontenelle dam, threatening the safety of the dam, was ascribed by Bellport[23] to a grouting failure. Because of the broken bedrock, grout acceptances had been very large, a total of 4 049 m³ (about 1 600 t) of grout on two lines of holes being used. On September 3rd 1965, after the reservoir had been filled for the first time (with interruptions by a number of incidents including smaller seepages) a major seepage developed near the right abutment adjoining the spillway. By the following morning, the seepage had increased to 600 litre/s (0·6 m³/s and 8 000 m³ of fill had eroded from the downstream slope of the dam. Rockfill was dumped into the hole in the dam and lowering of the reservoir commenced. In the afternoon of September 6th, part of the dam crest collapsed, exposing bedrock in a 10 m deep hole; water could be seen issuing from cracks in the bedrock. More rock was dumped and the dam was saved.

It was concluded that the grouting was not fully effective in preventing the flow of water through the abutment and into the dam. Hydrated sodium carbonate ('trona') was known to exist in the rock and it was surmised that this might have reacted with the grout, interfering with its setting process. It had been found by Bannister[24] that even 2·5% of added sodium carbonate in the form of soda ash reduced the setting time of Portland cement to less than 10 mins, while 10% produced a flash set.

Other failures may be from a misapplication of the technique rather than from failure of the grout itself; the following example supports Casagrande's views. The 45 m high Isola concrete gravity/arch dam in Italy was provided with a classical single-line cement-grout curtain, acceptance in primary holes being 61·7 kg of cement per metre of grout hole, and in secondary holes, 38 kg/m. During the first filling of the reservoir, uplift pressures just downstream of the grout curtain varied from 35% to 75% with an average of 55% of the reservoir head. Further cement grouting was therefore put in hand. Because of the low acceptance of 23 kg of cement per metre of grout hole on this second attempt, it was decided to try resin grouting as it was felt that there was insufficient evidence of the durability of silicate grouts. This further grouting made little difference either to the uplift pressures or to the seepage. Drainage holes, 10 to 15 m deep, were then drilled every 3 m. The uplift pressures were halved, although Gilg[25] says that seepage loss was approximately doubled to 70 litre/s.

Grouting may be damaged by a subsequent mechanical failure, as in the following example. Bissina is a hollow buttress dam, 84 m high, in the upper Chiese valley, Italy, which was provided with a double row curtain injected with cement/water grout mixes ranging from 4 : 1 to 1 : 1. In 1957, as the reservoir was impounding, the leakage was so small (approx. 1 litre/s) as to be incapable of accurate measurement. In 1958 when the water came within 18 m of the top of the dam, the leakage rapidly increased to 21 litre/s, and fine cracks appeared at the surface on the rock. After a study using elastic models of the dam behaviour under stress, it was concluded that the grout curtain had been ruptured by the deformations of the foundation. The reservoir was emptied and a further 130 t of cement grout injected into drillholes inclined upstream. Candiani and Govazzi[26] say this reduced the leakage to 2 litre/s.

The 34 m high Hales Bar dam on the Tennessee river was constructed in 1904.

In 1913, to reduce leakage, several thousand tons of cement were injected into its cavernous limestone foundations; in spite of this, heavy leakages continued and attempts to stop them with rags, old carpets, burlap and wire-reinforced cinder-concrete were unsuccessful. The presence of cavities up to 1 m deep was confirmed. In 1920, according to Christians[27], 2 000 t of bitumen were injected through pipes that were heated electrically with 6 kW/30 m of pipe, at pressures up to 14 MN/m$^2$. This was partly successful, but by 1941 the leakage had increased to 49 m$^3$/s. In 1963, according to Enry[28], the TVA finally abandoned the dam. In view of the record of successful performance of bitumen grouting at so many of the other dams in the area, it seems probable that the failure was due to further erosion of the bedrock rather than failure of the grouting.

## Testing

Testing the effectiveness of grouting for water stopping is best done by trying to circulate water within the grouted zone. It is sometimes overlooked that a control test should be performed by testing *before* grouting. Such a test may even show that grouting is unnecessary.

Water tests are usually done by pumping-in or pumping-out tests. When a pumping-in or pumping-out test is done at constant head, it is known as a *Lefranc* test. For a discharge $Q$ at an excess head $h$, the permeability is given by:

$$Q = Ckh$$

where $C$ is a coefficient depending on the form of the cavity in the ground. For example, for a spherical cavity of radius $r$:

$$C = 4\pi r$$

According to Cambefort[29] the form of cavity has little influence on the calculation of permeability. Pumping-in tests have the advantage that high pressures can be used simulating the head that will be applied across a grout curtain by the impoundment of a high dam. They have the disadvantage that the injected water may pick up particles from the sides of the hole or from fissures, even if it is initially clear, and such particles tend to clog up the injected ground by colmation, reducing its permeability. Pumping-out tests may cause some piping if too severe a reduction in head is used, but sensitive devices are now available for measurement, so that a reduction of a few centimetres is sometimes sufficient.

Lugeon[30] devised an empirical pumping-in test which has since borne his name. He developed the test in the light of his experience with concrete dams in the Swiss Alps in the 1920s. In descending stages of 5 m, he inserted a packer and applied water under a pressure of 10 kgf/cm$^2$ (approx. 1 MN/m$^2$) for 10 min; the drillhole was of unspecified diameter (but Lugeon probably intended that about 5 cm diameter should be used). The loss of water is expressed in litres per minute over a length of 1 m, called (incorrectly) by Lugeon the 'coefficient of porosity'. A pressure of 10 kgf/cm$^2$ (approx. 1 MN/m$^2$) is usually considered much too high to be used nowadays and it is customary to extrapolate from a test at a lower pressure. According to Lugeon, a loss of less than 1 litre/m min (unit Lugeon) could be tolerated and the rock did not require grouting. One Lugeon unit is frequently taken as equivalent to a permeability of $1 \times 10^{-5}$ cm/s. For dams less than 30 m high, Lugeon was prepared to accept water losses up to 3 litre/m min, although he thought the 1 litre figure always preferable.

## Other methods of exclusion

In the introduction to this chapter, other methods of exclusion were listed. Of these, the slurry-trench technique is probably the one which is evolving most rapidly.

If a trench is dug through a cohesionless soil like sand and gravel, the sides of the trench will begin to collapse once ground water is met. However, if a small addition of suitable clay is made to the water in the trench, this forms an impermeable cake on the exposed surface of the soil and the pressure of the clay slurry in the trench is sufficient to support its walls. Slurry losses roughly equal to the excavated volume are to be expected, so that the total volume of slurry which has to be supplied is about twice the excavated volume.

The idea of slurry (or 'mud') to support the sides of an excavation was probably first used in the oil industry to support the walls of deep boreholes sunk without casing. From this came the use of slurry in civil engineering construction to support uncased investigation drillholes, and then holes drilled for piles, from which evolved the slurry trench. The slurry-trench method was used by Kramer[31] in the USA in 1945 for forming trenches for cut-offs in flood levees along river banks. At first the trenches were backfilled with pulverised clay, but later it was found that sand and gravel could be used, because the slurry in the trench became incorporated in the sand and gravel as it was backfilled and converted it into an impermeable membrane. The next development was to tremie concrete into the trench, displacing the slurry and so forming a strong, relatively rigid, non-erodible membrane when the concrete set. Additions of bentonite to the concrete mix have been made to produce so-called 'plastic' concrete, which will undergo strains of several per cent without cracking.

A recent development is to incorporate cement with a retarding agent in the slurry itself to form a self-setting mix. When the excavation is completed the slurry sets and forms an impermeable membrane or grout-wall. At Gambsheim on the lower part of the Rhine near Strasbourg, France, the alluvial gravels were so permeable ($10^{-2}$ cm/s) that grouting would have been too expensive. Accordingly, to form the partial cut-off for the construction of a low-head hydro-electric station, the grout-wall system was used. The wall was 0·5 m wide and 29 m deep; the area of excavation was 76 m by 88 m. Two kelly rigs were used for the excavation, into which was continuously pumped a slurry containing 130 kg of blast-furnace cement, 46 kg of cement and 1–2 kg of lignosulphite retarder, to each cubic metre. The slurry took between 40 and 60 h for its initial set and several days to harden, its final strength being equivalent to a stiff or hard clay. Slurry losses in the permeable Rhine gravels were about twice the usual.

At suitable sites, where slurry trenches have been used for basement excavations, preformed concrete panels have been lowered into the trenches and exposed by subsequent excavation to form the permanent basement walls. Self-setting slurry is used. Precast concrete units of this type were introduced by Soletanche of Paris, but they are now used by others as well. At Boetie-Montaigne, Paris, France, ground-water level in the permeable alluvium was almost up to working level, below which the slurry trench was excavated 17·5 m into sandy clay. Precast panels, 35 cm thick and 11 m long, interlock to form the wall and are supported by grouted anchor ties at two levels (Fig. 4.5).

The thin continuous diaphragm formed by driving a steel structural shape, such as an 'I'-beam, and grouting the space so formed, is a kind of *in situ* sheet piling (it is also known as *membrane* or *screen* grouting). The method has been successfully used to cure leaky canal banks, according to Maillard and Serota[32], and for the pound at the Diddington Intake works. Figure 4.6 shows an improved method in which successive sections overlap.

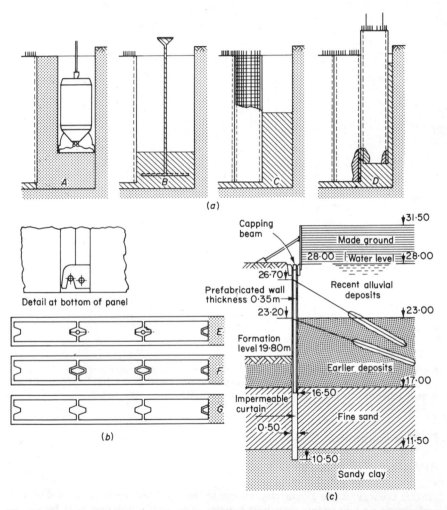

Fig. 4.5. Precast wall in slurry trench. (*a*) Excavating and placing; *A* excavating for a wall section using bentonite mud and the S.I.F. self-guiding grab, *B* introducing the grout through a spreader, *C* first panel in the sealing grout and *D* lowering the next panel. (*b*) Joint details—three examples of watertight joint between sections; *E* with a waterstop joint, *F* with a reinforced concrete key and *G* with sealing grout alone. (*c*) Boetie-Montaigne site: the sides of the excavation are retained by a Prefasif prefabricated wall made of 11 m deep sections, 2 m wide and 0·35 m thick, secured by two rows of S.I.F.–*TM* type anchors of 30 000–65 000 kg; the watertight wall is continued by an impermeable screen into the sandy clay (after S.I.F.–Bachy)

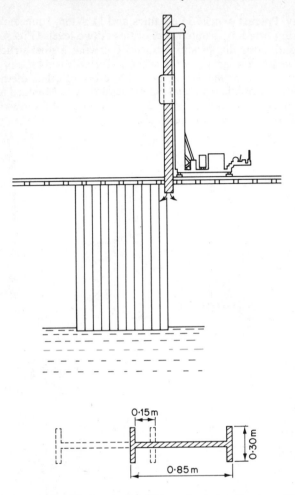

Fig. 4.6. Membrane grouting. The length of the 'I'-beam has to be at least equal to the depth of the cut-off to be constructed, this depth being generally determined by the level of the impervious substratum (after Soletanche)

## Further examples

### BRANCEPETH COLLIERY

At this colliery, a pre-glacial depression in the coal measures reduced the rock cover over an adit to less than half a metre. The depression had been backfilled with glacial silty clay so that the presence of the weak roof was unsuspected. After some years, a hole formed in the adit roof and soft silty clay of toothpaste consistency exuded into the tunnel (Fig. 4.7). Attempts at removal of the silty clay merely increased the quantity in the adit. Harding[33] describes an inspection on the surface, 36 m above which showed fir trees inclined from the vertical; a bar pushed into the ground disappeared. Shortly afterwards, a swallow-hole

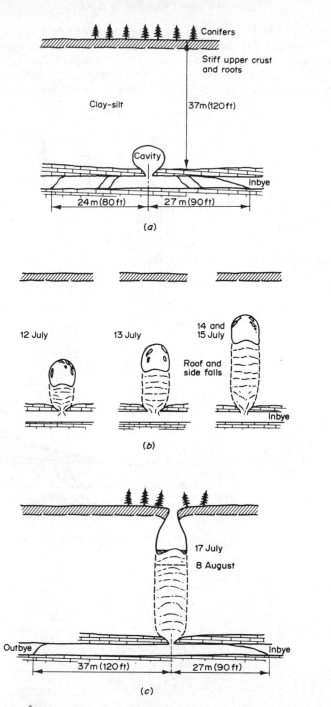

Fig. 4.7. Formation of cavity at Brancepeth colliery. (*a*) 11th July, 1949—collapse of roof and formation of cavity, (*b*) 12th–15th July—three stages of travel of cavity to surface and (*c*) 17th July—cavity exposed (after Harding[33])

appeared (Fig. 4.8). Material was excavated from the adit and $\frac{3}{4}$ in (approx. 20 mm) gravel tipped into the swallow-hole at the surface. Excavation continued and the swallow-hole surface was made up with more gravel until gravel began to appear in the adit. The gravel was then grouted through 50 mm pipes previously installed in the swallow-hole (Fig. 4.9); 100 t of cement were used and the run into the adit successfully checked.

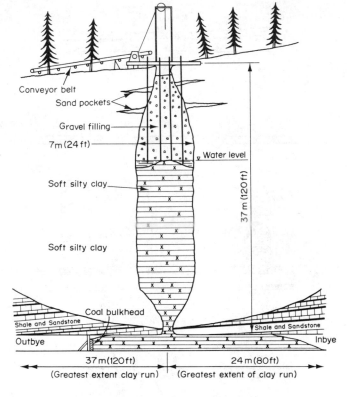

Conveyor belt
Sand pockets
Gravel filling
7 m (24 ft)
Water level
Soft silty clay
37 m (120 ft)
Soft silty clay
Coal bulkhead
Shale and Sandstone
Shale and Sandstone
Outbye
Inbye
37 m (120 ft)
24 m (80 ft)
(Greatest extent clay run)
(Greatest extent of clay run)

COMMENCEMENT OF FILLING

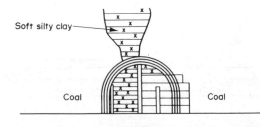

Soft silty clay
Coal
Coal

SECTION THROUGH BULKHEAD

Fig. 4.8. Silt-run into haulage way at Brancepeth colliery (after Harding[33])

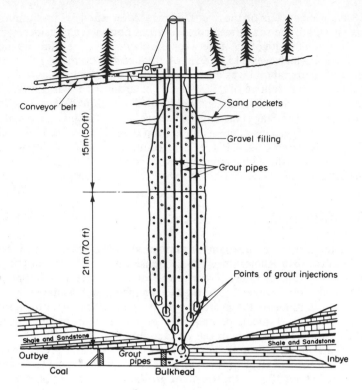

COMPLETION OF FILLING

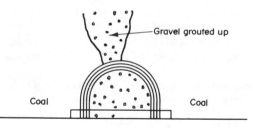

SECTION THROUGH BULKHEAD

Fig. 4.9. Completion of filling and section through bulkhead at Brancepeth colliery (after Harding[33])

## SERRE PONÇON DAM

Although the *tube-à-manchette* was invented at Bou Hanifia in 1933 and successful alluvial grouting was done for a cofferdam at Genissiat on the river Rhône in 1939 (this grouting surviving intact until after World War II), the first large-scale application of *tube-à-manchette* alluvial grouting was at the 100 m high Serre Ponçon dam on the river Durance. After extensive preliminary tests at two areas within the site, fifteen rows of grout holes were considered necessary across a contact width of 35 m, between the clay core of the dam and the foundation alluvium which was 115 m deep. A total of 49 700 m³ of grout containing 24 800 t of solid material was injected at pressures not exceeding $1 \cdot 5$ MN/m² to treat a theoretical volume of 97 000 m³. The grout used was a mixture of high liquid limit clay and a slag cement with a small addition of caustic soda (1–3%) as a setting reagent. Slag cement was used because of the aggressive nature of the ground water. These installations have been described by Ischy and Glossop[34] and by Chadeisson[35] (Fig. 4.10). Before grouting, the permeability was $5 \times 10^{-2}$ cm/s and it was reduced by grouting to $10^{-5}$ cm/s. The differential head across the grouted zone exceeds 120 m. The work was done between 1952 and 1958.

## RHINE GROUTING

Some of the largest applications of alluvial grouting have been in the alluvial deposits of the river Rhine. Since 1953, extensive hydro-electric works have been constructed to tap the latent power in the fall of the river, extending along the French bank from Switzerland to the German frontier. The upper stations were constructed first, inside the protection of a grouted box. At Vogelgrün, which may be taken as typical, permeability of the ground before injection was $10^{-2}$–$10^{-3}$ m/s. The bottom of the grouted box was about 40 m below normal ground-water level. Grouting was begun 8 m below water level and continued down to join the 5 m-thick grouted bottom of the box (Fig. 4.11). Ground water was lowered about 10 m to the top of the grouting and excavation done in the dry inside the box. Grouting was in two stages: firstly, clay-cement grout was injected through *tubes-à-manchette* at 3 m spacing to fill the large voids; secondly, this was followed by stabilised clay and silicate through tubes at 2 m centres. Sufficient material was left unexcavated over the grouted floor to counteract uplift pressures; 35 000 t of clay, 3 000 t of cement and nearly 3 000 t of silica gel were used to inject about 230 000 m³ of ground. Ischy and Glossop[34] say that flow into the excavation was reduced to 150 litre/s into the 16 000 m² excavation.

In later installations, slurry trenches have been used to form the vertical walls in place of grouting.

## DOKAN DAM

The 116 m high concrete arch Dokan dam across the Lesser Zab river in Iraq has one of the world's largest grout curtains. Rock at the site is mainly limestone underlain by dolomite, both of which were relatively permeable, and contained some large fissures and even caverns. In addition, the left abutment is narrow, offering a short leakage path. Grouting was from adits to reduce interference with other construction operations and to shorten the length of grout-hole drillholes, which in any case, were still a maximum of 200 m deep, amounting to the formidable total of 183 km. Grouting started with a mix of one of cement to eight of water, which was gradually thickened to 1 : 1; if no pressure could be recorded with the thicker mix, sand was added up to a maximum of 2 of sand to 1

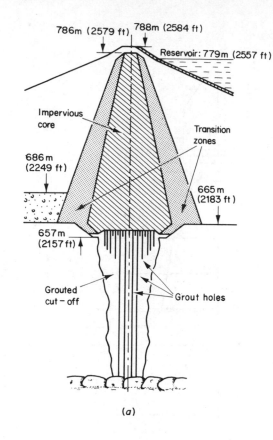

786m (2579 ft) 788m (2584 ft)

Reservoir: 779m (2557 ft)

Impervious core

Transition zones

686 m (2249 ft)

665 m (2183 ft)

657m (2157 ft)

Grouted cut–off

Grout holes

(a)

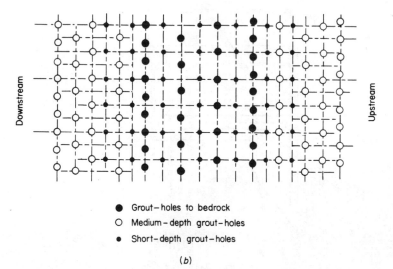

Downstream

Upstream

● Grout–holes to bedrock

○ Medium–depth grout–holes

• Short–depth grout–holes

(b)

Fig. 4.10. Serre Ponçon dam. (a) Typical cross-section and (b) distribution of grout holes in the central part of the grouted cut-off (after Soletanche)

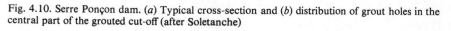

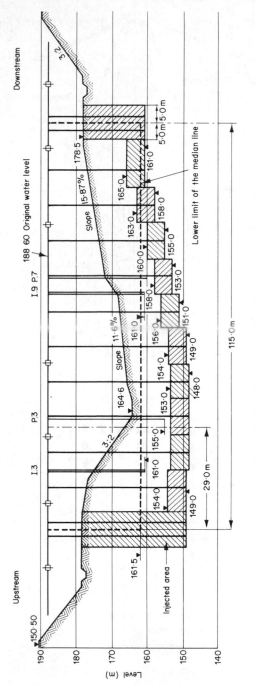

Fig. 4.11. Grouting at Vogelgrün (after Ischy and Glossop[34])

of cement. A total of 77 766 t of dry materials was used, an amount which, although large, has certainly been exceeded; for example, at the Camarasa dam, Spain, in 1926–1931 where 186 000 t of grouting materials were consumed, and more recently at Logan Martin dam, Alabama, USA, where Grant and Winefordner[36] say 84 000 m³ of solid material were injected. The cost of the grout curtain at Dokan was £2 400 000, according to Lancaster-Jones and Gillot[37], to which must be added £450 000 for the tunnels and left-abutment strengthening. The work was done between October 1955 and July 1957.

In 1960, serious leakage developed, amounting to 6 m³/s, and further grouting was done. To seal the worst leaks, a mix of 50 kg of bentonite, 30 litre of diesel oil and 0·5 kg of cotton flock, was used. This technique was proposed to the consulting engineers by the mud engineers of the Iraq Petroleum Co. The bentonite, in the presence of the diesel oil, swelled and set, forming with the flock an impermeable plug in the larger fissures. This was followed by sand/cement grouting with a calcium chloride additive. According to Perrot and Lancaster-Jones[38], and Clark[39], the addition grouting consumed 10 700 t of cement, 8 000 t of sand and 149 t of other products.

## AUREOLE GROUTING

*Aureole* or *umbrella* grouting is a useful technique when driving tunnels through unstable water-bearing ground. The technique entails drilling and grouting ahead of the tunnel in a cone embracing (but larger than) the tunnel[40].

The Roselend dam is an impressive, 150 m high arch and buttress dam in the French Alps of Upper Savoy. The more impressive technical feat is the way in which the tunnel negotiates the 'accident' of the Grande Combe, a zone between the crystalline rocks on either side of the rock affected by an old fault movement and under high water pressure. The zone consisted of 30 m of broken black Carboniferous schist, followed by 55 m of crushed Triassic quartzite and dolomite. It proved impossible to drive the pilot tunnel through the affected zone; even drillings were difficult, but they revealed the 85 m of broken and crushed rock and water pressures from 1·4–1·9 MN/m² (Fig. 4.12).

The first stage in aureole grouting was to inject sodium silicate with sodium bicarbonate as a reagent. The mixes used per cubic metre of gel were 170–210 litre of sodium silicate of s.g. 1·32–1·345 (35–37° Baumé), 23–25 kg of sodium bicarbonate and 860–830 litre of water, with a setting time of 30 min. The amounts for the second stage were 145 litre of sodium silicate, 25 kg of sodium bicarbonate and 880 litre of water, with a setting time of 15 min.

As the 6 m diameter tunnel approached the crushed Triassic rock in February, 1957, the Carboniferous schist in which it was being driven began to cave at about 25 m from the junction with the crushed quartzite. A concrete stop-end was built and cement was injected into the schist; holes were drilled 46 m ahead into the crushed Triassic quartzite and dolomite. The Trias was injected with silicate followed by cement or clay-cement to break-up and further compact the material. Grouting was continued until no more could be injected at a maximum pressure of 15 MN/m². This work took 4½ months. A timbered top adit was then driven (Fig. 4.13) which was enlarged to form the upper half of the tunnel, and was well supported with steel ribs (Fig. 4.14). The lower half of the tunnel was then excavated (Fig. 4.15), blasting being necessary in the schist, and it was

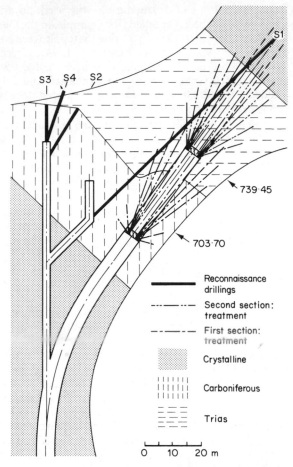

S1

S3  S4  S2

739·45

703·70

Reconnaissance
drillings

Second section:
treatment

First section:
treatment

Crystalline

Carboniferous

Trias

0    10    20 m

Fig. 4.12. Roselend pilot tunnels (after S.I.F.–Bachy)

similarly supported. Before advancing to the next stage, the reinforced concrete
lining was cast. The second stage, wholly through the crushed Trias, was a
repetition of the first stage with improvements as a result of experience. It was
found possible to use the more dilute silicate with fewer grout holes and use of
three times the quantity of clay, but it was found advisable to increase the
thickness of treatment in the tunnel roof. 4 700 m³ of silicate were injected along
with 1 775 t of cement and 130 t of clay, amounting to 25 t of dry materials injected per metre of tunnel. Grouting occupied 8 months with another 3 months to
construct the concrete stop-ends; tunnelling and lining took $5\frac{1}{2}$ months. The
work was completed by S.I.F. in 1958[41].

A similar treatment was used in 1965 for the crossing by the Mont Cenis
tunnel of a similar geological feature. The concrete stop-end was omitted,
carefully injected rock being used as a stop-end instead, the operation being
assisted by a careful pre-drainage operation involving 33 borings yielding 485
litre/s. A volume of 1 396 m³ of silicate gel and 363 t of clay and cement were
injected.

Fig. 4.13. Adit of Roselend pilot tunnels (courtesy S.I.F.–Bachy)

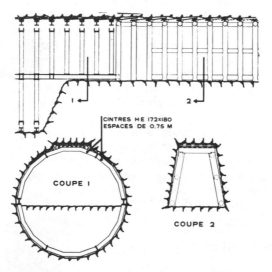

CINTRES H E 172x180
ESPACÉS DE 0.75 M

COUPE 1

COUPE 2

Fig. 4.14. Supports of Roselend pilot tunnels (courtesy S.I.F.–Bachy). *Coupe*—Cross-section, *Cintres HE*—steel arches and *Espacés de*—centres

Fig. 4.15. Main Roselend Tunnel (courtesy S.I.F.–Bachy)

## SHEK PIK DAM

At Shek Pik, Hong Kong, although the alluvium is only 12 m deep it is highly permeable. The presence of large boulders makes sheet piling out of the question and the advisability of a rigid cut-off was made doubtful by the variable but compressible nature of the decomposed rock foundations.

Following the successful alluvial grouting at Serre Ponçon it was decided to adopt the same system for the 55 m high Shek Pik embankment dam. However, because the alluvium had been partially decomposed by tropical weathering and there was some doubt about the efficacy of alluvial grouting under such conditions, it was decided to enclose the grouting within two rows, 6 m apart, of tangential bored piles, 560 mm diameter, which would, in themselves, form a partial cut-off. A 'test box' of piles and grouted alluvium was constructed; tests showed it to be very satisfactory, permeability after grouting being reduced to between 1 to $18 \times 10^{-5}$ cm/s compared with a permeability before treatment of about $10^{-1}$ cm/s. Local clay mixed with cement was used for the injections.

Carlyle[42] says that subsequent behaviour of the dam confirmed the correctness of the choice for the cut-off. Differential settlements, resulting from the varying compressibility of the foundations, caused extensive cracking of the clay core but there was no sign of distress from the cut-off.

The work was done from 1957 to 1963.

## CHAIN VALLEY COLLIERY

Inflows totalling 45 500 litre/h through badly fissured conglomerate threatened two new drifts in this New South Wales colliery. It was decided to use *AM9* chemical grouting to reduce the flow to acceptable amounts. Large fissures in the rock were caulked with wedges and sealed with cement. Relief holes were drilled to divert water flows and grout was injected. This had the effect of diverting water flow elsewhere and further relief holes became necessary. Using low pressures, the flows were then chased from areas of weak, badly broken rock to points where packers could be anchored in drill-holes and high pressures applied until the inflows were stopped. Gel times were adjusted so that the grout gelled as it emerged from the leak. In some places, after pumping *AM9* for 2 min to form a deep barrier, bentonite and cement were then added to the *AM9*.

The grouting, which was done in 1962, reduced the inflow in one particularly bad zone from a maximum of 18 200 litre/h to 3 400 litre/h (Janus[43]).

## AUBER METRO STATION

This station on the Réseau Express Régional (R.E.R.) runs beneath the Rue Auber with its tunnel crown about 18 m below street level and adjoins the Paris Opéra, a national monument. The station is 228 m long, 20 m high and 40 m wide. It lies almost entirely below the water table in Tertiary Lutetian marls, capped by old Seine alluvium and underlain by massive limestone. As an additional complication, Line No. 3 of the Paris Metro runs in the Seine alluvium above the station tunnel. In order to excavate the very large void for the station under these difficult conditions, Glossop[44] says extensive use was made of grouting for water stopping. This work is also reported by Janin and le Sciellour[45].

In the first stage, an adit was driven at the level of the tunnel crown; fortunately, only half the adit was below the water level. Clay-cement grouting from radial borings from this adit treated the ground beside and below the adit (Fig. 4.16). At

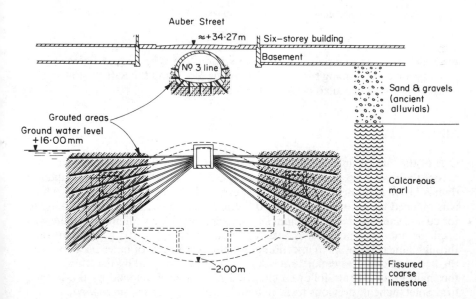

Fig. 4.16. Auber Station, first-phase treatment (after Janin and le Sciellour[45])

the same time, ethyl acetate gel was injected into the alluvium outside the Line No. 3 tunnel to stabilise it. Two further adits at about the level of the springing of the station arch were then driven through the grouted ground. Ground above and below these adits and above the first adit was grouted with clay-cement to provide a complete mantle of grouted ground in which to excavate the station (Fig. 4.17). Adjoining the Opéra, fine Beauchamp sand had to be treated with

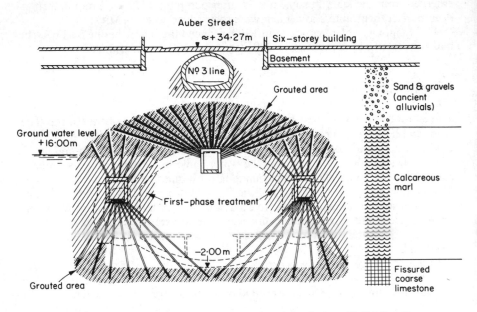

Fig. 4.17. Auber station, second-phase treatment (after Janin and le Sciellour[45])

phenolic resin. At one point outside the station, the very large Asnières sewer passed above the running tunnel of Metro Line No. 9 and the R.E.R. (Fig. 4.18). The work was executed between 1965 and 1968.

## ASWAN DAM

One of the largest and deepest alluvially grouted cut-offs is at the Aswan dam across the river Nile. The cut-off is taken to 220 m below the river bed and the dam is 110 m high. Before injection, the permeability was $2 \cdot 5 \times 10^{-2}$ cm/s which was reduced by grouting to $2 \cdot 3 \times 10^{-4}$ cm/s. Cement with local clay was used for coarse sand injections; sodium silicate hardened with sodium aluminate was used for fine sand pockets. A total dry volume of $2 \cdot 1 \times 10^{6}$ m³ was injected through nine rows of main injection holes plus eight rows of holes used to inject the fine sand only. Bowman[46] says that the method adopted by the Russians for the main grout curtain followed closely a procedure developed by the French firm Soletanche in previous tests including the use of *tubes-à-manchette*.

The work was completed in 1968.

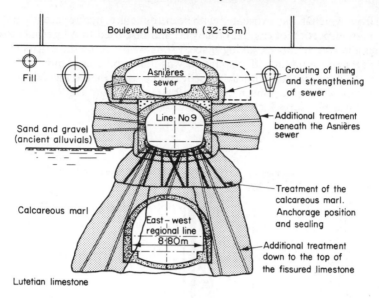

Fig. 4.18. Auber station (after S.I.F.–Bachy)

## BALDERHEAD

This 48 m high embankment dam across the headwaters of the river Tees was completed in 1964, and impounding then started. In 1967 swallow-holes developed in the upstream face and investigation disclosed extensive erosion damage in the core.

The swallow-holes were filled under gravity only, with a mix of 45 kg of water, 1 kg of bentonite, 16 kg of cement, 77 kg of fly ash and 18 g of aluminium powder. The damaged core was grouted with a mix of 45 kg of water, 5·4 kg of bentonite, 5·9 kg of cement and 20 g of aluminium powder. The amount of grout injected was limited to 0·42 m³ per sleeve. The sleeve grout was 133 kg of water, 54 kg of cement and 68·5 kg of bentonite. A total of 650 m³ of fly ash grout and 4 630 m³ of cement–bentonite was injected.

As described by Vaughan, *et al.*[47], after the grouting, an 0·6 m wide slurry trench wall, backfilled with plastic concrete, was constructed along the most damaged section of the core. Although the trench was up to 46 m deep, it landed with 99% accuracy on the 0·6 m wide top of the concrete spearhead (Fig. 4.19).

The work was done in 1968.

## LLUEST WEN

On December 23rd, 1969, a horseman taking a short cut at the head of the Little Rhondda Valley rode his horse across the crest of the Lluest Wen embankment. About three quarters of the way across, the turf gave way and the horse fell into a hole from which it was extricated with some difficulty, but apparently unhurt. A thorough inspection of the dam followed and disclosed that internal erosion of the puddle core had been taking place, probably for some time. An emergency was declared, some limited evacuation was done and a coal mine in the valley below the dam was temporarily closed. At the same time remedial works were put in hand. These have been described by Gamblin and Little[48]. Among other things, these measures included grouting.

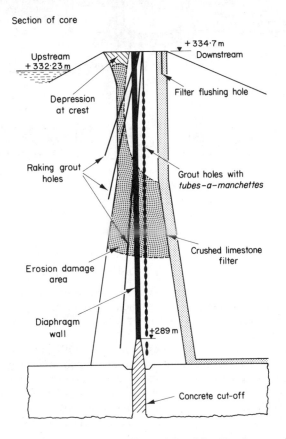

Fig. 4.19. Remedial work at Balderhead dam (after Vaughan, *et al.*[47])

The area most affected was in the vicinity of an old valve shaft, where the horse came to grief, and which was later proved to have a close connection with the erosion. Eleven holes were drilled between January 19th and 30th, nine of them on the presumed line of the puddle core of the dam, and 53 m³ of sleeve grout containing 45 t of cement and bentonite were absorbed. Considering that no pressure was used beyond the liquid pressure of the grout, this was a remarkable acceptance of grout by the supposedly impermeable membrane of the dam. The mix consisted of 50 kg of Portland cement, 2·3 kg of bentonite and 41 litre of water, making a batch volume of 0·058 m³. After the sleeve grout had set, injection grouting was started on January 21st using a mix containing either 50 or 25 kg of cement, 4·5 kg of bentonite and 54·5 litre of water, making batch volumes of 0·07 $m^3$ and 0·06 $m^3$, respectively. A small quantity of silicate was added to some batches. About 93·4 $m^3$ of additional grout was injected containing $6 \times 10^4$ kg of cement and bentonite. Subsequently, grouting was continued along the line of the dam with a weaker mix containing 15 kg of cement, 5 kg of bentonite and 50 litre of water, making a batch volume of 0·057 $m^3$. The total volume of grout injected was $1·1 \times 10^4$ $m^3$ (including 156 $m^3$ of sleeve grout) containing 300 t of cement and 83 t of bentonite.

The grouting was considered to be satisfactory as a first-aid measure, but check holes made after grouting disclosed so many imperfections in the dam puddle core that it was decided to construct a new plastic concrete cut-off in slurry trench along the entire length of the dam.

## Conclusion

With the introduction of more sophisticated grouts and injection techniques, grouting has taken great strides forward. Little[49] has compiled Table 4.1 showing the progress which has been made in forming grouted cut-offs for dams in alluvial deposits. The steady diminution, over the ten years 1957–1967, of quantity of grout injected per unit volume may be noted, as well as the reduction in the number of rows of grout holes thought necessary, especially in the core contact zone (six at Mont Genis compared with 15 at Serre Ponçon). Both these reductions are strong testimony to the growing efficiency of alluvial grouting and the confidence in it.

Although slurry trenches were first used for permanent works, their greatest use has been as temporary construction expedients.

With the introduction of large kelly rigs which are replacing the old cable-operated rigs, slurry trenches are now capable of reaching great depths and of being constructed rapidly in alluvial materials. On the Rhône, production increased from about 2 $m^2$/h in 1962–1964 at Pierre Benite where 14 rigs were needed for the 36 000 $m^2$ of trench to 8–9 $m^2$/h at Avignon in 1970, where two rigs completed 21 000 $m^2$ in three months[50]. This means a great reduction in cost, and slurry trenches have largely replaced grouting in vertical water barriers for temporary works. Slurry trenches for permanent works have also become commonplace; Little[51] has described a dam constructed at Singapore which relies on a grout-wall constructed in slurry trench for its permanent cut-off.

However, in special applications, and in hard materials, grouting remains useful. It is indispensable in tunnels, for instance, and is likely to continue in demand for permanent cut-offs beneath dams for the foreseeable future.

*Acknowledgements*

The author thanks the partners of Binnie and Partners and Mr. D. G. Gamblin, formerly Engineer and Chief Executive, Taf Fechan Water Board, for permission to use unpublished information. He also records his gratitude to the various grouting contractors who have supplied information.

**Table 4.1**  PROGRESS IN FORMING GROUTING CUT-OFFS FOR DAMS IN ALLUVIAL DEPOSITS

| Date of forming cut-off | Dam | Ht. of dam (m) | Depth of grouted alluvium (m) | Area of grouted alluvium (m²) | Core-zone contact width* (m) | No. of rows of grout-holes | General cut-off width* (m) | No. of rows of grout-holes | Theoretical volume treated (m³) | Volume grout injected (m³) | Ratio of grout volume to treated volume | Dry wt. of material injected (t) | Ratio of dry wt. to grout to treated volume (t/m³) |
|---|---|---|---|---|---|---|---|---|---|---|---|---|---|
| 1939 | Genissiat | 15 | 25 | 240 | — | — | 0·8 | 3 | — | — | — | — | — |
| 1943–46 | Cofferdam† Lac Noir | 6 | 15 | 2 475 | — | — | 10‡ | 5 | 24 750 | 392 (silica gel only) | — | 1075+ (silica gel) | — |
| 1957–58 | Serre Ponçon | 120 | 115 | 4 200 | 35 | 15 | 15 | 4 | 97 000 | 49 700 | 0·51 | 24 800 | 0·26 |
| 1957–58 | Sylvenstein | 45 | 100 | 5 200 | 25 | 7 | 12 | 2 | 60 000 | 40 200 | 0·66 | 13 000 | 0·22 |
| 1958–59 | Terzaghi (Mission) | 65 | 105¶ | 6 200 | — | — | 15 | 5 | 95 500 | 46 900 | 0·49 | 19 500 | 0·20 |
| 1960–61 | Notre Dame de Commiers | 45 | 44 | 7 200 | 10 | 5 | 8 | 2 | 90 000 | 32 400 | 0·36 | 15 800 | 0·18 |
| 1961–63 | Shek Pik | 55 | 12 | 4 200 | 20* | 4 | 6 | 2 | 25 000 | — | — | 1 900 | 0·07‖ |
| 1964–66 | Backwater | 45 | 45 | — | 12* | 5 | 9 | 3 | 104 000 | 18 700 | 0·18 | — | — |
| 1967 | Mont Cenis | 120 | 55 | 8 000 | 18* | 6 | — | — | 54 000 | 7 600 | 0·14 | 2 750 | 0·05 |

* Approximate values.
† Grouting survived until after World War II.
‡ Indicated average.
¶ Top of grouted cut-off 20 m below ground level.
‖ Within two rows of bored piles.

REFERENCES

1. Glossop, R., 'The Invention and Development of Injection Processes', *Geotechnique,* **10** No. 3, 91; **11** No. 4, 255 (1960)
2. Brown, R. H., 'The Use of Cement Grout at the Delta Barrage in Egypt', *Proc. I.C.E.,* **158,** 1 (1904)
3. Lauchli, E., 'Building the Mathis Dams', *Engineering News,* **74,** 529 (1915)
4. Vinson and Mitchell, 'Polyurethane Foamed Plastics in Soil Grouting', *Proc. A.S.C.E.,* **98** No. SM6, June (1972)
5. Soletanche, Personal communication (1974)
6. Benko, K. F., 'Instrumentation in Rock Grouting for Portage Mountain Dam', *Water Power,* 407, Oct. (1966)
7. van Asbeck, *Bitumen in Hydraulic Engineering,* Elsevier, Amsterdam (1964)
8. Little, Stewart and Fookes, 'Bedrock Grouting Tests at Mangla Dam', Symposium on Grouts and Drilling Muds, Butterworths, London, 91 (1963)
9. Cambefort, H., *Injection des Sols,* Vol. I: *Principes et Méthodes,* Eyrolles, Paris (1964)
10. Nicholson, A. J., 'Discussion on Session 2', Symposium on Grouts and Drilling Muds, Butterworths, London, 108 (1963)
11. 'Grout Curtain Seals Excavation', *Engineering News-Record,* **67,** Nov. 28 (1968)
12. Casagrande, A., 'Control of Seepage Through Foundations and Abutments of Dams; First Rankine Lecture', *Geotechnique,* **11** No. 3, 161, Sept. (1961)
13. Mayer, A., 'Quelques Réflexions sur l'Utilisation des Injections dans les Barrages', *Geotechnique,* **11** No. 4, 328, Dec. (1961)
14. Bolognesi, *et al.,* 'Behaviour of Single Line Grout Curtain', Sixth Int. Conf. on Soil Mechanics and Foundation Engineering, Montreal, **2,** 456 (1965)
15. Fergusson and Lancaster-Jones, 'Testing the Efficiency of Grouting Operations at Dam Sites', Eighth Int. Conf. on Large Dams, Edinburgh, Q28, R7, **1,** 121 (1964)
16. Sherard, J., Private communication (1972)
17. O'Brien, T. J., 'Tough Tunnel Requires Special Grouting Technique', *World Construction,* 32, Nov. (1965)
18. Skempton and Cattin, 'A Full Scale Alluvial Grouting Test at the Site of Mangla Dam', Symposium on Grouts and Drilling Muds, Butterworths, London, 131 (1963)
19. Fern, K. A., 'The Application of Polymerisation Techniques to the Solution of Grouting Problems', Symposium on Grouts and Drilling Muds, Butterworths, 146 (1963)
20. Terzaghi, K., Opening Discussion, Section M, 'Methods for Improving the Physical Properties of Soils', First Int. Conf. on Soil Mech. and Found. Eng., Harvard, **3,** 181 (1936)
21. Glossop and Skempton, 'Particle Size in Silts and Sands', *J.I.C.E.,* **25,** 81, Dec. (1945)
22. Cambefort and Caron, 'Le Délavage des Gels de Silicate de Soude', Fourth Int. Conf. on Soil Mech. and Found. Eng., London, **1,** 13 (1957)
23. Bellport, B. P., 'Bureau of Reclamation Experience in Stabilising Embankment of Fontenelle Dam', Ninth Int. Cong. on Large Dams, Istanbul, Q32, R5, **1,** 67 (1967)
24. Bannister, A., 'The Addition of Sodium Carbonate to Cement and Pulverised Fuel Ash Grouts', *The Consulting Engineer,* London, **25** No. 1, 55, Jan. (1964)
25. Gilg, B., 'Mesures Prises pour l'Amélioration de la Stabilité du Barrage D'Isola', Ninth Int. Cong. on Large Dams, Istanbul, Q32, R56, **1,** 923 (1967)
26. Candiani and Govazzi, 'Influence des Déformations de la Roche de Fondation d'un Barrage sur l'Écran d'Imperméabilisation', Eighth Int. Conf. on Large Dams, Edinburgh, Q28, R30, **1,** 571 (1964)
27. Christians, G. W., 'Asphalt Grouting Under Hales Bar Dam', *Engineering News-Record,* **96** No. 20, 798 (1926)
28. Enry, 'TVA Gives up on Hales Bar Dam', *Engineering News-Record,* **133** No. 16, 26, April 18 (1963)
29. Cambefort, H., *Forages et Sondages,* Eyrolles, Paris (1955)
30. Lugeon, M., *Barrages et Géologie,* Rouge et Cie, Lausanne (1932)

31. Kramer, H., 'Deep Cut Off Trench of Puddled Clay for Earth Dam and Levee Protection', *Engineering News-Record,* 76, June 27 (1946)

32. Maillard and Serota, 'Screen Grouting of Alluvium by the E.T.F. Process', Symposium on Grouts and Drilling Muds, Butterworths, London, 75 (1963)

33. Harding, H. J. B., 'Discussion on Bo-Peep and Arley Tunnels', *Proc. I.C.E.,* 36 No. 5, 93, March (1951)

34. Ischy, E. and Glossop, R., 'An Introduction to Alluvial Grouting', *Proc. I.C.E.,* 21, 449, March (1962)

35. Chadeisson, R. I., 'Results of Injections in Cohesionless Soils', *Consulting Engineer,* London, 425 (1963)

36. Grant and Winefordner, 'Grouting a Dam Cut Off in Cavernous Limestone', *Proc. Am. Soc. Civ. Eng.,* 92 No. CO3, Sept. (1966)

37. Lancaster-Jones and Gillot, 'The Dokan Project: The Grouted Cut Off Curtain', *Proc. I.C.E.,* 14, 193, Oct. (1959); discussion, 17, 79, Sept. (1960)

38. Perrot and Lancaster-Jones, 'Case Records of Cement Grouting', Symposium on Grouts and Drilling Muds, Butterworths, London, 80 (1963)

39. Clark, J. F. F., 'Discussion on Session 2 of Symposium on Grouts and Drilling Muds', Butterworths, London, 112 (1963)

40. Caille and Barbedette, 'Le Méthode d'Injection des Terrains à l'Avancement dans les Cas Difficiles de Percement d'Ouvrages Souterrains', Third Int. Conf. on Soil Mech. and Found. Eng., Zurich, 2, 157 (1953)

41. S.I.F., 'Aménagement de Roselend. Traversée de l'Accident de la Grande Combe', S.I.F., Paris (1961)

42. Carlyle, W. J., 'Shek Pik Dam', *Proc. I.C.E.,* 30, 557, March (1965)

43. Janus, Z. L., 'Chemical Grouting Cuts Water Flow in Colliery Drift', *Mine and Quarry Mechanisation,* Australia, 119–124 (1963)

44. Glossop, R., 'Eighth Rankine Lecture: The Rise of Geotechnology and Its Influence on Engineering Practice', *Geotechnique,* 18 No. 2, 107, June (1968)

45. Janin and le Sciellour, 'Chemical Grouting for Paris Rapid Transit Tunnels', *Proc. A.S.C.E.,* 96 No. C01, 61, June (1970)

46. Bowman, W., 'Record Grout Curtain Seals Nile's Leaky Bed', *Engineering News-Record,* 168, 22, Feb. 29 (1968)

47. Vaughan, Kluth, Leonard and Pradoura, 'Cracking and Erosion of the Rolled Clay Core of Balderhead Dam and the Remedial Works Adopted for its Repair', Tenth Int. Cong. on Large Dams, Montreal, Q36, R5, 1, 73 (1970)

48. Gamblin and Little, 'Emergency Measures at Lluest Wen Reservoir', *Water and Water Engineering,* 74 No. 889, 93, March (1970)

49. Little, A. L., 'Discussion on The Backwater Dam', *Proc. I.C.E.,* 56, 133 (1973)

50. Gemaehling and Mathian, 'Parois Moulées comme Écrans Étanches Provisoires sur les Chantiers Du Rhône', *Travaux.* Nov (1970)

51. Little, A. L., 'In situ Diaphragm Walls for Embankment Dams', Conf. Diaphragm Walls and Anchorages, I.C.E. (1974)

# Chapter 5

# Fundamental Conditions Governing the Penetration of Grouts

In the context of ground engineering the term *grouting* is used for the process of pressure injection of setting fluids into pores and cavities. The process is widely used in the construction of tunnels, shafts and dams for the purpose of either reducing percolation or increasing the mechanical stability in water-bearing soil or rock. If a useful engineering purpose is to be achieved, the sealing and strengthening actions must extend a considerable distance into the formation, and it is, therefore, general practice to inject the grout into a special array of boreholes drilled into the rock or the soil.

Current grouting methods are effective in sealing cavities and both coarse and fine fissures in rock, and in sealing pores in granular materials typical of all soils short of clays and very silty sands. However, the development of the present range and effectiveness of grouting has been a slow process. The first recorded use of grouting appears to be the work by Bérigny in 1802 on the gravels underlying the Dieppe scouring sluice. Bérigny used clay slurries and pozzolanic mortars as grouts. Later in the century these materials were replaced by hydraulic lime and by Portland cement mortars. All these grouts took the form of concentrated suspensions or slurries compounded to develop a well-defined set when in place in the ground. Such grouts were satisfactory for wide gaps and fissures and for very open gravels.

The development of methods for grouting fine rock fissures and for grouting porous soils came during the present century, and involved modified injection techniques as well as new materials of higher penetrating capacity.

The key developments in cement grouting were due to François, who found that cement particles could be transported into fine rock fissures for considerable distances before settling out, by using well-agitated dilute suspensions pumped into the formation continuously and often under high pressure. This technique is still widely used for rock grouting around shafts and tunnels and in dam foundations.

Grouting materials and techniques suited to the injection of soils have a more complex history. Chemical grouts in which reacting chemicals are injected into the ground in the form of solutions, first appeared towards the end of the 1800s. By 1910 François refers to the then current existence of grouts based on sodium silicate in combination with other reacting chemicals, and uses such materials as preliminary injections to improve the penetration of subsequently injected cement grouts. However, the development of a particular silicate grouting technique by Joosten in 1925 greatly advanced the application of grouting, particularly for the strengthening of sandy gravel formations.

The practical difficulties of controlling the rate of gelling of sodium silicate solutions led to two distinct methods of injection, generally known as *single-shot* and *two-shot* processes. In single-shot chemical grouting, the reacting materials are mixed before injection with the intention that setting is sufficiently delayed for pumping to be completed before setting commences. In early applications it was not uncommon for some gelation to occur before injection, in which case only low injection rates and limited acceptances were achieved. The Joosten process was a two-shot process: the reacting solutions were pumped in successive doses into the ground. Although precipitation commenced immediately on contact of the solutions, the reaction products could be forced about 0·5 m radially from the injection pipe, and the resulting impregnated soil quickly developed a considerable cemented strength, typified by crushing strengths of several tens of kilograms per square centimetre. The two-shot Joosten type of ground treatment is still in use for a restricted range of soil character. Single-shot grouts have a much wider application as the many different modern grouts give scope for high penetration rates, high set strength and delayed and controlled gelation.

### Penetration rate for grouts with true fluid properties

While it will be clear that grouts containing suspended particles cannot be regarded as having the normal flow properties of true fluids, those chemical grouts that are used in single-shot formulations can generally be considered as viscous forms of ground water, and therefore amenable to the type of flow-net analysis used in well and borehole calculations. In the related calculation of rates of penetration of grout from, for example, a cylindrical section of an injection hole, the hydraulic resistance to local flow must be increased in the ratio of the viscosity of the grout to ground water for those parts of the formation in which the advancing grout has displaced ground water. Expressions for spherically radiating displacement flow have been given by Raffle and Greenwood[1], and the results are embodied in Fig. 5.1. The curves illustrate how the radius of the grout boundary increases with time for each of three specified ratios of the respective viscosities.

At the late stages of the injection, at which time the grout-water interface has moved well away from the injection hole, a much simpler and yet reasonably accurate estimate of penetration rate can be made using well-flow formulae (e.g. Hvorslev[2]) applicable to short sections of open cylindrical hole, but with the reduced coefficient $k_G$ in the place of the conventional water permeability coefficient $k$. If the open section has a length of $L$ and a radius of $a$, the relation between flow rate $q$ and injection pressure represented by a differential hydraulic head $H$, is of the form:

$$q/H = \frac{4\pi k_G L}{\alpha} \tag{5.1}$$

where $\alpha$ depends on the cell dimensions and the extent of confinement of the aquifer. Fig. 5.2 illustrates the flow patterns and the corresponding values of $\alpha$ for the two typical categories of confinement often occurring in practice. Fig.

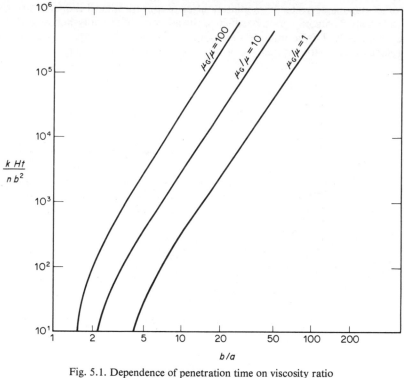

Fig. 5.1. Dependence of penetration time on viscosity ratio

| | |
|---|---|
| $k$ = soil permeability (m/s) | $a$ = radius of source (m) |
| $H$ = hydraulic head (m) | $b$ = radius of grout at time $t$ (m) |
| $t$ = time (s) | $\mu_G$ = viscosity of grout |
| $n$ = porosity of soil | $\mu$ = viscosity of water |

5.2$a$ represents an open section of injection hole in unrestricted porous ground. Fig. 5.2$b$ represents an injection hole that completely spans a stratified water-permeable zone extending laterally for a considerable distance.

In the case presented in Fig. 5.2$a$, the length of the injection cell usually extends to ten times the radius, and therefore $a$ approaches 2 ln $L/a$ and commonly lies between 5·5 and 8. For the stratified aquifer of Fig. 5.2$b$, the value of $b$ is often indefinite and unknown, but effective values of $b$ usually range between 100 and 100 000 and lead to a range of 9 to 18 for $a$.

An adequate estimate of flow rate can be made covering a wide range of hole dimensions and aquifer conditions by assigning the approximate value of 10 to the factor $a$. Indeed, the flow resistance $q/H$ is largely determined by the product $k_G L$. An example will illustrate the level of flow achievable. A typical injection hole may have a diameter of 40 mm and an 0·5 m length of hole exposed at any one time to the ground. If the water permeability of the ground is taken as $10^{-5}$ m/s, corresponding to a clean fine sand, the flow-rate for a grout of water-like viscosity is given by a $q/H$ value of about $0·6 \times 10^{-5}$ m²/s and the flow rate for an injection pressure equivalent to 100 m of waterhead becomes 0·0006 m³/s, i.e. 0·6 litre/s. In practice the most fluid chemical grouts are between $1\frac{1}{2}$ and 3 times as viscous as water immediately after preparation, and the viscosity rises considerably during injection because of the advance of the polymerising process (the grout *AM-9* is a notable exception). The grouting rates obtaining are therefore one half to one quarter of the rate calculated for water.

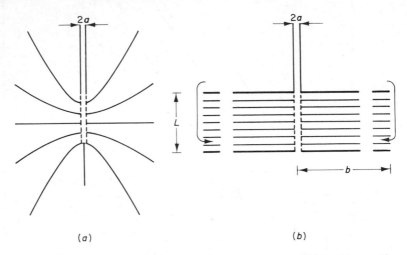

(a)                                    (b)

Fig. 5.2 Flow patterns for injection into (a) uniform ground and (b) stratified aquifer

$$a = \frac{2L}{(L^2 - 4a^2)^{\frac{1}{2}}} \ln \frac{L + (L^2 - 4a^2)^{\frac{1}{2}}}{2a} \qquad a = 2 \ln (b/a)$$

The application of flow-net theory to the flow of true fluid grouts in a system of interconnected rock fissures is clearly somewhat artificial. Essentially, however, equation 5.1 represents the consequence to the value of the flow resistance of the diverging nature of the flow as it leaves the injection source. It can be shown that equations of the type in 5.1 may still be usefully applied in many practical cases by substituting for the permeability a parameter dependent on the characteristic width and mean spacing of fissures (see, for example, Snow[3]).

In the rock tunnelling and shaft sinking it is not uncommon for a single open joint or fissure to carry a major flow of water into the excavation. It is clear that flow in such a water passage can be expressed by some appropriate hydraulic resistance, at least where the Reynolds number is low enough for viscous dissipation to be dominant.

It can be shown on simple physical grounds, as for example by Vaughan and Ambraseys[4], that for a uniform flat fissure of width $T$ penetrated by a hole of radius $a$ and connecting with an open reservoir or sink at a radial distance $b$ from the hole,

$$q/H = \frac{\pi \gamma_w g T^3}{6\mu \ln b/a} \qquad (5.2)$$

where $\gamma_w$ is the density of water and $\mu$ the viscosity of the injected fluid. As the logarithmic term changes very slowly with the value of $b$, this dimension can be considered in the case of rock formations as the order of distance away from the hole at which the fissure merges with a more open structure, such as might be constituted by multiply-interconnected open fissures and joints.

Equation 5.2 provides estimates of flow either for grout flowing through a fissure into the formation or for influx of ground water into an open hole. It will be clear that flow is largely determined in both cases by $T^3/\mu$ and that other dimensions have relatively a minor influence. As an example of flow, consider a single fissure 0·1 mm wide (100 $\mu$m) grouted with an injection pressure equivalent to 100 m of hydraulic head from an injection hole of 40 mm diameter. If ln $b/a$ is taken as about 5, the flow rate for grout of water-like viscosity becomes about $10^{-3}$ m$^3$/s, i.e. 1 litre/s. As the fissure size decreases, the flow resistance falls rapidly according to the third power law, and a 10 $\mu$m wide fissure subject to the same injection pressure as mentioned above would accept the most fluid grouts at the almost negligible rate of about 0·001 litre/s.

## Penetration and blockage for particulate suspensions

The penetration characteristics of cement and of clay grouts are very different from those of true fluids. When such grouts are injected into porous soil or fissured rock there may be a pronounced filtering action in which the larger particles in the suspension tend to separate out at the entrance of the passage. A further limitation in penetration, even in passages large enough to accept the grout particles, arises from the complex fluid properties of suspensions; many concentrated suspensions, including slurries of cement or clay, behave like weak solids rather than fluids when the driving pressures are small. This special property can severely limit the injection rate.

## CRITERIA OF BLOCKAGE

When dilute suspensions such as thin cement grouts are pumped through fine passages at very low velocity, the particles tend to gravitate towards the bottom face of the passage, and in due course to build up what is often a strongly adherent layer of settled material. An aim of cement grouting is to carry the cement particles to a considerable distance from the injection hole and thereafter to allow steady deposition to fill the fissure or void system. If the flow rate is maintained at a moderately high level, the fluid velocity, at least near the point of injection, is so much higher than the settling velocity that small particles are transported readily provided the particles are all substantially smaller than the cross dimension of the passage. Particles of one third or less of the passage width are carried smoothly; marginally larger particles, even though smaller than the passage width, can initiate a blockage and the determining factor in fissure grouting can involve the roughness of the surface of the passage and the cohesion and adhesion between individual particles or between particles and the wall. In relatively concentrated suspensions the individual particles tend to form flocs or loose aggregates in which case pore passages and fissures need to be even larger in relation to individual particles for free transport to be maintained (Fig. 5.3). This aggregation is pronounced both for cement and for clay suspensions; however, aggregation can be reduced by suitable dispersing agents.

The commercial cements and clays tend to have a wide range of particle size. In Portland cement the mean particle size is about 30 $\mu$m, with a maximum rising usually above 100 $\mu$m. Montmorillonite clay mineral has a particle size well below 1 $\mu$m, but silts of 50 $\mu$m and more are invariably to be found as impurities in the commercial grades of bentonite.

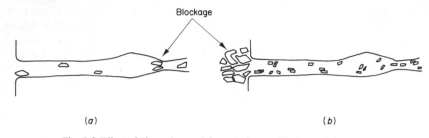

Fig. 5.3 Effect of dispersion and flocculation on blockages in passages

It is the larger particles, even though in small number, that determine blockage. The coarse particles are caught at the entry of the narrow passages, and thereafter finer material is trapped in the remaining very restricted gaps flanking the trapped coarse particles. Injection experiments show that cement particles build up at the mouth of a narrow artificial fissure between metal or stone plates when the width of the passage is smaller than about 200 $\mu$m. Similar filter-cake formation is found in attempts to inject uniform sands of less than 2 mm in grain size with cement; the injection limit of clay grouts is not much lower.

For soils that are not uniformly graded, a useful estimate of the condition for blockage by a particulate grout can be gained by applying the Kozeny relationship

$$R = \left(\frac{8\mu k}{\gamma_w g n}\right)^{\frac{1}{2}} \tag{5.3}$$

to find the diameter 2R of the average pore passage, where $\mu$ is the viscosity, $k$ the permeability and $\gamma_w$ the density of water, and where $n$ is the soil porosity (see, for example, Dallavalle[5]). If the average pore diameter is taken to equal in size the 100 $\mu$m particle of cement, positive blockage can be expected on this basis for a soil permeability of about $10^{2\cdot5}$ m/s.

## LIMITATIONS OF PENETRATION ARISING FROM COMPLEX FLOW PROPERTIES

True fluids have a simple proportional relationship between the rate of strain in the flowing fluid and the shear stress applied. However, many concentrated suspensions do not begin to flow until a certain limiting shear stress $\tau_f$ has been imposed. At higher shear stresses than the limiting value flow commences and thereafter the flow is directly proportional to the excess of applied shear stress. Fluids which are covered by this law are named *Bingham* fluids. The flow behaviour of both clay suspensions and cement suspensions is approximately of the Bingham type. Fig. 5.4 illustrates the typical flow laws for a true fluid such as water and a Bingham fluid represented in the example by 5% Wyoming bentonite. The critical shear strength $\tau_f$ exhibited by typical cement or clay grouts is in the range $1-20 \text{ N/mm}^2$. In engineering terms such a level of strength would imply an extremely weak material, but in permeation flow the modest shear stresses acting must be summed over the very considerable surface area of the pore passages. In consequence, quite considerable pressures are required to maintain

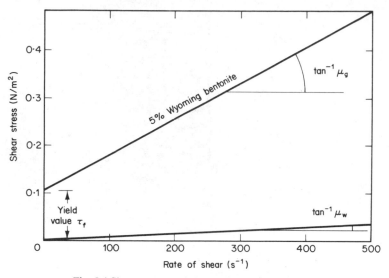

Fig. 5.4 Shear stress needed to maintain flow in fluids

flow of grout in passages of the size encountered in fine-grained soils. Raffle and Greenwood[1] deduced that an extra pressure gradient of $2\tau_f /R$ must be applied at all parts of the advancing grout to overcome the shear strength during injection, where $\tau_f$ is the Bingham yield stress for the grout and $R$ is the effective radius of an average pore passage assessed as before from the Kozeny relationship (equation 5.3). The situation during injection at a time when all the injection pressure is absorbed in overcoming $\tau_f$ is illustrated in Fig. 5.5. The conclusions are illustrated in Table 5.1 which shows the calculated minimum hydraulic gradient needed to maintain flow for soils of given permeability and yield value.

If this reasoning is applied to a simple clay suspension containing 5% of Wyoming bentonite having a yield value of approximately $1.5 \text{ N/mm}^2$, a grouting pressure equivalent to a 60 m head of water must be applied for each metre of grout penetration simply to offset the inherent yield strength. In shallow alluvium the maximum pressure allowable if ground disturbance and heave are to be avoided may be no more than a few tens of metres and penetration is then much less than 1 m.

## Character of the progressing boundary between injected grout and ground water

As the grouting proceeds in a water-bearing porous soil or rock, the boundary between grout and ground water moves progressively outwards. Whether the

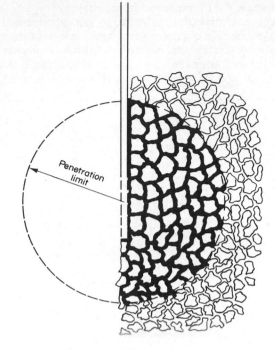

Fig. 5.5. Limited pore penetration caused by yield value of grout

**Table 5.1**  HYDRAULIC GRADIENT TO MAINTAIN FLOW IN NON-NEWTONIAN GROUTS

| Soil permeability (m/s) | Yield value (N/m²) | Hydraulic gradient |
|---|---|---|
| $10^{-2}$ | 1 | 1·2 |
| | 10 | 12 |
| | 100 | 120 |
| | 1 000 | 1 200 |
| $10^{-3}$ | 1 | 4 |
| | 10 | 40 |
| | 100 | 400 |
| | 1 000 | — |
| $10^{-4}$ | 1 | 12 |
| | 10 | 120 |
| | 100 | 1 200 |
| | 1 000 | — |
| $10^{-5}$ | 1 | 40 |
| | 10 | 400 |
| | 100 | 4 000 |
| | 1 000 | — |

boundary is smooth and the displacement of water regular and complete depends on the respective viscosities and densities of the grout and the ground water, and also to some extent on the rate of pumping. The commonly used chemical grouts are both denser and more viscous than water. A volume of dense grout already placed in wet ground tends to fall slowly through the soil on account of inadequate buoyancy of the surrounding water. The sinking movement is irregular; the lowermost boundary becomes distorted and as the grout sinks, local pendular zones are formed. In due course, descending tongues of material break away from the main body of the grout.

For sinking grouts the fingers move down at approximately the same rate as would characterise Darcy flow of the grout under the differential hydraulic gradient of $(\gamma_G/\gamma_w) - 1$, where $\gamma_G/\gamma_w$ is the ratio of densities of grout and water. Using the previous notation, the velocity of fall $V_F$ is given roughly by:

$$V_F = \frac{k(\gamma_G - \gamma_w)\mu}{\gamma_w \mu_G n}$$

Saffman and Taylor[6] have analysed the physical problem for sinking movement, and also for pumped flow in which the advancing fluid and the displaced fluid have different viscosities of $\mu_G$ and $\mu_w$. The criterion for stability under the combined influence of pumping and sinking is that

$$\frac{\mu_G - \mu}{\mu} \frac{V}{k} - \frac{\gamma_G - \gamma_w}{\gamma_w} > 0$$

for stable downward movement of the boundary at velocity $V$. In the absence of any difference in density the advancing grout boundary is stable if the viscosity of the grout is greater than that of the ground water. In contradistinction, the sinking movement of the dense fluid is unstable except when the pumping rate is high enough to make the full expression positive (see Fig. 5.6). An interesting and

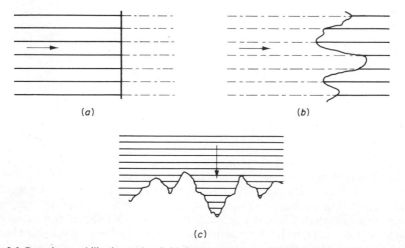

(a)                              (b)

(c)

Fig. 5.6. Boundary stability in moving fluids in porous ground. (*a*) Viscous displacing less viscous fluid, (*b*) less viscous displacing more viscous fluid and (*c*) dense fluid sinking through less dense fluid

important deduction from this theory is that with the more common grouts, which are both denser and more viscous than water, the whole boundary remains stable during pumping provided the hydraulic gradient associated with the pumping of the grout is greater just inside the grout boundary than just outside it by at least an amount equal to $(\gamma_G - \gamma_w)/\gamma_w$. For spherical flow this can be written as:

$$\frac{\mu a H}{b\mu_G(b - a) + \mu ab} > \frac{\gamma_G - \gamma_w}{\gamma_w}$$

for a grout boundary a distance $b$ from the source, moving under the action of an injection hydraulic head of $H$ and displacing void water. This condition is readily met in most practical cases provided the ratio $H/b$ of injection head to radius is greater than $50(\gamma_G - \gamma_w)/\gamma_w$. This conclusion can be confirmed readily by observation of the shape of grouted balls of sand, produced by injection from an open pipe. If the grout gels soon after the completion of pumping, the balls have good spherical form. If gelation is delayed, the lower, intrinsically unstable surface first becomes rough, and sinking movement takes place thereafter in irregular fingering flow (see Fig. 5.7).

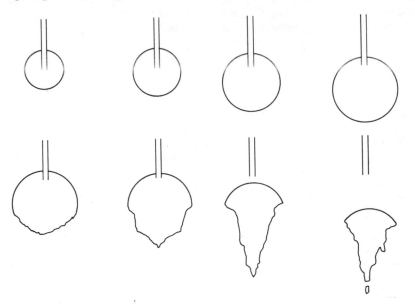

Fig. 5.7. Smooth displacement during injection and irregular sinking on cessation

As a considerable proportion of soil and rock grouting is applied in zones of ground well below the water table it is natural to consider grouting as generally involving the displacement of ground water. However, there are circumstances in which grout is injected into dry ground. It is clear from earlier considerations that for dry ground the viscosity ratio of the fluids on each side of the grout boundary favours stability and a smooth interface during the injection phase. Nevertheless the absence of the strong buoyant action of ground water increases the tendency of the grout to sink, and therefore to break up in the period between injection and gelation. The risk is greatest in open soil, and an obvious safeguard is to use relatively viscous grouts or grouts with significant shear strength.

In very fine dry soil, capillarity assists or retards penetration according to whether or not the grout wets the soil particles. Capillary heads are usually much smaller than injection heads even in soil of permeability as low as $10^{-5}$ m/s.

## Intrusive penetration in grouting technology

There are several special techniques encountered in grouting, as outlined below, where the injected grout has a lower viscosity than the fluid already existing in the porous ground, and for which the injected grout therefore tends to penetrate with an intruding or channelling action.

### Injection prolonged beyond the gelation time

Karol[7] has shown that if flow of fresh grout is maintained by positive displacement at a time when gelation is approaching, and the placed grout is growing rapidly more viscous, the fresh grout intrudes through the older grout and emerges with an erupting action into the untreated ground beyond. This intrusive action might be expected from the Saffman[6] and Taylor analysis. As the fresh grout is urged forward by the injection pump, fingers or tongues of grout move

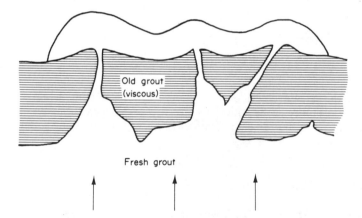

Fig. 5.8. Channelling of fresh grout through partially set grout

forward through the rapidly stiffening older grout. The channels so formed allow the fresh grout to pass freely, and regular permeation continues in the more distant medium (Fig. 5.8).

### Two-shot injection techniques

The effective action of single-shot grouts is associated with the tendency of simple chemical grouts to displace the ground water at a smooth progressing interface. Two-shot grout systems appear at first sight to present an anomaly as the successive grouting solutions must intermix extensively if the products of reaction are to be well distributed in the pores of the soil. However, the type of two-shot grouting represented by the Joosten process is undoubtedly successful, and it is evident that its success depends on grouting under conditions favouring intrusive penetration. In practice the first component fluid injected (sodium silicate) is much more viscous than the second component fluid (e.g. calcium

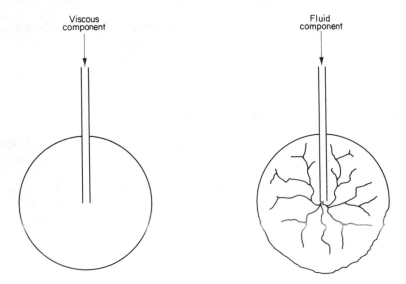

Fig. 5.9. Two-shot grouting; intrusive character of second injection

chloride); the calcium chloride tends, therefore, to invade the silicate solution and reaction takes place at the numerous interfaces where the branching network of injected calcium chloride comes into contact with the viscous sodium silicate. The process is depicted in Fig. 5.9.

### Injection to consolidate compressible silts and clays

The intrusive flow associated with the pumping of free-flowing fluids into relatively immobile fluids is made use of for the injection treatment of compressible clays and silts, which occur, for example, in cavities and in fault zones encountered in tunnelling and mining. These clays and silts have too low a permeability to be regularly permeated at acceptable speed. However, a common and successful procedure is to inject a chemical grout, using a considerable pressure where practicable; the grout tends to intrude into the soft masses of clayey material, in a network of branching passages. The injection pressure applied to the grout subjects the clayey material to localised high-pressure gradients. This high local gradient can, where conditions are suitable, be maintained for periods of an hour or more. During this time the silt or soft clay is consolidated by the mechanical pressures. The grout permeates a small way into the material, and then set grout both encases and reinforces the previously unconsolidated material. By this action the material may be considerably hardened and strengthened. The consolidated material remains confined tightly in the rock formation as the space originally occupied by surplus pore water is filled out by hard-set grout.

## Mechanical strengths of grouted soils

### RESISTANCE OF SET GROUT TO EXTRUSION

A grout which has been successfully injected must develop sufficient rigidity once in place to resist forces tending to move it out of position. Grouts which fill pores and fissures adjacent to an open excavation must, therefore, be able to resist the hydraulic pressure exerted, for example, by ground water which has been sealed off by the grouting operation. If the thickness of the grouted zone of soil is small in relation to the height of the water table above the base of the excavation, the hydraulic gradient acting in a direction to extrude the grout into the excavation can amount commonly to ten and often to one hundred and more. These gradients are comparable with the hydraulic gradients acting to force the grouts into the ground during injection itself. It is clear, therefore, that when in place the grout must develop resistance to flow very many times greater than it possesses at the time of injection.

In the case of the clay grouts used by Bérigny and with the simple clay slurries that have sometimes been recommended for use as grouts, the decreased fluidity of the placed grout arises from the thixotropic character of the clays. This decrease is small and may amount to a factor of no more than two. Clay slurries are, therefore, not very suitable for pre-injection of ground in which a deep excavation is to be made.

The chemical grouts, however, involve a specific chemical interlinking action associated with a distinct gelation time. The majority of such grouts set to form weak solids. If such grouts are injected into wide fissures or pores, and a sufficiently high hydraulic force is applied, there is sometimes a tendency for the set gels to extrude bodily. If the gel moves through shear failure near the walls of the passages the criterion for the shear strength required of the set gel to resist extrusion is given by the expression given earlier for the hydraulic gradient needed to maintain flow in Bingham fluid. If $\tau_F$ is the shear strength of the set gel, extrusion from a pore of radius $R$ will be expected when the extruding gradient equals $2\tau_F/R\gamma g$.

Since the results of this calculation are already embodied in Table 5.1, it will be seen that the minimum shear strength for a soil of given permeability is simply related to the applied hydraulic gradient. The demand for a high shear strength in a set grout is greatest in soils of high permeability. By way of example, a grout with a set shear strength of 120 N/mm² is just strong enough to resist an extrusion gradient of 100 in a fine gravel characterised by a permeability of $10^{-2}$ m/s.

When grouts are used for the sealing of coarse fissures preparatory to the sinking of deep mine shafts, the demand for shear strength in set grout is again very high. In a shaft the grout may extend only 3 m from the shaft wall, and yet need to withstand immediately after excavation an hydraulic head of 1 km. Some chemical grouts with high qualities in respect of fluidity will not support the necessary high shear stress and extrude slowly out of fissures when subject to such very high gradients. When the hydraulic gradient is very high the choice of suitable grout must take into account the creep properties of the set grout.

## MECHANICAL STRENGTH ENDOWED BY INJECTION OF GROUT

In considering the reaction of set grouts to extruding forces it has been implied that some gelled grouts are not necessarily strong enough always to prevent extrusion from pores and fissures. However, grouts range very widely in mechanical qualities and not least in their capacity to give cohesive strength to otherwise incohesive soils. Grouts which are primarily developed to have very low viscosities generally have moderately low strength as they usually consist of dilute aqueous solutions of organic or inorganic monomers which polymerise to form hard jellies. When injected into sandy soil of conventional internal friction angle, the unconfined compressive strength commonly lies between $0 \cdot 2$ and 4 $N/mm^2$. Several experimenters have carried out programmes of triaxial testing on soil impregnated with selected chemical grout, and conclude that typical weak aqueous gels lead to Mohr envelopes typical of a cohesive material with an internal angle of friction not much changed by the grouting operation—at least for soils with a moderately high relative density (see, for example, the work on the grout *AM-9* by Schiffman and Wilson[8]. Figure 5.10 illustrates a range of results

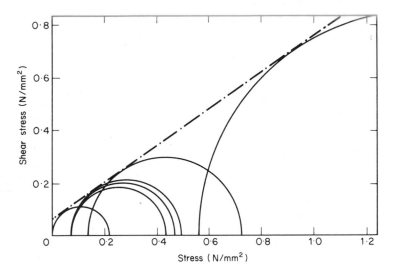

Fig. 5.10. Triaxial tests on sand grouted with chrome-lignin grout

of undrained triaxial tests on a chrome lignin grout. The value of the cohesion intercept increases with concentration of the active constituents of the grout. Triaxial tests carried out at conventional relatively fast straining rates tend, however, to exaggerate the strength of weak aqueous gels formed from the very fluid chemical grouts. This reflects the viscoelastic nature of the gels.

Some special-purpose grouts containing high concentrations of polymerising components set to form very rigid products, although at the expense of fluidity during injection. Crushing strengths typical of strong concretes can be produced by injection of sand with grouts based on epoxides or polyesters.

REFERENCES

1. Raffle, J. F. and Greenwood, D. A., 'Proceedings of the 5th International Conference on Soil Mechanics and Foundation Engineering', **2,** 789 (1961)
2. Hvorslev, J., Bulletin No. 36, Waterways Experimental Station, U.S. Corps of Engineers (1951)
3. Snow, D. T., *Journal of Soil Mechanics and Foundations Division,* A.S.C.E., **94,** 73 (1968)
4. Vaughan, P. R. and Ambraseys, N. N., Symposium on Grouts and Drilling Methods, Butterworths, London, 54 (1963)
5. Dallavalle, J. M., *Micromeretics,* Pitman (1948)
6. Saffman, P. G. and Taylor, G. I., *Proc. Roy. Soc.,* Lond., **A245,** 312 (1958)
7. Karol, R. H., Chemical Grouting Technology Seattle Conference on Structural Engineering, A.S.C.E. (1967)
8. Schiffman, R. L. and Wilson, C. A., *The Mechanical Behaviour of Chemically Treated Granular Soils,* **58,** A.S.T.M. (1958)


BIBLIOGRAPHY

Glossop, R., 'The Invention and Developments of Injection Processes: 1802–1850', *Geotechnique,* Institution of Civil Engineers, Sept. (1960)
Proceedings of I.C.E. Symposium on Grouts and Drilling Muds in Engineering Practice, Butterworths, London (1963)
Scheidegger, A. E., *The Physics of Flow Through Porous Media,* University of Toronto Press (1960)

Chapter 6

# Classifiction of Grout: Classification by Engineering Performance for Grout Selection

## Summary

Provision is made for the selection of grouts by consideration of the engineering performance demanded and the permeability of the formation. Grouts which are technically acceptable are distinguished from those whose performance is inadequate. Final choice of grout, taken on the overall cost of the grouting works, follows after grout selection.

Grouts are positioned within the classification on the basis of their physical properties as fluid grout and as set within the voids. The classification is capable of extension to include the ranges of grout properties available by modification of the formulation of individual grouts, such as clay–chemical (bentonite–silicate–phosphate) or chrome–lignin, and the associated ranges of grout materials costs.

The physical properties of grouts are discussed in relation to the changes in molecular structure which bring about transformation from the freshly mixed fluid to the fully hardened or set state. The chemical and physical pathways to the three-dimensional micro-structures of the set state are examined so as to reveal the progressive nature of the changes in properties as reaction continues, and the relationships between 'setting time', defined for purposes of grout control, 'limiting injection time', 'zero displacement time' and 'fully cured time' are outlined.

Illustrations show how the relationships between grout formulation, setting time and temperature may be displayed. General comment on the magnitudes of permeabilities and strengths is included. An outline of the general procedure of economic evaluation concludes the chapter.

## Introduction

Grouting is a technique for the improvement of the engineering properties of soils and rocks by injection of material into naturally occurring pores and fissures, or into voids which have been created in the course of injection. The former, known as *permeation* grouting, is the principal concern of this chapter. The rate, and even the possibility, of grouting a particular formation with a specific grout can be predicted only following detailed consideration of both ground and grout. For fissuring or 'claquage' grouting the process is not so dependent on the fluid

84

properties of the grout, though it brings problems additional to those of treatment by permeation. Figures 6.9 to 6.12, which take into account both formation and grout properties, relate specifically to treatment by permeation.

It has not been usual for grouts to be selected by technical appraisal of all the materials available, because of the impossibly difficult task that this would be if it were to be undertaken in relation to a particular job, and for other reasons. Choice of grout has been much influenced by the conservatism of engineers whose everyday materials are concrete and steel. The contrast between the physical properties of these traditional materials and those of most grouts is extreme. Absolute differences in strength have probably been more influential than the knowledge that a mobile suspension of a few per cent of bentonite clay in water could set to a gel which, within the pores of a soil, would resist displacement under any hydraulic gradient likely to be encountered in the field. In addition the chemistry of many grouts has inhibited their wider use, despite the universal use of concrete, whose chemistry is far more complex than that of most grouts. It is surprising that so many engineers, confident of their ability to utilise correctly the subtle mixture of chemicals that constitute ordinary Portland cement, should hesitate before the straightforward *AM-9*. When comparative evaluation of grouts has been attempted, technical and economic factors have often been insufficiently clearly differentiated, with the result that the outcome has been either inconclusive or has been seen in retrospect to have been predetermined in a way which could have been anticipated.

The costs of grouting are determined primarily by the nature of a job, its size and its location. The grout materials almost always make up only a small proportion of the total cost of the grout *in situ*[1]. Most of the cost is contributed through the geology of the formation and the depth to which the treatment is to be carried, since these determine the spacing of grout holes and the time taken to complete the treatment.

Accordingly, grout selection is approached here by a consideration, firstly, of technical potential of all possible materials. It is to be followed, when a grout has to be selected for a specific job, by economic evaluation of all those grouts which the initial process of selection has indicated are likely to be technically acceptable.

The chemistry of individual grouts is discussed only in so far as it determines their physical properties. The physical properties are discussed in terms of their significance in determining the engineering performance of grout in the ground. It is the aim of the following paragraphs to facilitate preliminary selection by consideration of engineering performance alone. The engineer should not need to know anything of the chemical nature of the grout or of its transformation from the fluid to the set state.

## How grouts interact with the ground

Grouts may be placed in the voids of soil or rock to reduce the permeability or to increase the strength of the formation, for impermeabilisation, consolidation or both. Whatever the reason for their use, their presence within the soil structure will inevitably result in alteration of both permeability and strength. Account must always be taken of this when the job design requires modification of only one of these properties. This is particularly the case when grouting below the water table, when there may be substantial changes in hydraulic gradient as a consequence of grouting, bringing additional stresses within a weak formation.

In the majority of applications when a grout has been placed by permeation and the micro-structure of the formation has not been altered in the course of injection, the properties of the treated formation are determined by those of the formation and of the grout, and by their interaction. The properties of the composite material cannot safely be predicted from a knowledge of the behaviour of formation and grout properties, considered separately. They must almost without exception be determined by conventional soil mechanics testing of treated specimens.

A qualitative prediction of properties, such as would be desired in the screening of a large number of potential grouts for a specific application can, however, generally be made if the nature of the interaction between soil particle and grout is known (Fig. 6.1). Three factors contributing to this interaction are important:

1. The volume and location of grout within each void between soil particles.
2. The properties of the set grout.
3. The interaction between grout and the surface of the soil particles.

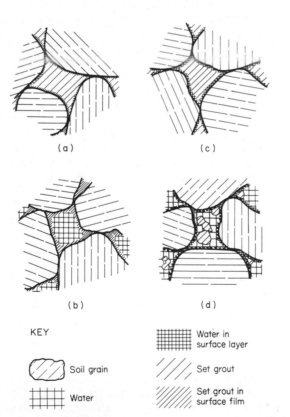

(a) Set grout fills the pores and adheres to the surface of the soil grains, having completely displaced the ground-water.

(b) Set grout coating the soil grains, but leaving water occupying most of the pore volume. Soil, set grout and water are each continuous in three dimensions. A substantial part of the original permeability may be retained after treatment. Accumulation of grout at points of contact under the influence of surface tension may give high strength with a strong grout.

(c) The pores filled by a grout with poor wetting ability for the soil surface, or by one which has formed only a weak bond and has subsequently undergone syneresis.

The water film is continuous. The overall permeability is low when the water film thickness remains low around the grain contacts.

(d) Grout particles loosely held within the pores may reduce permeability, so long as they are not themselves displaced by ground-water flow. This type of product is generally to be avoided.

*Note*: Pores drawn in two dimensions, as in these illustrations, appear discontinuous. In reality they constitute a continuous network (*cf.* Reference 19, page 2021) in: terpenetrating the solid structure of soil particles. It is particularly important that this should be remembered when the probable level of residual permeability which would result from a particular grout-soil combination is being considered; water flowing through the soil will typically have component velocities in the plane of the diagram and perpendicular to it.

KEY

▨ Soil grain

▦ Water

▤ Water in surface layer

⧄ Set grout

⧄ Set grout in surface film

Fig. 6.1. Interaction between grout and ground: alternative microstructures resulting from grouting by permeation

A grout may or may not completely fill the void; it may or may not adhere to the surface of the individual soil particles; it may be strong or weak. Within the pore or fissure a particular grout may exhibit any combination of these properties.

In a saturated or nearly saturated soil or rock the solid particles are in point contact. The contacts provide a continuous, three-dimensional skeleton, which is interpenetrated by the continuous volume of water in the pores and fissures. The strength and deformation of the soil under load are determined by the friction and cohesion between grains, and by the permeability, which controls the rate of response of ground-water to changes in stress. Replacement of ground-water by set grout further complicates the pattern of response to stress.

At one extreme is void filling by inert solids, and at the other is void filling by a high-strength resin such as an epoxy. Injection of a sand into an open gravel will improve the grading and increase the relative density, with consequent improvement of properties as is well known from conventional soil mechanics. An epoxy resin filling the pores of a siliceous material bonds well to the surface of the grain and is itself of very high strength; the whole behaves as a high-strength concrete.

Chemical grouts which set by gelation in the pores are altogether different in their action. There may be little bonding between gel and the solid surfaces of the grains. Particularly in the case of hydrogels prone to syneresis, a microscopic film of water may separate gel and soil surface. Strain of the solid matrix is initially resisted by elastic deformation of macroscopically continuous gel, and the elasticity, creep and strength of the gel are all important.

## Materials for grouts

Two things are required of any grout: firstly, it should confer on the formation the desired properties, and secondly, it should be capable of being injected into the formation. In order that both requirements should be met, it is necessary for a grout to undergo a change of state, by chemical or physical reaction, from the fluid to a set condition. With most grouts, the transition is gradual though there are a number of different types of flash set which have been exploited. As chemical reaction proceeds, so the physical properties of the grout are gradually transformed from the fluid state obtained on mixing the grout components together to the final state on cessation of reaction. The progress of the reaction affects the ease of injection in the period following initial mixing, and the ability of the grout to resist displacement from the fissures and pores under the stress imposed by the hydraulic gradient in the interval between completion of injection and attainment of the final 'fully hardened' state. The overall performance of a grout is thus determined by the initial fluid state, the set state and by the transition between them.

All conceivable physical forms of fluid grout have been described and most have been used. The range includes molten solids (sulphur), pure liquids (epoxy resin), gases (silicon halides), aqueous solutions (silicate–aluminate, chrome-lignin), suspensions of solid in water (cement) or non-aqueous liquid (clay–petroleum oil), emulsion of liquid in water (bitumen) and foamed grouts (polyurethane). The range of materials is vast. Hundreds of different chemicals have been patented or otherwise described as being suitable for use as grouts[2,3]. The set state, and the interaction between grout and ground have been commented on in the previous paragraphs. The fundamental requirement of the setting reaction is that it shall yield a stable three-dimensional micro-structure. There are only a small number of pathways to such structures. All chemical types of grout, of all initial physical forms, must follow one or other of them. From a knowledge of the pathway followed by a particular grout, several aspects of its performance can be predicted, including constraints on injection arising from changing fluid properties, and the time delay between initial setting and attainment of final properties.

The grouts of greatest practical importance are those based on hydration of cement and those which yield hydrogels from aqueous solution. Their setting mechanisms are outlined below. An understanding of the setting reaction is not essential to the use of a grout, but it will assist towards ensuring efficient exploitation of the grout's potential and in preventing failures. In every case, the strength and stability of a set grout are determined by the chemical nature, by concentration, and by the density of cross-linking. Stable products of widely differing strengths can often be obtained from a single chemical type.

## Setting of grouts: pathways to 3-D molecular structures

### SETTING BY CHEMICAL CHANGE

The many small molecules present in the grout at mixing have to combine together into a few giant ones. All these monomer molecules are incorporated into the growing polymer by the formation of new chemical bonds. This may only involve rearrangement of electrons within the molecules. In this case, reaction is simple and fast. Alternatively, some part of the monomer molecule may be broken off, the residues combine, and the material lost from the monomer appears as a by-product in the set grout. Because these changes involve groups of atoms they proceed far more slowly than those involving only electron rearrangement.

The engineering significance of the two setting mechanisms lies in the very different rates of reaction, and the manner in which the fluid properties change between mixing and setting of the grout (Fig. 6.2). They are commonly called *polymerisation* and *condensation*, respectively. In both cases the product is a polymer. The basic chemistry is the same whether the grout is a pure fluid, or if it is in a diluted form as a solution in water or some other solvent. In solution grouts, the interaction between the grout chemical and the solvent changes as the monomer reacts and gradually attains the final polymer structure.

### Polymerisation

In polymerisation the monomer grout chemical has within its structure a double bond with a pair of electrons which can be uncoupled. Each forms an association with a similar electron on another monomer molecule, and the monomers combine. The 'dimer' formed in the initial reaction retains two uncoupled electrons, and the addition of further molecules proceeds rapidly in a chain reaction until all the monomer is combined into a few very long molecules.

Inclusion of a small proportion of a chemical whose molecules contain two double bonds which can react, allows the chains to cross-link and so grow into a three-dimensional network.

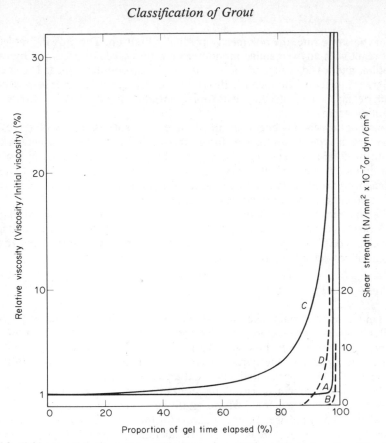

Fig. 6.2. Fluid properties of grouts by gelling by polymerisation and condensation. Changes in grout viscosity (continuous line) and shear strength (broken line) are shown during (1) addition polymerisation (*A* and *B*) and (2) condensation polymerisation (*C* and *D*) (courtesy American Cyanamid Co.)

Reaction is initiated by an activator. By appropriate use of inhibitors, initiation may be postponed for as long as is necessary for injection to be completed. Initiation is followed by rapid setting. Polymerisation grouts may consequently exhibit near ideal properties: a constant low viscosity or, in aqueous solution, water-like viscosity, and instant transformation to the fully hardened state.

During polymerisation in aqueous solution, the hydrophilic groups which are responsible for the solubility of the monomer are retained unchanged. The polymer holds the water within its structure and the product is a hydrogel; *AM-9* is an example of a polymerisation grout.

## Condensation

The rate of reaction is determined by the energy required for two molecules to pass through a transition state, from which the molecular fragments appear in new combinations with one another as the desired product and one or more by-products. The product has similar reactivity to the original reactants but is of greater molecular weight. By stepwise reaction, in which each step proceeds at about the same rate, the polymer is gradually built up. The growing molecules may react with any remaining monomer or with molecules produced by earlier reaction, and a wide range of molecular weight is soon developed. The effect of the larger molecule is to increase the viscosity. The gradual increase in viscosity which begins to make itself evident shortly after mixing is observed with all condensation grouts.

Some of the reacting chemicals must have the ability to react with three other molecules in order to produce a stable three-dimensional polymer network.

During condensation some grouts lose as by-products, or directly by reaction, hydrophilic groups of atoms which were responsible for their solubility. Sufficient hydrophilicity must be retained if a hydrogel is to be obtained, rather than a precipitate together with an aqueous fluid.

For this reason condensation grouts are generally more sensitive to dilution and other changes in the detailed chemistry than is *AM-9* (Fig. 6.6). Phenol-formaldehyde grouts (including polyphenolic- and resorcinol-formaldehyde) are typical of condensation grouts.

### Cement grouts[4,5]

Portland cement remains the most widely used grouting material. It is readily available, gives reproducible performance and yields high strengths. Pound for pound, it is far cheaper than any chemical grout. Its disadvantages are a slow gain of strength, and the particle size which precludes permeation into soils whose coefficient of permeability is less than $10^{1/2}$ mm/s.

The cement grains are crystalline, containing four principal chemical compounds (the cement minerals) whose relative proportions are determined by the mix of raw materials used in manufacture of the cement. Two of these cement minerals, dicalcium silicate $(C_2S)$ and tricalcium silicate $(C_3S)$, are responsible for the strength of the set cement through formation of the same hydrated calcium silicate, commonly known as *tobermorite* gel. Hydrated lime is also liberated as a by-product, $C_2S$ giving about three times as much as $C_3S$, weight for weight. The reactions between these minerals and water are:

$$C_2S: \quad 2(2CaO.SiO_2) + 4H_2O \rightarrow 3CaO.2SiO_2.3H_2O + Ca(OH)_2$$

$$C_3S: \quad 2(3CaO.SiO_2) + 6H_2O \rightarrow 3CaO.2SiO_2.3H_2O + 3Ca(OH)_2$$

The remaining two cement minerals are both calcium aluminates. One of them, tri-calcium aluminate $(C_3A)$ tends to react rapidly with water, and can lead to a flash set of the cement. In order to eliminate this possibility, a little gypsum is added to the cement, which reacts with the $C_3A$ forming an almost impervious coating over the $C_3A$ so that the rate of reaction becomes comparable with the rate of hydration of the calcium silicates.

Reaction takes place on the surface of the solid particles. As it proceeds the tobermorite gel grows out from the surface as fine sheets, which may occur rolled as acicular needle-like forms[6]. Interaction between the gel growing out from adjacent particles of cement causes setting and hardening. The same reactions lead to initial set, then final set and ultimately to the fully hardened state. As reaction proceeds the gel accumulates around the cement particles; water is used up, and the residual water has less and less access to the remaining unhydrated cement. The rate of reaction consequently diminishes rapidly, though reaction does not completely cease for several months at ambient temperature.

In concrete, the cement particles are small compared with both coarse and fine aggregate. Its structure is that of a cement paste heavily filled with larger, inert particles. The interaction between growths of tobermorite gel, and therefore the strength of the mix at any instant, is determined by the distance between cement particles, and this in turn is governed by the amount of water separating them, i.e. by the water : cement ratio.

The simplest grouts, consisting of cement–water slurry, are injected at high water : cement ratio. When the cement particles are trapped, excess water usually is able to escape by further permeating the pores or fissures, and a cement paste of much lower water : cement ratio is left. This can then set, giving the possibility of high strength.

*Cement–bentonite*   Cement particles have a high density of $3·1$ g/cm$^3$ and quickly settle from aqueous suspension. The practical problems arising from this may be alleviated by the use of a small percentage of bentonite (sodium montmorillonite) in the grout, to confer a little shear strength on the fluid. Provided that the percentage of bentonite is low, adequate strength is achieved and penetration is improved by lubrication of movement of cement particles within the voids.

*Cement–clay and clay–cement*   Clay particles are small compared with the cement. As the clay content is increased and that of the cement reduced, the structure of the cement paste is modified by the gradual introduction of clay together with water in the pores between cement particles. The clay soon interferes with interaction of the developing tobermorite gel, and strength rapidly falls.

On a further increase in the proportion of clay, the separation of the cement particles is increased until the grout consists of cement particles randomly distributed within a matrix of clay. Strength is no longer at all comparable with that afforded by cement and cement–bentonite. The cement imparts a little strength and, more importantly, confers a setting action on the clay-based grout.

*Cement/p.f.a.*   Pulverised fuel ash (p.f.a.) particles are predominantly spherical, and of similar size to the cement. During the first stages of setting and hardening, the p.f.a. dilutes the cement, increases the average separation between cement grains and reduces their interaction. Strengths are consequently lower than those of cement grout. The p.f.a., however, has a high content of active silica, which is able to undergo a pozzolanic reaction with lime liberated as a by-product of the cement hydration. The product of these reactions is similar to that obtained from the cement, and has the same cementitious action:

$$3Ca(OH)_2 + 2SiO_2 \rightarrow 3CaO.2SiO_2.3H_2O$$

Long-term strengths comparable with those from cement grouts are given by mixes containing a substantial proportion of p.f.a., at lower cost.

In some circumstances cement–p.f.a.–bentonite grouts may be preferred to straight cement–bentonite.

## SETTING BY PHYSICAL CHANGE

Ground freezing is in principle the simplest means of ground stabilisation. Apart from water itself, only the freezing of molten sulphur which yields a hard rock appears to have obvious potential for some specialised applications. There are two other physical setting processes which find limited applications, emulsion breaking and the gelation of active clays.

Emulsions of organic fluids in water are most commonly encountered in the form of bitumen emulsions. They afford high concentrations of high viscosity bitumen by close packing of spherical globules of bitumen in a smaller proportion of water, but have a viscosity in bulk which is determined by that of the continuous phase, i.e. the water. In use, provided that the voids into which the emulsion is injected are sufficiently large in comparison with the bitumen micelles, their performance is limited by the extent to which a controlled break can be achieved. In so far as emulsion break is controlled by a progressive change induced by addition of other chemicals, the differences in practice between the use of an emulsion grout and grouts setting by chemical reaction *in situ* may be negligible. The ideal emulsion is that which remains stable for a predetermined time, then breaks rapidly.

Bentonite is an important constituent of many cement grouts, where it acts as a suspending agent and lubricant, and of clay chemical grouts. It may also be used as a simple suspension of clay in water; the suspension is thixotropic. The clay mineral is plate-like, with opposite electrical changes on face and edge. Gelation is the result of face-edge electrostatic attraction between the plates, which carry with themselves a layer of bound water, giving a random, house-of-cards structure.

In contrast to emulsion breaking, bentonite gelation is a purely physical process. The gel may be liquified by shearing, and will gel again on standing, and the cycle may be repeated indefinitely. Gels may be obtained with active clays at concentrations down to as little as $2\% {}^V/_V$ (or $5\% {}^W/_W$) and at $5\% {}^V/_V$ stiff gels are formed within a very few minutes of mixing. Because of the possibility that bentonite gels are liable to liquefy under shear at any time subsequent to placing and gelation, bentonite is more commonly used in the form of clay-chemical grout, in which the bentonite gel is combined with an irreversible silicate gel. A potential which does not appear to have been exploited, and which is not possessed by clay-chemical or other grouts, is the self-healing capacity of straight bentonite grouts. A related use of bentonite grouts which exploits this property, is the temporary sealing of boreholes[7].

## Setting time and its control

### DEFINITIONS

For all grouts which undergo a setting reaction by some chemical change, the rate of reaction has to be capable of being controlled. At any temperature, a reproducible change must be obtainable for a given grout formulation, and it is desirable that a range of setting time should be available by alteration of formulation.

Between initial mixing of the grout and attainment of final set (the fully hardened state) a number of intermediate times may be distinguished which correspond to successive physical states of the grout (Fig. 6.3). In most cases, the same chemical reaction proceeds from mixing to final set and the times are distinguished for convenience. They have no fundamental physical or chemical significance. They may be arbitrarily defined, as are, for instance, the initial and final setting times for concrete:

1. *Limiting-injection* time, at which time the effective viscosity has increased to the extent that injection becomes uneconomically slow.
2. *Zero-displacement* time, when the grout has achieved sufficient strength for displacement under the influence of hydraulic gradients in the formation to be negligible. Injection pressure has to be maintained up to this time if grout movement is likely to be significant.
3. *'Setting'* time, defined by some empirical test, and used for control of grout formulation, on site and during laboratory development work.
4. *Fully cured* time at which time final properties have been developed and chemical reaction has virtually ceased.

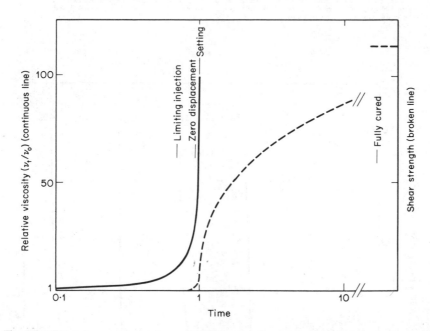

Fig. 6.3. Change in grout properties as the setting reaction proceeds. These curves represent a grout setting to a gel within an hour after mixing and attaining a strength close to that of its fully cured state within about a day

The delay between limiting-injection time and zero-displacement time needs to be short. As both conditions are the result of the same progressive chemical change, there is a tendency for this delay to relate to the limiting injection time, so that it increases in almost direct proportion (Table 6.1 and Fig. 6.4). When injection is slow and the time of injection long, the delay between cessation of injection and the fully cured time may, in extreme cases, become critical. An example could be the treatment of a lens of silt from an advancing tunnel face.

The advantages of polymerisation grout such as *AM-9*, for which times 1–4 are identical, are obvious.

No single definition of setting time has been attempted. Different laboratories

94

**Table 6.1** LIMITING-INJECTION TIME AND ZERO-DISPLACEMENT TIME FOR GEOSEAL $MQ$-5, GELATION AT $10°C$ ($50°F$) (FROM VISCOSITY/TIME DATA, COURTESY BORDEN CHEMICAL CO.[8])

| Grout concentration (% solids) | Limiting-injection time, $T_{10}$ (min) | Zero-displacement time, $T_{100}$ (min) | $\dfrac{T_{100} - T_{10}}{T_{100}}$ |
|:---:|:---:|:---:|:---:|
| 14 | 200 | 285 | 0·30 |
| 15 | 160 | 227 | 0·29 |
| 17 | 120 | 172 | 0·30 |
| 22 | 72 | 116 | 0·38 |

*Note* 1. The time intervals between grout mixing, cessation of injection and the time when any grout movement becomes negligible, are determined for a given grout by the nature of the formation and by the hydraulic gradient.

*Note* 2. Limiting-injection time and zero-displacement time are here taken as the time at which viscosities of 10 cSt and 100 cSt respectively, are attained. Zero-displacement time is very close to the gel time. The proportion of the setting time during which the grout is sufficiently mobile for injection to continue tends to be constant with this grout.

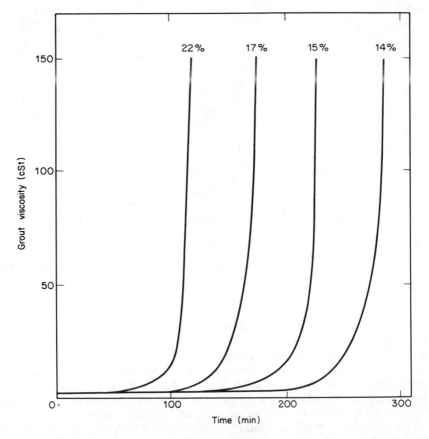

Fig. 6.4. Gelation of a grout setting to a hydrogel by condensation; reaction at $10°C$, grout solids concentrations as shown (Geoseal $MQ$-5, courtesy Borden Chemical Co.). (*See also* Table 6.1[8])

have adopted different techniques and different standards, and have even used different criteria for describing the state of set of different grouts. The definition is bound to be somewhat arbitrary if the diverse conditions of use of grouts are taken into account, as well as their various patterns of development of Newtonian viscosity and fluid shear strength.

For setting time to be of direct relevance to field applications, it should clearly be synonymous with zero-displacement time. For the purpose of comparison between grouts, some arbitrary definition is needed. With *AM-9*, and a number of grouts which undergo transformation from Newtonian fluid to a hydrogel, the time of development of a significant shear strength is well defined. It can be detected on slow withdrawal of the end of a rod from the fluid, when a stable thread is drawn from the surface: prior to this point the fluid coalesces into droplets and falls from the rod. For most practical purposes the time after which the effective viscosity has increased a hundredfold over its initial value may be taken as the setting time. For these grouts, the setting time is generally referred to as the 'gel' time.

## THE INFLUENCE OF GROUT TEMPERATURE ON SETTING TIME

Very nearly all grouts set more quickly at higher temperature. For most, it is found that the rate of reaction is doubled, and the setting time halved by a rise of about 10°C (Fig. 6.5). Usually, the thermal capacity of the formation being

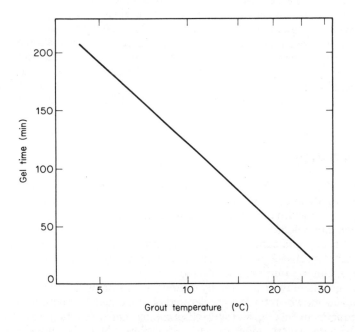

Fig. 6.5. Response of a solution grout to changes in temperature at which the setting reaction takes place (Geoseal *MQ-5*, concentration 22% w/v; courtesy Borden Chemical Co.). Soluble polyphenolic compouds yield a hydrogel on reaction with formaldehyde and a metal salt

grouted greatly exceeds that of the grout, so that the grout is soon cooled or warmed to near formation temperature. The rate of setting should be taken as that at formation temperature.

When held under adiabatic conditions, most grouts heat up as reaction proceeds and the heat of reaction is evolved. Heating accelerates the reaction, and setting rapidly follows. The temperature may exceed the boiling point of the fluid grout, or may pass 100°C after setting—when some gels are blown apart by the internal steam pressure. Care must be taken to avoid this situation when it is decided to inject batches of the fully mixed grout, rather than to mix the grout continuously close to the point of injection as injection proceeds.

The temperature of samples taken for control purposes should always be maintained constant.

## GROUT CONCENTRATION AND THE EFFECTS OF DILUTION

Increase in grout concentration in most cases gives greater strength and faster setting. Dilution of the whole grout may be used as a means of adjusting setting time.

If, after injection, the grout is mixed with ground-water, similar behaviour will occur: a progressive lengthening of setting time until a threshold concentration is reached, below which the grout will never set. When this occurs, not only is the grout wasted and the formation left untreated, but the formation is contaminated with dilute grout which may be highly toxic. Several alternative approaches may be employed to overcome this hazard. Even where dilution is unlikely, a grout concentration substantially above the threshold concentration should be used. Where the risk is higher it may be possible to use a short gel time that is much shorter than the injection time[9]. For treatment of fissures, recourse may be made to chemicals which undergo a flash set on contact with water for initial flow reduction, this being followed by more conventional treatment as required.

## CONTAMINANTS

Grouts vary very greatly in their sensitivity to contaminants. Setting may be accelerated or delayed by the presence of dissolved salts in the ground-water, by chemical reaction with the formation or by contact with the metals of the mixing or injection equipment.

Oxygen has a significant retarding effect on the setting of certain polymerisation grouts, including *AM-9*. Mixing techniques which entrain air should be avoided with *AM-9*. Other grouts are not affected.

Several grouts may be affected by dissolved salts or by the pH of the mixing water. Grouts may be retarded, accelerated or weakened by reaction with metals used in equipment mixing, storage and pumping. On-site testing will usually be found adequate, except under extreme conditions when laboratory evaluation may be needed so as to take into account possible changes in strength.

Acidic grouts may fail to set altogether if injected into limestone or any other formation containing calcium carbonate. Cement grouts based on ordinary

Portland cement should not be used in ground containing gypsum or more soluble sulphates, so that physical breakdown due to sulphate attack on the aluminate in the cement may be avoided.

$$3CaO.Al_2O_3.6H_2O + 3CaSO_4 + 32H_2O \rightarrow 3CaO.Al_2O_3.3CaSO_4.32H_2O$$
<small>Hydrated calcium aluminate        Gypsum</small>

## CONTROL OF SETTING TIME BY GROUT FORMULATION

The setting time required for a particular job may be anything from a few seconds to several hours at temperatures from around freezing to in excess of 40°C. Large changes in grout formulation are necessary in order to accommodate this variation within a single grout type. It is indeed desirable that considerable alteration in concentration and in the proportions of the different chemical constituents should be necessary, in order that the setting time should not be too sensitive to slight variations in concentration such as are inevitable under site conditions.

Large changes in concentration are likely to have a significant effect on grout viscosity, on strength and stability after setting, and on cost. Grout evaluation for particular circumstances of use must take into account the setting time required and the temperature of reaction. It is only with grouts in which the setting time is controlled by low concentrations of catalysts or inhibitors, such as *AM-9*, that viscosity, strength and cost are substantially independent of setting time.

The setting time of many grouts is influenced by the concentration of more than one component. There may accordingly be several different formulations of the same grout which will give the same setting time at a particular temperature. It is desirable in these cases to know the sensitivity of setting time, and of viscosity, strength and stability, to changes in the concentration of each component separately.

Figure 6.6 shows the variation of gel time of *AM-9* with concentration of inhibitor over a wide range of temperature, for fixed concentrations of the other constituents[10]. Figures 6.7 and 6.8 have been constructed from the manufacturer's data for a Terranier grout[11]. This grout is based on low-molecule-weight polyphenolic polymers which set by reaction with formaldehyde in the presence of a metal salt (ferrous sulphate or sodium dichromate) to yield a hydrogel.

A number of approximations have been made, and the performance indicated by Figs. 6.7 and 6.8 is not consistent everywhere with single points taken from the published performance graphs. A set of such figures, one for each concentration of Terranier, would provide a description from which a better understanding of possible alternative formulations could be gained. The information published for most proprietary grouts is, regrettably, insufficient for presentation in a similar manner. For field use, when setting time is being regulated by variable proportioning of grout components, graphs relating setting time to volume ratio are required. When, in the course of injection, a change in gel time is sought so as to meet the requirement of ground of different permeability, the possibility of significant change in grout viscosity must be taken into account.

## Classification

### TYPES OF GROUT AND THEIR GROUPING

In 1952 the American Society of Civil Engineers appointed a Committee on Grouting 'with the aim of advancing the art and supplying information on grouting to the engineering profession.' Task committees were set up to cover four groups of grout materials, i.e. soil, cement, bitumen and chemical. The task

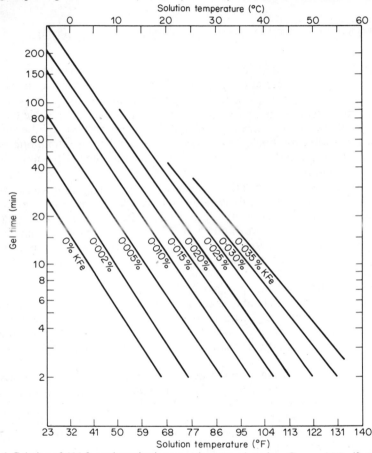

Fig. 6.6. Gelation of *AM-9*, a polymerisation grout (courtesy American Cyanamid Co.[10]). The constituent chemicals are *AM-9* (a mixture of acrylamide and methylene bis-acrylamide, *DMAPN* (dimethylaminopropionitrile), *KFe* (potassium ferricyanide) and *AP* (ammonium persulphate). All percentages are w/w in aqueous solution. The gel time is relatively insensitive to change in *AM-9* concentration. Similar graphs to these may be constructed for other concentrations of *DMAPN* and *AP*. For the grout containing *AM-9* 10%, *DMAPN* 0·40% and *AP* 0·50% w/w, the gel time is given by:

$$\log_{10} G = 3·61 + 0·812 \log_{10}C - 0·044T$$

where $G$ = gel time (min),
$C$ = *KFe* concentration (% w/w) and
$T$ = temperature (°C).

This equation is in good agreement with the manufacturer's data within the ranges $C = 0·002–0·020\%$, T = 0–20°C

committee on chemical grouting had to systematise a formidable volume of literature. This covers a great diversity of chemicals, excluding only those specific types of grout which were the concern of the other task committees. Their work was made all the more difficult since, 'Articles on chemical injection are sometimes written by people, not to inform the profession, but to promote their own interests. These articles usually avoid precise scientific descriptions, numerical data and stoichiometric equations.' Their approach was to distinguish physical aspects of grouting from the types of chemical applicable to injection processes, as 'procedures' and 'processes' respectively[2].

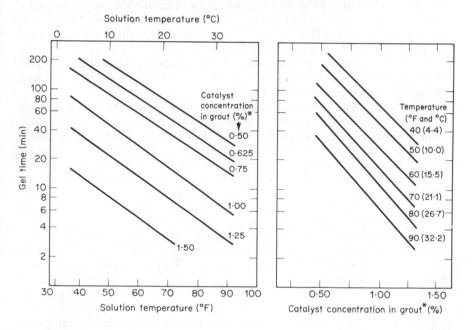

For 12% Terranier C the gel time $G$ (min), catalyst concentration $C$ (%) and temperature $T$ (°F) are related by the equation:

$$\log_{10} G = 4\cdot09 - 1\cdot33C - 0\cdot0222T$$

Terranier sets by a slow progressive condensation reaction, in contrast to *AM-9* which undergoes rapid polymerisation after a controlled period during which reaction is completely inhibited.

Gel time and limiting injection time are the same for *AM-9*. With Terranier regard must be paid to both setting (gel) time and the shorter time available for injection (*cf.* Table 6.1).

*Note*: Figs. 6.7 and 6.8 are derived from experimental data supplied by the grout manufacturers. The two sets of figures are in broad agreement within the temperature limits given above. Discrepancies may, however, be sufficiently great to be important in practice. Reference should be made to the manufacturer's data for all field use of Terranier grout.

* Concentrations are those in the grout (whereas the manufacturer's data are in terms of a nominal concentration of Terranier—that in the stock solution used with a proportioning pump). (Both figures courtesy Rayonier Inc.[11])

Fig. 6.7. Variation of gel time of a Terranier C(1) polyphenolic grout with temperature at several catalyst concentrations, and a solids content of Terranier C of 12% in the grout

Fig. 6.8. Variation of gel time of the same Terranier grout with catalyst concentration at several temperatures between 40° and 90°F (5° and 35°C)

Ten processes were distinguished: dissolution, ion exchange, soil structure alteration, cooling of thermoplastic or molten materials, pore water freezing, metathetical precipitation, polymers, emulsion breaking, suspension separation and particle hydration. Whether a grout was one- or two-shot was included under 'procedures'.

This amounts to classification of grouts by the type of setting reaction involved. It takes no account of the physical nature of the fluid which is injected, or of the set grout. Whilst the interaction between grout and soil particles is referred to, it is not made a basis for the grouping of grouts. It does, however, serve to emphasise that grouts may be logically grouped together on some basis other than by chemical type or by the chemical detail of the setting reaction.

Subsequent authors have not followed the task committee's approach. They have grouped grouts by the chemical type of grout components[12], by the nature of the setting process[13] or by the physical nature of the set grout[14]. Others have attempted to match the fluid property of the grout with the particle size of the soil to be grouted[15], or have listed favoured grouts[16].

Kravetz[3] relates grout type (clay, cement, chemical, etc.) to function (impermeabilisation or consolidation) and the range of soil particle size and rock dimensions over which they may be used.

When there are so many approaches to grout selection, which is the purpose for which classification schemes are designed, when authors may leave their readers in a greater state of perplexity than before[17] and when some of what is published may be positively misleading, it is not surprising that attempts are made to use grouts which are wholly inappropriate to their intended application.

Systematic grout selection, as exemplified in Einstein and Schnitter's account[18] of their work for Mattmark dam, demands a great deal of experimentation. From all the grouts available, they chose four which they believed from previous experience were likely to be technically acceptable. One material they eliminated on the grounds of physical stability, and a second was too viscous. The remaining pair of grouts were similar chemically, and performed in almost an identical manner. It can be seen in retrospect that the outcome was predetermined by the choice of grouts for evaluation. It should have been possible for Einstein and Schnitter to have selected four grouts from which their final choice could have been made on overall cost rather than on purely technical grounds: where selection came down, for example, to the balance between injection time and materials cost. The outcome would have been more acceptable if the doubts about syneresis and leaching of the selected grout had been resolved by comparison with others, but by this stage in their evaluation there were no others remaining.

Most of the attempts at classification of grouts are of some value in categorising the mass of information available and in assisting towards some general understanding. They provide little assistance at best, however, if their purpose is to assist grout selection. Selection based on consideration of fluid properties or on the nature of the setting process does less than half the job. What is required is a systematic classification which takes into account both fluid and set properties and which relates these to the formation to be grouted, i.e. a classification based on engineering performance.

## TECHNICAL POTENTIAL AS THE BASIS FOR A CLASSIFICATION

The complete description of a soil or rock for which grouting is to be evaluated must include geological and physical location, depth below surface and height of the water table, permeability, porosity and the size distribution of fissures. The chemical nature of the minerals present will occasionally be important, and the presence of dissolved salts in the ground-water should be noted. The design requirements for the soil or rock after alteration of properties by grouting will include final permeability, and strength and deformation characteristics.

In order that a grout may effect the desired transformation of properties it is necessary that it should have fluid properties such that it can be introduced to the formation, that the set properties of the treated formation satisfy the design specifications, and that the transformation between the fluid and final set states shall be sufficiently rapid for displacement of the grout to be unlikely under the stresses to which it will be exposed.

A full description of the grout to be evaluated in conjunction with the particular soil or rock will include initial density, fluid viscosity and shear strength, particle size distribution of any solids, and the change of these whilst injection is in progress. The tolerance of the grout for mixing or dilution with water, and the effect of the chemical nature of the grout on its tolerance of the chemicals of the formation and ground-water, also need to be known. In addition, regard must be paid to the toxicity of the fluid grout in relation to possible contamination of ground-water, as well as towards ensuring the safety of operatives handling the grout or grouted soil.

Set properties, in addition to those composite properties of the treated formation, will include volume stability against syneresis in the case of hydrogels, and structural stability under wet/dry cycling.

## THE PRESENT APPROACH: GROUT CLASSIFICATION BY ENGINEERING PERFORMANCE

To the twenty or so factors already listed, all of which are relevant to the success of any attempt to improve engineering properties of soils and rocks by grouting, may be added others which are important in particular circumstances, e.g. the rate of flow of ground-water in a fissure system, or the chemical stability of grout components and their solutions under exceptionally high or low site temperature.

Hundreds of different chemicals have been proposed as potential grouts; many have been used at least for the purpose of demonstration and several have found wider application. The general character and physical properties of every grout are determined by the chemical constitution. Within each chemical type there is, however, a considerable range of variation of properties which may be achieved by alteration of the concentration and proportion of the individual constituents.

The present classification provides a means whereby grouts are presented systematically on the basis of the engineering performance typical of a range of formulation which will be likely to be used in the field. It makes possible the selection of those grout types which are potentially of use, and eliminates those whose properties are such as to render them technically unsuitable for the particular need.

The classification is achieved by selection of the most important factors from those listed, the factors which most influence the ability of a soil to accept grout, i.e. the injectability of grout and the engineering properties of the treated formation. By ranking within each of these, appropriate grouts are indicated.

*Set properties*   The strength of a grouted soil is a composite property, depending on the nature of the soil, the interaction between soil and grout, and the structure of the grout. Two ranges of strength are distinguished, low ($L$) and high ($H$).

The residual permeability of a grouted soil depends primarily on the structure of the set grout. When the soil voids are completely filled low permeability is inevitable. When the grout only partially fills the voids, as a result of the use of only a little grout or due to the separation of a fluid phase during the setting process, complete impermeabilisation will not result; the reduction in permeability will depend, for a given soil, on the percentage of voids filled and on the position of the grout within the voids.

Two ranges of residual permeability are distinguished, i.e. a low range, associated with complete solidification of grout in the soil voids, and a higher, broad range, associated with the presence of a fluid phase ($F$) in the set grout. Grouts are thus separated into four groups on the basis of their set properties:

$$H, HF, L \text{ and } LF$$

*Fluid properties*   'Viscosity' is used here as a composite term to sum the effects of viscosity, shear strength and their change whilst the fluid is in motion during injection. It determines the rate of injection, and places a lower limit on the soil permeability which it is practicable to treat.

Viscosity is divided into two ranges, high and low, designated viscous ($V$) and mobile ($M$). Viscosity, in the absence of shear strength, places an economic lower limit on soil permeability which can be treated; a Newtonian fluid will permeate any soil, however fine, if given long enough. The presence of solid particles in the grout immediately places an absolute limit; the soil pores must be sufficiently large for the solid particles to pass through. In practice, for continuous flow without blocking of the capillaries, the diameter of the solid must not be more than about one tenth of the $D_{10}$ size of the soil.

The presence of a solid in the grout is indicated by $S$ written after the $V$ or $M$. In this way four groups of grouts are differentiated on the basis of their fluid properties. They are described respectively as $V$, $VS$, $M$ and $MS$.

A set grout in any of the groups $H$, $HF$, $L$ and $LF$ may be derived from any one of the types of fluid grout, $V$, $VS$, $M$ or $MS$. Thus all actual or potential grouts are completely described by their inclusion within one of sixteen types, each type having a unique combination of fluid and set properties. Figure 6.9 shows the groups diagrammatically, and is so arranged that grout properties may vary continuously within any one quadrant, thus providing for the entering of grouts by consideration of their relative properties. The 'solids in the fluid grout-' ( or $S$-line) and 'fluid phase in the set grout-' (or $F$-line) emphasise the discontinuity across the diagram: the $S$-line separates those grouts whose injectability is controlled by 'effective viscosity' only from those where the filtering out of solid particles may ensue on attempted injection, and the $F$-line separates those grouts giving a continuous set grout from those which result in the voids being partially filled with a fluid after final setting of the grout.

The sixteen groups are presented as in Fig. 6.9 in order to emphasise the symmetry and continuities and discontinuities of properties; it will be evident that the top and bottom lines of the block are identical, and that if they are superimposed fluid properties vary across this second $S$-line. Similarly, the two edges are identical with one another and constitute a second $F$-line.

## THE SHORT CLASSIFICATION

The complete classification may be simpled by the elimination of two sets of grout types:

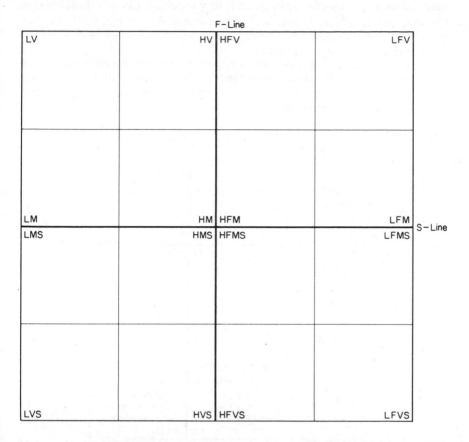

Fig. 6.9. Full classification and its 16 subdivisions. *L:* Grout confers low set strength. *H:* grout confers high set strength. *M:* fluid grout of low viscosity (mobile). *V:* fluid grout of high viscosity (viscous). *S:* suspended solids present in fluid grout. *F:* fluid phase present within grouted formation after grout setting and hardening

1. Those grouts which neither confer strength nor significantly reduce the permeability, i.e. the *'LF'* grouts; *LFV, LFM, LFVS* and *LFMS* fail to satisfy either of the main requirements of a grout. They neither increase the strength nor significantly reduce the permeability of the soil.
2. Grouts which in the fluid state contain a solid phase possess shear strength, and will not normally be described as mobile. The *'MS'* grouts, *LMS, HMS, LFMS* and *HFMS* can therefore be dismissed as having an unlikely combination of fluid properties.

The short classification is shown in Fig. 6.10 together with the *S-* and *F*-lines.

## Use of the short classification

Measurement of the properties of grouts, in 'typical' formulations as fluids and in the set state in combination with a typical soil which has been grouted by permeation, allows the placing of grouts within the classification as has been done for a number of grouts in Fig. 6.11. This is derived from Fig. 6.10, the short classification, by the addition of three strip charts. An extension of the use of the classification is shown in Fig. 6.12.

The strip charts illustrate the consequences of the physical properties of the grouts as manifest in the three generalised properties: injectability in relation to initial permeability of the formation $(A)$, and the strength $(B)$ and residual permeability $(C)$ after treatment.

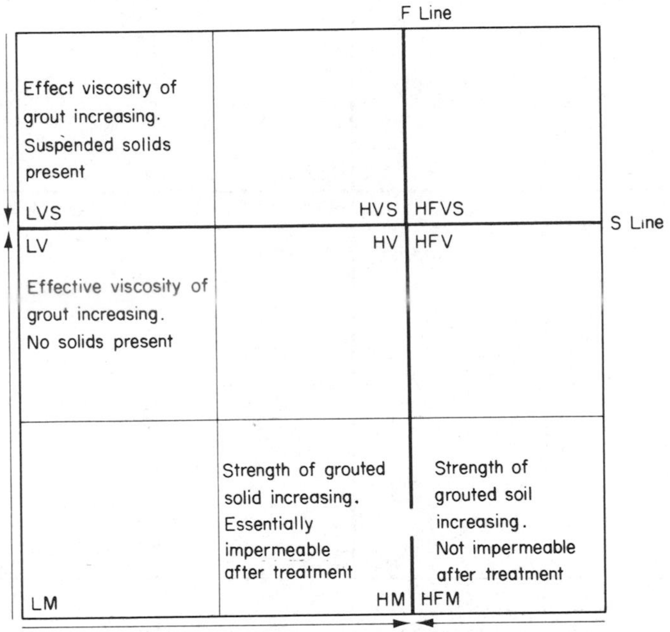

Fig. 6.10. Short classification of nine subdivisions. Seven groups of grouts have been eliminated from the full classification (Fig. 6.9) as having combinations of properties which are either of little value (the *LF* grouts, i.e. *LFM LFV, LFMS* and *LFVS*) or which are improbable (the *MS* grouts, i.e. *LMS, HMS, LFMS* and *HFMS*)

*Chart 1: Initial soil permeability (permeation)*   The range of initial soil permeability over which grout may be introduced by permeation is indicated by the shaded area, the range for any particular grout within the classification being read horizontally across from the position of the grout.

*Charts 2 and 3: Strength, and residual permeability of grouted soil*   The broad bands show the general level of property when read vertically above or below the grout as it is placed in the classification. The band breadth is some measure of the range of variability which will follow from use of the grout in a variety of soils and for different grout concentrations. Residual permeability in the case where the set grout does not completely fill the pores reveals the wide variation possible.

The final permeability will be determined by the volume fraction of fluid in the set grout and by the interaction between set grout and the soil particles (*see* 'How Grouts Interact with the Ground', pp. 85–87). Strengths, initial and residual permeabilities are not shown numerically.

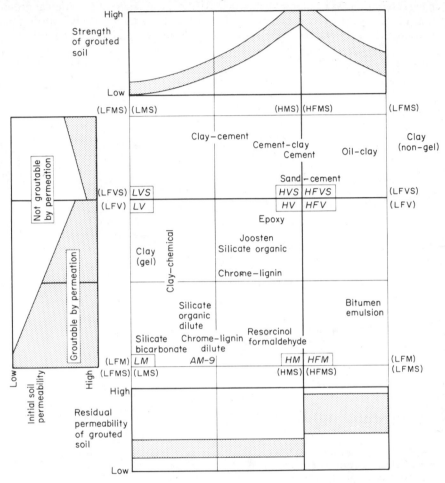

Fig. 6.11. Classification system for grouts, and the engineering properties of soils before and after grouting.

1. Initial Soil Permeability. The range of permeability of soils which may be grouted by permeation with particular grouts (to be read horizontally from grout position within the classification).
2. Strength of Grouted Soil. The variation in ultimate strength (after wet curing, i.e. below the water table) by grout type (to be read vertically).
3. Residual Permeability of Grouted Soil. The ranges of residual permeability of the grouted formation by grout type (to be read vertically).

Use of the classification: named grouts are here placed within the classification as typical examples for purposes of illustration. Grouts additional to those named may be placed within the classification on measurement of their physical properties. Thereafter preliminary selection of grouts may be made on consideration of engineering specification alone, without specific reference to physical properties or chemical nature of the grouts

*Strengths*     Strengths of the weakest gels may be between 0·1 and 1 kN/m². A suitable soil treated with a strong grout may achieve a strength exceeding 7 MN/m² (1 000 lbf/in²). The strength of a grouted formation depends on the type and degree of treatment, and on the extent to which fissures and pores have been filled. The strengths available by alteration of the formulation of a particular grout may range over an order of magnitude. It is necessary to describe fully both the formation, the treatment and the grout if strength figures are to be meaningful.

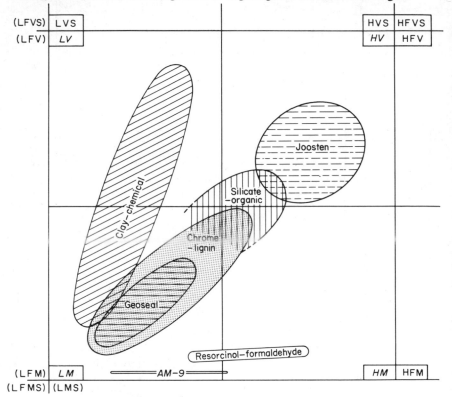

Fig. 6.12. Use of the classification: a section of the engineering classification which is shown in full in Fig. 6.11 is here extended to reveal the overlaps in grout performance which are available by formulation changes within each grout type.

Zones in which the grout stability is suspect, or where the grout is unduly sensitive to moderate dilution by ground-water should be distinguished from the main zone for each grout. Chemicals and grout preparation costs associated with the particular formulations could be added to the classification. Further refinement, extending these additions by the use of stability and cost contours within the area occupied by each grout, may be of value as a means of further reducing the number of grout formulations to be considered in the final stage of appraisal and selection.

In comparative evaluation of grouts by means of tests on grouted sand samples, the sand grading and the relative density must be known and standardised.

*Initial permeability*     The relationships between soil and grout properties and injectability are discussed fully in Chapter 5. High initial permeability may be taken as that of formations which can be permeation grouted by cement ($k \geqslant 10^{1/2}$ mm/s). The rate of acceptance of grout by soils in the fine sand range ($k \approx 10^{-2}$

mm/s) is such that high injection pressures are desirable. Silts with $k \approx 10^{-3}$ mm/s represent the lowest permeability which it is usually practicable to treat by permeation.

*Residual permeability*    The water permeability of set grout may be $10^{-9}$ mm/s or below. Within the formation, the solid particles of which are completely impervious, such low final permeabilities are not observed. In general, a final overall permeability for the mass of treated ground of $10^{-4}$ mm/s is low. The overall efficacy will depend primarily on the location and extent of treatment of pores and fissures rather than on the permeability of the set grout. Uniform soils of high to medium permeability can be grouted easily and completely. Their residual permeability is likely to be minimal. Soils of lower permeability initially are more difficult to treat. Their residual permeability may be greater than that of the more permeable soils. A fissured rock may sometimes accept grout more readily than a porous formation of the same overall permeability.

These patterns of behaviour are illustrated in Fig. 6.13. This figure cannot of

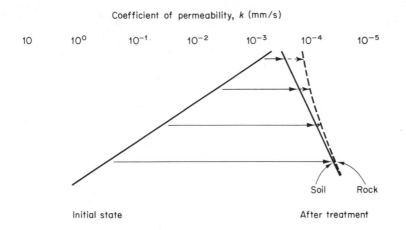

Fig. 6.13. Grout efficacy and the relationships between initial and residual permeabilities (diagrammatic)

course be used to predict the residual permeability which will be obtained in any particular grouting job.

## Economic evaluation for final grout selection

Once the group of grouts which are potentially acceptable has been distinguished from those which are eliminated on purely technical grounds, economic evaluation may follow.

It is necessary first to define the zone to be treated. From the detail of its geology, and particularly the permeability and porosity, the time taken for treatment by permeation at each stage may be calculated. In the particular case of grouts with water-like viscosity, such as *AM-9*, the calculation is simplified by the volume rate of injection being constant through time. For these grouts it is possible to optimise the overall volume of ground grouted in order to ensure

efficient treatment over the volume of the design zone and the number of drillholes employed for grouting, provided only that the unit costs for grout in place,
and drilling and grout-hole preparation (lining, *tube-à-manchette*, etc.) are
known (Fig. 6.14).

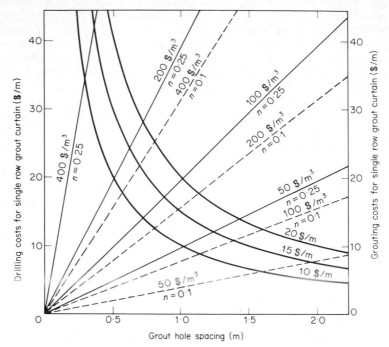

Fig. 6.14. Cost optimisation in use of *AM-9* and other grouts whose viscosity is constant up to setting, for a single row grout curtain with adjacent injections tangent. For this configuration, the cost of
grouting works is at a minimum when the grout hole spacing is that indicated by the intersection
between the appropriate drilling costs and grouting costs lines.

— Drilling costs per metre of single-row grout curtain for rates of $10, $15 and $20 per metre of
  hole.
--- Grouting costs for porosity treated, $n = 0.1$, and
— grouting costs for porosity treated, $n = 0.25$, for rates of $50, $100, $200 and $400 per cubic
  metre of grout in place.

"There are no conditions where such a pattern would be the most desirable choice. The main
utility of such data is in establishing a design value for the radial spread of grout in the major line of
a closed grouting pattern. . . . In a closed pattern two rows of holes are sufficient to make a complete
cut-off. The volume of grout used per inner hole can be considerably less than in the major line,
though not necessarily so. The volume of grout used in each hole in the major line would be as com-
puted from a chart such as this. The spacing, however, would be increased to almost double the
value indicated. Spacing in the inner row would be the same as in the outer row. The distance
between the centre lines of the rows would be about one third of the hole spacing" (after *AM-9
Field Manual*[10])

For other grouts which are somewhat more viscous than water, the volume
rate of injection diminishes as injection proceeds; under saturated conditions the
whole of the initial resistance to flow of the grout is that of the ground-water
being displaced. As the ground is wetted by the grout, an increasing proportion
of the total resistance is contributed through the viscosity of the grout. The

volume rate of injection falls off until it reaches a constant value related inversely to the initial rate through the viscosity ratio of grout to ground-water.

As an example, consider a grout which is a Newtonian fluid of viscosity 10 cP, being injected into a soil of permeability $k = 0 \cdot 1$ mm/s under a head of 100 ft (30·5 m) of water and from a 3 ft (0·9 m) length of 1·5 in (38 mm) dia hole (Fig. 6.15)[19].

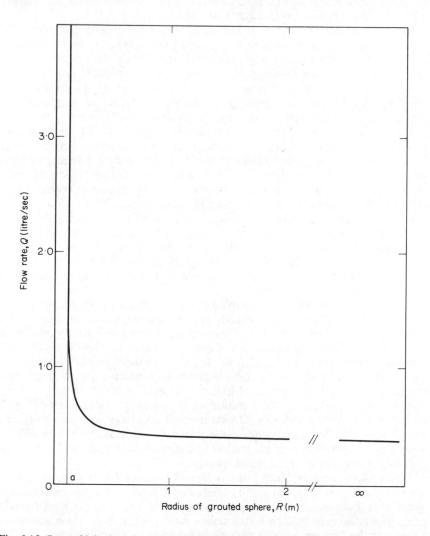

Fig. 6.15. Rate of injection of a Newtonian grout of viscosity 10cP into a soil of coefficient of permeability k = 0·1 mm/s, under an injection head of 30 m of water from a source of equivalent spherical radius 100 mm (after Raffle and Greenwood[19])

When the grout has permeated only 0·3 m beyond the periphery of the injection source (equivalent spherical radius 102 mm) the instantaneous rate has fallen from 3 900 cm³/s to below 500 cm³/s, that is, within 25% of the ultimate rate of 390 cm$^3$/s. Because of the considerable change in the rate of injection with increasing penetration shown by grouts a few times more viscous than water, the unit cost of grout in place is not constant for different radii of grout penetration, and injection time, grout cost and hole costs must be taken into account individually. Grouts which have substantial viscosity attain rates close to their lower limiting rate of injection at small radii of penetration, so that for practical purposes the rate can be taken as constant. This rate can be used for cost calculation in the same manner as that for water-like grout.

Most grouts may be compounded in different ways to give viscosities and strengths varying over a considerable range. For grouting by permeation, the lowest viscosity grout which yields adequate strength will be selected for use in formations of moderate to low initial permeability. The initial viscosities of two grouts of the same chemical type may differ by a factor of ten or more. It is therefore essential that the actual grout viscosity at formation temperature is used in calculations of rate of grouting, rather than some 'typical' figure.

For maximum rates of grout acceptance the formulation of lowest viscosity should be used. A low viscosity when the grout is a true solution may be sought in two ways: by using only solutes of low molecular weight, in water or some other solvent of high mobility, or by having a low concentration of larger molecules in solution. In the latter case, the minimum acceptable concentration will generally be conditioned by the need for physical and chemical stability, for adequate strength and creep characteristics of the set grout and stability in the chemical environment of the ground, and also by the safety factor in concentration judged necessary to ensure against accidental dilution of grout by groundwater. In general, it will be desirable to adopt minimum grout concentrations for field use substantially greater than those which are just sufficient to produce a stable gel from aqueous solution.

When large quantities of grout are being used, materials costs are such that a small saving in unit costs may yield considerable benefit during the course of the contract. Expenditure on testing of local materials and on site formulation of grouts, and the setting up of a system of quality control, may then be justified. On small contracts, grouts prepared from fine chemicals or ordinary Portland cement offer the advantage of reproducibility of performance from a given grout formulation. Proprietary grouts of known viscosity, setting time and stability, can be used on many jobs with a minimum of preliminary testing and of expenditure on site control facilities. On both small and large jobs as complete a knowledge of the permeability and allowable grouting pressures as is possible is needed if the overall cost of the job is to be minimised through selection of the best combination of grout and hole spacing.

When solution grouts which yield hydrogels are used in permeation grouting, the volume of ground which will be treated by injection of a known volume of grout is fairly accurately known. This is not the case with cement grouts and with other grouts injected at high water:solids ratios. Water from these grouts escapes into the finer passages in the soil or rock which the solid particles are too coarse to enter, and the trapped grout particles pack more closely into the voids. Whereas the gelling solution or resin grouts fill a cubic metre of voids for every cubic metre of grout injected, the yield from cement grouts may be much lower. Comparative costing must take into account both differing rates of injection as a result of differences in fluid properties, and also the fact that the volumes of grout to be pumped may not be at all comparable.

REFERENCES

1. Karol, R. H., Contribution to discussion on paper by Perrott, W. E., 'British Practice for Grouting Granular Soils', *Proc. Am. Soc. Civ. Engrs.,* **92,** SM4, 106–107 (1966)
2. Lambe, T. W., *et al.,* 'Chemical Grouting', progress report of the Task Committee on Chemical Grouting, *Proc. Am. Soc. Civ. Engrs.,* **83,** SM4, Paper 1426, 1–106 (1957)
3. Kravetz, G. A., 'Cement and Clay Grouting of Foundations. The Use of Clay in Pressure Grouting', *Proc. Am. Soc. Civ. Engrs.,* **84,** SM1, Paper 1546, 1–30 (1958)
4. Czernin, W., *Cement Chemistry and Physics for Civil Engineers,* Crosby Lockwood and Son Ltd., London (1962)
5. Elston, J. P., *et al.,* 'Cement Grouting', Progress report of the Task Committee on Cement Grouting, *Proc. Am. Soc. Civ. Engrs.,* **88,** SM2, Paper 3098, 49–98 (1962)
6. Brunauer, S., and Copeland, L. E., 'The Chemistry of Concrete', *Scientific American,* **210** No. 4, 80–92, April (1964)
7. Hilton, I. C. and Howell, F. T., 'Is the Cementing-up of Boreholes too Drastic?', *Water and Water Engineering,* **71,** 95–96 (1967)
8. *Geoseal Resin Grouts,* Borden Chemical Co. (1972)
9. Karol, R. H., 'Chemical Grouting Technology', *Proc. Am. Soc. Civ. Engrs.,* **94,** SM1, Paper 5748, 175–204 (1968)
10. *AM-9 Chemical Grout Field Manual,* American Cyanamid Co., 4th ed (1973)
11. *Terranier Grouting Process,* Rayonier Incorporated (1969)
12. Neelands, R. J. and James, A. N., 'Formulation and Selection of Chemical Grouts with Typical Examples of Their Field Use', Proc. Symposium on Grouts and Drilling Muds in Engineering Practice, May 1963, Butterworths, London, 150–155 (1963)
13. Jones, G. K., Contribution to discussion, Proc. Symposium on Grouts and Drilling Muds in Engineering Practice, May, 1963, Butterworths, London, 164, 165 and 170 (1963)
14. Skipp, B. O. and Renner, L., 'The Improvement of the Mechanical Properties of Sand', Proc. Symposium on Grouts and Drilling Muds in Engineering Practice', May, 1963, Butterworths, London, 29–35 (1963)
15. Advertisement, copyright N. G. Reid, in 'Grouting Design and Practice', supplement to *The Consulting Engineer,* **33,** 1–40, Oct. (1969)
16. 'Grouting Design and Practice', supplement to *The Consulting Engineer,* **33,** 1–40, Oct. (1969)
17. Pozament Cement Ltd., 'Principles of Grouting Selection', *Civil Engineering and Public Works Review,* **66,** 1137 and 1142 (1971)
18. Einstein, H. H. and Schmitter, G., 'Selection of Chemical Grout for Mattmark Dam', *Proc. Am. Soc. Civ. Engrs.,* **96,** SM6, 2007–2023 (1970)
19. Raffle, J. F. and Greenwood, D. A., 'The Relation Between the Rheological Characteristics of Grouts and Their Capacity to Permeate Soil', Proc. 5th International Conference on Soil Mechanics and Foundation Engineering, Paris, 1961, 789–793 (1961)


BIBLIOGRAPHY

Hilton, I. C., 'Grout Selection: A New Classification System', *Civil Engineering and Public Works Review,* **62,** 993–995 (1967)
Seaman, W. K., *et al.,* 'Guide Specifications for Chemical Grouts', *Proc. Am. Soc. Civ. Engrs.,* **94,** SM2, 345–352 (1968) and discussion, SM2, 640–655 (1969)
Werner, J., 'Strength Properties of Chemically Solidified Soils', *Proc. Am. Soc. Civ. Engrs.,* **98,** SM11, 1163–1185 (1972)
Code of Practice for Foundations, CP2004: 1972, Section 6; Leonard, M. W., *et al.,* 'Geotechnical Processes for Dewatering and Treatment of Substrata', British Standards Institution, 79–84 (1972)

# Chapter 7

# Ground Conditions in Mining Areas

The need for urban redevelopment on a large scale together with the increase in the rate of construction due to increasing mechanisation and the increasing scarcity of suitable sites has meant that in recent years areas formerly regarded as unsuitable have been, and are being, considered for building purposes. Most of the large industrial centres of the UK, in all of which redevelopment is going on, are underlain by rocks of Coal Measures age. Therefore an added factor as far as redevelopment in such areas is concerned is the problem of past or existing mineral workings. Indeed land over old coal workings has, in some cities, been considered unsuitable for development with heavy buildings because of the presence of old uncollapsed voids at shallow depth. It must not, however, be assumed that the frequent problems associated with mining in these areas are only related to the extraction of coal, for other materials have been and are won from the Coal Measures. These include fireclay; gannister; ironstone; clays, shales and mudstones for bricks; sandstones for building purposes, etc. Such materials have been both mined and quarried. Ground covered by discard from old mines is now being developed with increasing frequency. Mine waste may be poorly compacted, with a low strength. If heavy structures are founded upon it they are likely to undergo appreciable settlement.

## The character of the Coal Measures

The term *Coal Measures* is given to those rocks which occur in the Carboniferous system above the Millstone Grit, or Namurian as it is now known. The Carboniferous system is divided into lower and upper divisions, the Namurian and Coal Measures being in the latter. As can be inferred from the name 'Coal Measures', this sequence of rocks contains workable coals. Workable coals with associated rock types, however, are found in other parts of the Carboniferous of the UK, e.g. in the Scremerston Coal Group and the Limestone Group of the Lower Carboniferous of Northumberland, and in the Edge Coal Group of Scotland. Furthermore the uppermost strata of the Coal Measures, known as the Stephanian, are barren, i.e. they do not contain coals workable by underground methods. That part of the Coal Measures which does contain workable coals is referred to as the Westphalian. Coal occurs throughout the world in every system from the Devonian onwards.

A characteristic feature of Coal Measures sedimentation is its rhythmic deposition with the consequent development of cyclothemic stratal sequences. A cyclothem has been defined as a multiple repetition of beds of different lithology which are recognisably similar in internal sequence, showing usually minor variations both in thickness and precise sequence of components. In the UK the simple 'classical' cyclothemic unit in the Coal Measures usually consists of:

One cyclothem
$\begin{cases} \text{Coal} \\ \text{Seatearth} \\ \text{Sandstone} \\ \text{Non-marine shale or mudstone} \\ \text{Marine band} \\ \text{Coal} \end{cases}$

Little reliance, however, may be placed on the standard pattern in any particular coalfield as a means of predicting rock types at various levels within the sequence. Marine bands are generally thin and indeed in most units are absent. Coals may also be absent. Individual cyclothems vary in thickness usually ranging between a few metres up to a few tens of metres. Fine-grained sediments form the major part of a cyclothem, the ratio of shale, mudstone and siltstone to sandstone being about 3:1. It follows that the thickest members of a cyclothemic unit are generally the mudstones and shales, but massive bedded sandstones may be important locally. These, however, are often lenticular and laterally impersistent. The coal in a given thickness of coal-bearing strata will usually form from 2 to 5% of the total thickness, inclusive of thin, unworkable seams. The coal seams themselves vary in thickness from mere films to a couple of metres or so thick; exceptionally they may be very thick such as the Ten Yards Coal of Staffordshire.

Most coal seams have a composite character. At the bottom the coal is often softer and is sometimes simply referred to as 'bottom' coal. In the centre of the seam, bright coal is often of most importance whilst dull coal may predominate in the upper part of the seam.

Most coals can be broken into blocks which have three faces approximately at right angles. These surfaces, along which breakage takes place, are termed *cleat*. The cleat direction is usually pretty constant and frequently influenced the direction of underground working, for it was easier to hew across the cleat than along it. Within a single seam, the cleat is best developed in the bright coals and less prominent in the dull. Cleat partings may be filmed with mineral matter, commonly calcite, ankerite and occasionally gypsum. Cleat is not developed in anthracite.

Argillaceous rocks account for about three quarters of the thickness of a sequence of coal-bearing strata. Their occurrence is often widespread and uniform and they may be traceable over large areas of a coalfield. The individual beds may be over 30 m in thickness. These argillaceous rocks are usually some shade between black and pale grey although blue-grey is a common colour, and brown and red mudstones and shales occur, particularly in the upper part of the Coal Measures. There are several types of black shales, e.g. carbonaceous shales are soft, finely laminated and feel rather soapy. As their name suggests they contain plant remains. Marine shales may also be black in colour but these are not nearly so frequent in occurrence as non-marine shales.

There is no sharp distinction between mudstones and shales, one grading into the other. Shales, however, are characterised by their fissility, which in some cases may be very thin, as in 'paper' shales, whilst mudstones are relatively massive and may break either along joints or with an irregular, conchoidal fracture. Clays, like mudstones, are relatively massive but they lack induration.

The plasticity of a typical clay from the Coal Measures is due to the presence of a sufficient quantity of clay minerals and of colloidal material with their marked affinity with water. Some marine shales may be impregnated with carbonate material, which makes them appreciably stronger, and they may grade into impure limestones.

Clay ironstone may be found in the mudstones and shales of the Coal Measures. Nodules frequently occur in a recognisable layer and in some instances they may be replaced by a continuous band of ironstone. The shales in which they occur are typically iron stained and brittle.

Seatearths are almost invariably found beneath coal seams although they may occur at other levels in a sequence. The character of a seatearth depends on the type of deposits which were laid down immediately before the establishment of plant growth. If they were muds then a fireclay underlies the coal, on the other hand if they were silts and sands then it is a gannister. Seatearths can be regarded as fossil soils and as such are characterised by the presence of fossilised rootlets. These rootlets extended downwards and tended to destroy the lamination and bedding of the seatearths. A typical fireclay is pale grey in colour and consists of clay minerals with fine quartz grains. Fireclays with a low content of quartz are typically highly slickensided and break easily along randomly orientated listric surfaces. A gannister is a fine-grained quartzose rock, often the quartz grains are angular and of rather uniform size. Many gannisters are pure siltstones and because they are usually well cemented with silica they are hard and strong. They are usually light grey in colour although the presence of carbonaceous matter may give darker shades. Individual beds of gannister only infrequently exceed 2 m in thickness. The bulk of all the true gannisters occur in the Lower Coal Measures. Fireclays tend to replace gannisters as seatearths in the Middle Coal Measures.

Siltstones grade imperceptibly into rocks of clay grade. Some are massive although many are laminated. The individual laminae may be picked out by the presence of darker layers which contain carbonaceous matter and/or mica. They vary in thickness from less than 1 mm up to a few millimetres. Micro-cross bedding is frequently present and in some siltstones the lamination may be convoluted. Siltstones have a high quartz content with a predominantly siliceous cement, they are therefore grey in colour and are hard, tough rocks. Frequently siltstones are interbedded with shales or fine-grained sandstones, the siltstones occurring as thin ribs.

Sandstones are the most inconsistent members of Coal Measures cyclothems. They are generally lenticular in shape and vary rapidly in thickness. Some of the sandstones are composed almost entirely of quartz and usually have a siliceous cement. These are white or pale grey in colour and are amongst the strongest rocks of the Coal Measures. Other sandstones may have a carbonate cement or argillaceous matrix or an admixture of both. Iron oxides may also act as a cementing material.

Most of the inter-seam sandstones are fine-to-medium grained though occasional coarse varieties do occur. These coarse-grained sandstones may merge into conglomerates and breccias. Generally speaking, Coal Measures sandstones may be subdivided into two groups, namely the thick-bedded massive or coarsely cross-bedded types on the one hand, and the fine-grained thinner and less persistent types on the other. The latter type may exhibit cross bedding on a macro- or micro-scale, they are frequently laminated, notably the micaceous varieties, and ripple marks may also be present.

Many of the rocks of the Coal Measures have been worked besides coal. Both gannister and fireclays are worked for refractory purposes and have been either quarried or mined. Many between coal shales, the so-called bastard fireclays, although not refractory enough for firebricks, have been worked for sanitary ware. Shales, mudstones and clays are extensively worked for brick making. Ironstones were formerly quarried and mined on an extensive scale, although none are exploited at the present time. Many sandstones have also been quarried and mined for flags, building stones, moulding sands and grindstones. Consequently the engineer who is involved in construction in an area of Coal Measures should bear in mind that problems may arise not only due to the extraction of coal but also due to the exploitation of other materials, whether in the past or the present. Past exploitation will usually provide more headaches than that going on at the present.

Foundation design and construction in Coal Measures areas not only has to consider the problem of old mine workings but also the varying lithology of the cyclothems which comprise the formation. As far as the rocks of the Coal Measures are concerned, in unconfined compression at right angles to the bedding planes, sandstones tend to be stronger than siltstones and these in turn are stronger than mudstones, shales and coals (Table 7.1). The compressive strengths of sandstones with siliceous or ferruginous cements are usually greater than those with carbonate cements or clay matrix, i.e. if the amount of cement is approximately equal. When subjected to compression parallel to the bedding, a rock fails at a lower loading. Thus flaggy sandstones are weaker than massive varieties and shales weaker than mudstones. Generally there is a decrease in compressive strength with increasing porosity, this is particularly true in the case of sandstones. The saturation moisture content can also effectively reduce the compressive strength of well lithified rock by 25–50%, and fireclays may soften in the presence of water. The strength of siltstones is largely dependent upon the relative amounts of quartzose and clayey material they contain, in other words the more quartz they contain the stronger they are. It has been shown that there is a general tendency for the compressive strength of coal to increase with increasing rank. Little laboratory testing has been carried out on fireclays but very large variations in bearing capacity have been recorded when underground plate loading tests have been carried out on them.

When rocks are subjected to bending, shearing takes place along the bedding plane direction. Thus the more parting planes there are in a rock, the weaker it is when so loaded. Massive sandstones and siltstones are again stronger than laminated varieties, bending strengths of mudstones are greater than those of shales. The amount of bending for a given span and thickness is least in the case of sandstones. Siltstones bend less than mudstones and shales whilst these bend less than coal.

Creep tests performed on Coal Measures rocks have suggested that both instantaneous strain and primary creep under load are not completely recoverable and that this irrecoverable strain is possibly related to the level of stress applied. It has been shown that a linear relationship exists between load and the rate of

**Table 7.1**   STRENGTH OF COAL MEASURES ROCKS (DATA AFTER HOBBS, PRICE, AND EVANS AND POMEROY)

| Rock type | Description | Crushing strength (MN/m²) | Tensile strength (MN/m²) |
|---|---|---|---|
| 1. Pennant Sandstone | Massive, fine-grained sandstone | 168·9 | 18·9 |
| 2. Parkgate Rock | Massive, fine-grained sandstone | 111·7 | 8·6 |
| 3. Tupton Rock | Massive, friable medium-grained sandstone | 62·1 | 4·5 |
| 4. Markham Sandstone | Slightly bedded, fine-grained sandstone | 108·9 | 10·8 |
| 5. Snowdown Siltstone | Laminated, fine-grained sandstone | 93·1 | 6·6 |
| 6. Chislet Siltstone | Well-laminated fine-grained siltstone | 90·3 | 7·9 |
| 7. Seven Foot Mudstone | Slightly bedded mudstone | 88·3 | |
| 8. Dunsil Mudstone | Carbonaceous, shaley mudstone | 44·8 | |
| 9. Barnsley Hards Coal | | 55·7†* 34·1‡* | 4·1† 2·8‡ |
| 10. Deep Duffryn Coal | | 18·2†* 16·1‡* | 0·9‡ 0·7† |
| 11. Shale Cumbernauld | Laminated | 20·4 | |
| 12. Sandy shale Cumbernauld | Finely interbedded sandstone and shale | 25·8 | |

* Crushed cubes (25·4 × 25·4 × 25·4 mm).
† Load applied across bedding planes.
‡ Load applied parallel to bedding planes.

secondary creep in the case of some sandstones, and some sandstones and siltstones which failed did not exhibit tertiary creep prior to fracture. Sandstones generally produce 'S'-shaped stress–strain curves, typical $E_{t50}$ values falling within the range 21 000 MN/m² to 56 000 MN/m². The range for mudstones is 14 000 MN/m² to 35 000 MN/m², with fireclays about 7 000 MN/m².

Swelling of rocks is associated with weathering. Clays, shales, mudstones and marls are most prone to swelling; however, small amounts have been recorded in some sandstones. The clay mineral content of argillaceous rocks plays an important role as far as swelling is concerned, e.g. kaolinite is not expansive whilst montmorillonite is. When a rock swells it does so due to the absorption of water which allows the development of pore pressures high enough to overcome its inherent strength. Rocks which have an unconfined compressive strength of 41 MN/m² and above are not subject to swelling[1].

In a study of the disintegration of Coal Measures shales in water, Badger, Cummings and Whitmore[2] concluded that this was brought about by two main processes, namely, air breakage and the dispersion of colloid due to the disassociation of ions. It was noted that the former process only occurred in those shales which were mechanically weak, whilst the latter appeared to be a general cause of disintegration. It was found that the variation in disintegration of different shales in water was not usually connected with their total amount of clay colloid or the variation in the types of clay mineral present. Rather, it was controlled by the type of exchangeable cations attached to the clay and on the accessibility of the latter to attack by water which, in turn, depended on the porosity of the shale. Air breakage could assist this process by presenting new surfaces of shale to water. It was also suggested that like coal, shale may also have a rank and that low-rank shales were associated with low-rank coals. The low-rank shales disintegrated most easily.

After an exhaustive investigation into the breakdown of Coal Measures rocks, Taylor and Spears[3] concluded that the disintegration of sandstones and siltstones was governed by their fracture pattern and that after a few months of weathering the resulting debris was still greater than cobble size. After that the degradation to give component grains took place at a very slow rate. The major part of their work, however, was devoted to a consideration of the breakdown of mudstones and shales. Both latter types of rocks, as well as seatearths, are rapidly broken down to a gravel-sized aggregate. The mudstones and shales which were considered possessed a polygonal fracture pattern normal to the bedding, possibly due to syneresis. These fractures were regarded as the principal factor causing breakdown in non-laminated argillaceous rocks. Such fractures, together with laminations and joints, contribute towards the degradation of shales and mudstones within a matter of months. Listric surfaces in seatearths may mean that they disintegrate within a few wetting and drying cycles. Nevertheless it was noticed that a simple behaviour pattern did not exist, e.g. some rocks like the Brooch and Park seatearths, after being desiccated, disintegrated very rapidly in water (the former was literally 'explosive' and the latter broke down in less than 30 min). Although the expandable clay content in these two rocks is high and leads to intra-particle swelling, the authors maintained that this alone was not responsible for their rapid degradation. Taylor and Spears found that breakdown could largely be arrested by the removal of air from the samples under vacuum. Thus they concluded that air breakage was a principal disintegration mechanism in the weaker rocks. These two authors did not dismiss the physico-chemical ideas of Badger, Cummings and Whitmore[2] but suggested that breakdown in this case was primarily due to intra-particle swelling in rocks with a high expandable mixed-layer clay content (mica-montmorillonites with relatively high $Na^+$ cation-exchange capacities).

In a later paper, Spears and Taylor[4] discussed the effect of weathering on *in-situ* Coal Measures rocks. They found that minor evidence of weathering extended to depths of approximately 6 m below the surface. On testing the highly weathered equivalents of siltstone and shale, they noted that the values of compressive strength were reduced to about one tenth of those values of the unweathered parental rocks. The values of $\phi'$ and $c'$ for weathered siltstone, fragmental mudstone and seatearth varied from 36 to 45·5°, and from 131 to 179 kN/m² respectively. The intergranular friction values are apparently similar to those of jointed shales and siltstones whilst the values of cohesion approach those of soft rocks. As far as the shear strength parameters are concerned, they quoted a decrease in $\phi$ of up to 37%, and in cohesion of approximately 93%.

## Mining methods

Coal is by far the most important material mined in the UK. It appears to have been worked at least since Roman times and the exploitation of many coalfields dates from the twelfth century. The last one to be developed in the UK was the small Kent coalfield, a totally concealed field, which was opened after World War I.

Most of the early workings were at surface outcrops. By the fourteenth century outcrop workings had largely given way to bell pits and drifting. The shafts of bell pits rarely exceeded 12·2 m in depth and their diameter was usually about 1·3 m. Extraction was carried on around the shaft until such times as roof support became impossible. Another shaft was then sunk so that a series of bell pits frequently occur near the outcrop of a seam. These shafts may or may not have been back-filled. If they have the material may be poorly compacted. The scarcity of timber during Elizabethan times led to an increase in the demand for coal and by this time the pillar and stall method of extraction had been evolved. Underground workings were shallow and not extensive, e.g. they may only have penetrated 40 m from the shaft. Indeed, when such limits had been reached, it was usually less costly to abandon a pit and sink another shaft nearby. Workings extending 200 m from the shaft were exceptional even at the end of the seventeenth century, the shaft itself very often being less than 60 m deep.

In very early mining the remnant pillars were rather haphazard in size and arrangement, but mining development rapidly became more systematic and pillars of more or less uniform shape were formed by driving intersecting roadways in the seam. Also there was a general tendency for the size of stalls to increase, e.g. in Elizabethan times they were usually less than 2 m wide whereas in the eighteenth century they began to exceed 3 m in width. Wardell and Wood[5] noted that in the nineteenth century the normal width of stall varied from 1·83 to 4·57 m, the extraction ratio varying from 30 to 70%. Several variations of the room and pillar method were devised, perhaps to overcome particular local problems, but in all cases the method had to be related to the thickness and quality of the seam, the character of the roof and floor rocks and the dip of the seam, e.g. Staffordshire squarework was developed to work the Ten Yards Coal seam, in the Sheffield area ribs of coal were generally left to support the roof rather than pillars.

With the development in the eighteenth century of steam power and the use of coal to smelt iron, the demand for coal accelerated. The miner, however, was faced with a number of problems which limited the size and depth of his pit: drainage, ventilation and haulage being three of the most important. Developments such as steam pumps, the Buddle fan, the safety lamp and wire ropes, allowed mines to become more extensive and go to greater depths. In addition longwall working evolved in the eighteenth century, probably first originating in the Shropshire coalfield. The panels were developed from an initial drivage within the seam and as the working face advanced so the support was withdrawn allowing the roof to collapse. Thus coal mining gradually developed to become one of the most important industries in the UK, reaching its peak production in 1913.

Subsidence is an inevitable consequence of mining; under some circumstances it may be small or it may be delayed for several years. It can be regarded as the vertical component of ground movement although there is also a horizontal component. Subsidence can and does have serious effects on buildings, services and communications, can be responsible for flooding, lead to the sterilisation of land or call for extensive remedial measures or special constructional design in site development.

Subsidence at the surface reflects the movement which has occurred in the mined-out area. As a consequence, small deformation in the workings is associated with insignificant subsidence whereas total closure of the workings can give rise to severe subsidence at ground level. A number of questions concerning the stability of the surface above mine workings require answers, these include:

1. Will subsidence occur and if so, what will be its magnitude?
2. When will it happen and how will it develop?
3. What form will the subsidence take?
4. Is it practical and economic to prevent or reduce its effects?

As already mentioned, mining methods in which pillars of coal are left as the main support for the overlying rocks have been employed over several centuries. In present-day workings the pillar-support system can be designed for long-term stability if it is important to protect the surface or to minimise damage to the roof[6], e.g. the mining engineer can control the pillar dimensions and the percentage extraction. The dimensions of a pillar, which in turn influence its stability, are influenced by the depth of the workings, the seam thickness, the strength of the roof rock (including its fracture pattern) and local conditions; they must be adequate to prevent the development of creep and thrust. Floor heave and the piling of bulk material, which has collapsed from the roof, against pillars provides a confining effect once an area has been abandoned. The consequences of interaction between beds of widely different properties can be significant, e.g. if a soft layer occurs within a pillar or near the roof or floor, it can have a weakening effect on the more rigid adjacent rock. Materials which display creep properties or are susceptible to deterioration on exposure to air or moisture do not form ideal permanent supports.

Pillars have to sustain the redistributed weight of the overburden which means that they and the rocks immediately above and below are subjected to added compression. Stress concentrations tend to be located at the edge of pillars and the intervening roof beds tend to sag. The effects on ground level are normally insignificant unless the floor is unusually soft. In such cases the pillars may penetrate the floor and give rise to a general lowering of the surface. Obviously this becomes more significant with increasing depth or high extraction ratio since these impose greater loads upon the pillars. Although such subsidence is often slow it may be quickened by the ingress of water into the workings. In addition minor strain and tilt problems occur around the periphery of the basin thereby produced.

From Fig. 7.1 it can be seen that $a$ is the pillar width whilst $b$ is the width of the stall. The extraction ratio $r$ can therefore be derived from the following expression: expression:

$$r = \frac{2ab + b^2}{(a + b)^2}$$

According to Wardell and Wood[5] determination of the loading on pillars is best approximated by averaging the load on a given pillar due to the weight of overburden. The latter is equal to the weight of the column of strata over an area equal to $(a + b)^2$. It is assumed that the load acts vertically and is uniformly distributed over the cross-sectional area of the pillars. It can be shown that the average loading $p$ on a pillar is given by:

$$p = \frac{d}{1 - r}$$

where $d$ = depth and $r$ = extraction ratio. The total load on a pillar determined in this way is probably greater than the true load. In addition the distribution of the load over the area of the pillar is not uniform for stress is concentrated at pillar edges. When a structure is to be built over an area of old pillared workings the additional load on the pillars can be estimated simply by adding the weight of the appropriate part of the structure to the weight of the column of strata supported by a given pillar. It can be seen from this expression that although the intrinsic

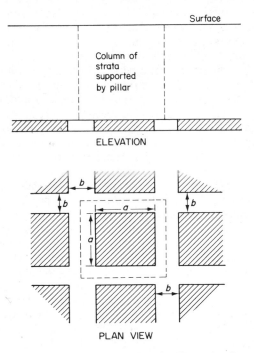

Fig. 7.1. Plan view of loading on pillars in pillar and stall working

strength of coal varies, the important factor in the case of pillars is that their ultimate behaviour is a function of seam thickness to pillar width, the depth below ground and the size of the extraction area. The mode of failure also involves the rock character of the roof and floor. The greatest stress occurs at the edges of pillars. Pillars in dipping seams tend to be less stable than those in horizontal seams since the overburden produces a shear force on the pillar.

Recent work on pillar stability has been carried out by Wilson[7]. He suggested that a pillar was surrounded by an outer yield zone in which the stress distribution varied in linear fashion from zero at the surface to failure point at the surface of the pillar core. The constraint given to coal in the pillar core can increase its strength appreciably. The strength of the pillar core was given by the following expression:

$$\sigma = \sigma_0 + \sigma_3 \tan \beta$$

where $\sigma_0 =$ the failure stress in the unconfined condition,

$\tan \beta =$ angle of shearing resistance of the coal (which was shown to approximate to 4),

$\sigma_3 =$ the confining pressure and

$\sigma =$ stress required to cause failure.

If it is assumed that the confining pressure is due to a hydrostatic state of stress then this equation can be simplied thus:

$$\sigma = \sigma_0 + 4\rho h$$

where $\rho =$ average density of rock and $h =$ thickness of overburden.

Wilson[7] went on to give empirical expressions for the loads which both wide and narrow, square, rectangular and long pillars can carry. It must be remarked, however, that these expressions take no account of the strength of the material involved and although they may be admissable for *deep* workings they possibly give significant underestimates of the strength of pillars at shallow depths.

Pillars often experience local failures whilst mining is taking place. If a pillar is highly jointed then its margin may fail and fall away under relatively low stress. Such action reduces and ultimately removes the constraint from the core thereby subjecting it to increasing stress. This could lead to pillar failure. Collapse in one pillar can bring about collapse in others in a sort of chain reaction because increasing loads are placed on those remaining. This has never been a significant problem in the UK. Collapse of a whole pillar district, however, has been known to happen, e.g. in Coalbrook, South Africa. The Coalbrook Colliery disaster occurred at 7.30 p.m. on January 21st, 1960, and lasted for only 5 min[8]. It resulted in the loss of 437 lives and the collapse extended over at least 3 km$^2$. The seam in which the collapse took place was 7·6 m thick and at an average depth of 143·3 m. In such cases the surface suffers substantial rapid subsidence, possibly shock damage, often a zone of fracture, and severe local strain and tilt damage.

Slow deterioration and failure of pillars may take place years after mining operations have elapsed, although observations at shallow depth and the resistance of coal to weathering suggests that this is a relatively uncommon feature at depths less than 30 m. However, old workings affect the pattern of ground-water drainage which in turn may influence pillar deterioration. On the other hand the small pillars of earlier workings may be crushed out once the overburden exceeds 50 or 60 m. Old pillars at shallow depth have occasionally failed near faults and they may fail if they are subjected to the effects of subsequent longwall mining. Nevertheless the dimensions of pillars are often such that at shallow depth stability is unlikely to be further reduced by structural surcharge.

Where old mine workings underlie a site it is necessary to determine the size of the pillars and extraction ratios; very often pillars were robbed on retreat. Extraction of pillars during the retreat phase simulates the longwall surface condition although it can never be assumed that all pillars have been removed. As already noted, at moderate depths pillars, particularly pillar remnants, are probably crushed and the goaf compacted, but at shallow depths lower crushing pressures may mean that closure is variable. This causes foundation problems when large or sensitive structures are to be erected above. Indeed the behaviour of shallow pillar and stall workings presents one of the most difficult problems a foundation engineer has to face because of the difficulty in quantifying their behaviour.

Even if pillars are relatively stable the surface can be affected by void migration (Fig. 7.2)[9]. This can take place within a few months of or a very long period of years after mining and in the UK is a much more serious problem than pillar collapse. Void migration develops when roof rock falls into the worked-out area.

Fig. 7.2. Void migration in shaley roof rocks above the Five-Quarter seam at Pethburn Open-cast site, County Durham (Courtesy Taylor[9])

When this occurs the material involved in the fall bulks, which means that migration is eventually arrested, although the bulked material never completely fills the voids. The factors which influence the height above the workings to which migration proceeds include:

1. The width of the unsupported span.
2. The mechanical properties, particularly the tensile strength, of the roof rock.

3. The thickness of overburden.
4. The seam thickness and height of the room.
5. The dip of the seam.

The height to which a void will migrate can be determined by using Tincelin's expression[10]:

$$H = t\left[\left(\frac{\gamma_1}{\gamma}\right) \div \left(1 - \frac{\gamma_1}{\gamma}\right)\right]$$

where: $t =$ thickness of the seam,
 $\gamma =$ bulk density of the roof rocks,
 $\gamma_1 =$ bulk density of collapsed roof materials and
 $H =$ height of migration.

The self-choking process may not be fulfilled if dipping seams are affected by copious quantities of water which can redistribute the fallen material. Nevertheless it has been suggested that generally speaking void migration will not produce crown holes at the surface where the seam concerned is located at a depth in excess of approximately six to eight times the seam thickness. Even so, voids just below the surface create just as awkward a problem. Void migration, however, will be confined beneath a thick, competent rock unit.

In longwall mining the coal is exposed at a face of 30–200 m between two parallel roadways. The roof is supported only in and near the roadways and at the working face. After the coal has been won and loaded the face supports are advanced leaving the rocks, in the areas where coal has been removed, to collapse. Subsidence at the surface more or less follows the advance of the working face and may be regarded as immediate. The curve of subsidence which precedes a working face first causes surface structures to undergo tension, then tilt, and finally compression (Fig. 7.3). This differential subsidence can cause substantial damage (Fig. 7.4), the tensile strains usually being the most effective in this respect. Although subsidence does not cease entirely when the face stops, only small changes then take place.

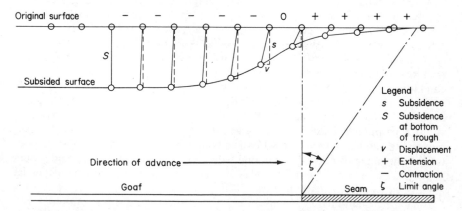

Fig. 7.3. Diagrammatic representation of subsidence trough indicating areas of tension, tilt and compression as well as vertical subsidence

An important feature of subsidence due to longwall mining is its high degree of predictability. Usually movements parallel and perpendicular to the direction of face advance are predicted. Although adequate for many purposes, such treatment does not consider the three-dimensional nature of ground movement. For instance, recent observations have shown that individual points move on approximately helical paths, the pitch and radii change from point to point and the direction of rotation is different on opposite sides of the subsidence basin. Methods of subsidence prediction are provided in the *Subsidence Engineer's Handbook* (see Bibliography).

Fig. 7.4. Damage due to mining subsidence at Elsecar, near Barnsley. Many of the houses in this street were no longer habitable

A number of factors influence mining subsidence due to longwall extraction, however, evidence suggests that the major factors are geometrical rather than geological. Seam thickness is an obvious one. Maximum vertical subsidence may equal 90% of the thickness of the coal seam extracted. If more than one seam is simultaneously worked beneath the same area then the subsidence effects are cumulative. Usually, however, there is an appreciable difference between the volume of mineral extracted and the amount of subsidence at the surface, which can largely be attributed to bulking effects.

One of the most important factors influencing the amount of subsidence is the depth and width of the panel removed. In fact it has been shown that maximum subsidence will begin at a depth to width ratio of 1 : 1·4. This is the critical condition above and below which maximum subsidence is, and is not achieved, respectively. The angle of draw, or limit angle, defines the outer limit of ground movement, this extending beyond the limits of the goaf. In most coalfields in the UK the angle of draw approximates to 35°.

It has been found by field measurements that subsidence is transmitted to the surface almost instantaneously. This, however, does not mean that all subsidence is transmitted to the surface at the same time. Usually it will continue for a given point whilst the face is being worked within the critical area. The amount of subsidence which occurs after the working face has passed out of the critical area is referred to as the *residual* subsidence. This rarely exceeds 5% of the total subsidence at any given point, but such movements may continue for up to two or so years afterwards.

The lithology of the strata between the surface and the coal seam under extraction does not necessarily show a relationship to the amount of subsidence produced. Superficial deposits may allow movements to affect larger areas than otherwise, but on the other hand thick deposits of till tend to obscure tensile effects. Some surface rocks, such as the Magnesian Limestone, have been badly fractured by subsidence and these fractures have a profound affect on the intensity of differential displacements.

Faults tend to be locations where strain is concentrated and unfortunately their exact location at the surface is not always easy to determine. What is more, many coalfields are heavily faulted. If a fault is encountered during seam extraction and its throw is large, then the workings may terminate against the fault, thus permanent strains will be induced at the surface probably accompanied by severe differential subsidence in the zone of influence of the fault. Indeed a subsidence step may occur at the outcrop of such a fault, sometimes with disastrous effects. The most notable steps occur when the coal is worked beneath the hade of the fault, faces in other positions being much less likely to cause differential movement. Steps are usually down towards the goaf but if old workings exist then steps may occasionally occur away from the face. The size of steps is on average one third of the maximum subsidence which takes place, but this value varies appreciably. Their extent is very much limited to the area worked. Because of the significance of faults the *Report on Mining Subsidence* prepared by the Institution of Civil Engineers[11] recommends that structures be set back at least 16 m from their line of surface outcrop. On the other hand, faults sometimes act as a barrier to strains generated by subsidence.

When the dip of the strata is less than 20° it has little influence on mining subsidence. The subsidence profile, however, may be shifted towards the deeper end of the working panel.

Finally, the amount of subsidence may be reduced by filling the goaf with waste material, either by strip packing or by solid stowage. These methods can prove costly and they cannot completely eliminate subsidence. For example, stowing may reduce subsidence by up to 50%.

Centuries of coal mining have meant that there are a great number of old shafts left behind. These are now the responsibility of the National Coal Board. Unfortunately the location of many, if not most, of these old shafts is unknown and the location of those which are supposedly recorded is not always accurate. It was not until 1872 that legislation was introduced making it compulsory to keep plans of mine workings. The location of a shaft is of great importance as far as the safety of a potential structure is concerned. Moreover from the economic point of view the sterilisation of land due to the suspected presence of a mine shaft is unrealistic.

The oldest and shallowest shafts were timber lined, but these were quickly superseded by brick linings. The continuing stability of a shaft lining is obviously important, particularly in the uppermost section, for there its collapse may lead to cratering, i.e. an in-rush of surface soils into the shaft to form a depression several times the shaft diameter (Fig. 7.5). A consideration of the long-term stability of shaft linings is therefore required as well as the effects of increased lateral pressure due to the erection of structures nearby.

Filling of shafts in the past was frequently undertaken in a haphazard manner without regard for the future, e.g. a wooden scaffold may have been constructed just below the surface of a shaft and then topped up with fill. With time the wood decayed to expose an open shaft. Many shafts were filled with unsuitable material and usually no attempt was made to seal them off from the workings, which after the mine was abandoned became waterlogged. In such instances fine

Fig. 7.5. Collapsed mine shaft giving rise to cratering at the surface (Courtesy *Western Mail and Echo Ltd.*)

fill is likely to flow into the workings with the result that a cavity is produced in the shaft. Again with time the plug above the cavity is denuded until eventually the remnant collapses down the shaft. Usually any material at hand was used to fill a shaft: rails, timbers, bogies, scrap metal and mine waste. As can be imagined this rarely meant that the shaft was properly filled, bridging and the formation of voids usually occurred. Such fills are potentially capable of sudden collapse.

Although shaft collapse is fortunately not a frequent event its occurrence can prove disastrous. For instance, in April 1945 an old filled shaft suddenly collapsed and cratered in a railway sidings at Abram, near Wigan. Immediately after this a train with 13 wagons was shunted across the site and these together with the engine and driver were lost down the shaft. In 1956 in Northwood playing fields, Stoke-on-Trent, two previously filled shafts collapsed taking their reinforced concrete cappings with them. Before these shafts were filled they con-tained water almost to their surface. The filling material had obviously proved unsuitable and the mouthings had not been sealed allowing the fill to move into the workings.

The location of shafts is obviously of paramount importance. If the position of a shaft is shown on a number of plans but not in the same location, then Taylor[9] has suggested that its position can be assessed by drawing equivalent circles of likely shaft dimensions about the plan locations. The overlap of the circles then provides a probability zone for detailed examination. Geophysical methods have been used to try to locate shafts, the proton magnetometer probably proving one of the most useful methods to date. Seismic reflection and current-path elec-tromagnetic methods would also appear to have had some success. A recent review of geophysical methods in areas of mining subsidence has been given by Burton and Maton[12]. Confirmation of the existence of a shaft must always be done by excavation. This may be accomplished by exposing the top of the shaft by a drag-line securely anchored on the outside of the area of probable position. If this is unsuccessful then the shaft will have to be exposed by boring, suitable safety precautions having been taken. A boring should go down the shaft into bedrock and another should be located next to the shaft to determine the thickness of overburden.

If this is not excessive and the shaft is open then it can be filled with suitable granular material. If, as is more usual, the shaft is filled with debris in which there are voids then these should be filled with pea gravel. Dean[13] suggested that if the exact positions of the mouthings in an old shaft are known then these areas could be filled with gravel, the rest of the shaft being filled with mine waste. However, the latter will tend to consolidate much more than will gravel. Dean[13] also supplied details concerning the concrete cappings needed to seal mine shafts. Such information is also available from National Coal Board offices. Where the depth of overburden is excessive then the problem of cratering in this relatively soft material exists if a shaft is open or badly filled. In such instances the shaft should be filled with gravel to the surface and this then grouted, e.g. with a cement-fly ash mix. The concrete capping should take the form of an inverted cone.

The easiest way of dealing with mine shafts is to avoid locating structures in their immediate vicinity. For instance, a suitably capped but unfilled mine shaft was located within a building site at Hoyland Common, near Barnsley. Unfor-tunately the shaft was near a fault and much of the area was going to be under-mined at some future date. This would possibly mean that the shaft would be affected and perhaps the cap dislodged. The overburden consisted of mine waste overlying till, approximately 6 m in total thickness. It was recommended that the shaft should be filled and re-capped, and that no building or structure should be located within 15 m of the shaft (in such instances the minimum distance should be twice the overburden thickness up to a depth of 15 m, unless the overburden is exceptionally weak). Protective sheet pile or concrete walls can be constructed around shafts to counteract cratering.

### A note on the geotechnical character of mine discard

As remarked at the beginning of this chapter, the pressing needs of urban development have meant that sites formerly considered unsuitable are now being used for constructional purposes. In mining districts such sites are frequently covered with mine waste.

There are two types of colliery discard: coarse and fine. Coarse discard, which we are concerned with here, consists of both run-of-mine material and the waste associated with the coal itself. It reflects the various rock types which are extracted during mining operations. It contains various amounts of coal which has not been separated by the preparation process, and in older tips it may be considerable. Fine discard consists of either slurry or tailings from the washery which may be pumped into lagoons.

After the Aberfan disaster of October, 1966, extensive investigations were made into the mineralogical and geotechnical properties of mine waste. Obviously the characteristics of colliery discard differ according to the nature of the spoil. The method of tipping also appears to influence the character of coarse discard. In addition many tips, particularly those with relatively high coal contents, may also be burnt or burning and this affects their mineralogical composition.

The most recent investigations concerning the geotechnical character of mine waste have been carried out by McKechnie and Rodin[14], Taylor and Spears[15] and Taylor[16]. Some of the results of their testing programmes are summarised in Table 7.2.

**Table 7.2**    THE GEOTECHNICAL PROPERTIES OF COLLIERY TIP SPOIL

|  | *Yorkshire Main** (unburnt) range | *Brancepeth†* (partly burnt) range |
|---|---|---|
| Moisture content | 8·0–13·6% | 5·3–11·9% |
| Bulk density | 1·667–2·196 Mg/m³ | 1·266–1·875 Mg/m³ |
| Dry density | 1·506–1·936 Mg/m³ | 1·058–1·683 Mg/m³ |
| Specific gravity | 2·04–2·63 | 1·81–2·54 |
| Plastic limit | 16–25 | Non-plastic to 35 |
| Liquid limit | 23–44 | 23–42 |
| Permeability | 1·42–9·78 × 10⁻⁶ m/s | |
| Size, >0·002 mm | 0·0–17·0% | Most material of |
| Size, >2·0 mm | 30·0–57·0% | sand size range |
| Shear strength, $\phi'$ | 31·5°–35·0° | 27·5°–39·5° |
| Shear strength, $c'$ | 19·44–22·41 kN/m² | 3·65–39·03 kN/m² |

* After Taylor and Spears[15].
† After Taylor[16].

The moisture content of tip spoil would appear to increase with increasing content of fines and the range of specific gravity depends on the relative proportions of coal, shale, mudstone and sandstone in the waste. In the latter case coal is of particular importance. The argillaceous content also influences the grading of spoil although most tip material would appear to be essentially granular in the mechanical sense. This is reflected in their low to medium plasticity, indeed certain samples which were tested were virtually non-plastic. As far as effective shear strength is concerned $\phi'$ usually varies from 25 to 45°. The strength of unburnt coarse discard does not seem to be seriously affected by long-term weathering, but the angle of shearing resistance increases in that material which has been fully burnt.

Although coarse discard may reach its level of degradation within a matter of months, once it is buried within the tip it suffers little change. For instance, Taylor and Spears[15] showed that no major changes in the physical and mechanical properties have occurred within the Yorkshire Main spoil heap since its inception over 50 years ago. They noted that the zone of oxidation did not extend beyond 1 m in depth, but that the breakdown of pyrite may take place within the upper 3 m. The first effect of degradation is the relatively quick breakdown of large particles to gravel and sand size, further reduction to silt size being a much slower process. In some old tips surface weathering has produced a relatively impermeable mantle, protecting the material beneath. When tip material is burnt it becomes much more stable as far as weathering is concerned.

Pyrite is a relatively common iron sulphide in some of the coals and argillaceous rocks of the Coal Measures. It is also an unstable mineral, breaking down quite quickly under the influence of weathering to give ferrous sulphate and sulphuric acid. For example, pH values of four and less were recorded in several small pools on an old spoil heap at Beighton, Sheffield. This meant that the culvert which was to carry a small stream, which ran adjacent to the heap, was of Armco construction rather than concrete. In order to avoid the deleterious attack of such acid and sulphate on concrete a safe maximum limit of 1·0% of sulphate (and 0·25% in the case of cohesive soils) has usually been adopted as far as construction in soils is concerned. Above these limits foundations may be protected by bituminous coatings or constructed with sulphur-resisting cement. Incidentally, burnt colliery waste usually has a high sulphate content.

The problem of combustion in tip material has sometimes to be faced when reclaiming old tips. In 1973 work started on the reclamation of the Wharncliffe, Woodmoor spoil heap at Barnsley. During earth-moving operations a number of hot spots were noticed. These normally had temperatures of around 600°C but at certain locations temperatures as high as 900°C were recorded. At such temperatures tyres on earth-moving equipment melted and their engines often seized; rescue was hazardous. Where excavation was still in progress it was decided to remove a layer 300 mm deep from these hot spots and compact the ground with a vibratory roller towed behind a tractor. This lowered the temperatures by one half within 1 or 2 h.

## Site investigations

The object of a site investigation is primarily to assess the suitability of a site for construction purposes and to provide information for the design team. It first of all generally involves a survey of the relevant literature, ordnance survey and geological maps and possibly aerial photographs. The latter are not usually of much use in built-up areas, and geological maps and memoirs may be inaccurate as far as older urban areas are concerned. If subsidence is at all suspected then a visit must be paid to the local National Coal Board offices; local authorities, libraries and museums may also prove of help. Nonetheless in some cases it may be more economic to obtain the required data directly from the site investigation rather than proceed with extensive and costly searches which may yield little information.

In areas of productive Coal Measures, if no record of mining activities is unearthed then it should not be assumed that mining has not taken place. Indeed, old shallow workings close to outcrop should be expected in any urban area where exploitable beds were not covered by thick superficial deposits. As already noted, mining has gone on in many coalfields for several centuries, but the first statutory obligation to keep mine records only dates from 1850 and it was not until 1872 that the production and retention of mine plans became compulsory. Many old mine workings were built over.

An investigation of a site for an important structure requires the exploration and sampling of all strata likely to be significantly affected by the structural load. The location of sub-surface voids due to mineral extraction is of prime importance in this context. In other words an attempt should be made to determine the extraction ratio, the pattern of the layout and the condition of old pillar and stall workings. The sequence and type of roof rocks may provide some clue as to whether void migration has taken place, and if so, its possible extent. The assessment of past and potential future collapse is obviously important.

For sub-surface examination at shallow depths, and where conditions prove suitable, trial pits and trenches allow visual inspection as well as mapping and sampling from continuous areas. Such excavations can be quickly made with mechanical diggers, but due regard must be paid to safety precautions. Their location and number is largely governed by the nature of the site and the type of structure to be erected.

The location and depth of boreholes also depends upon the nature of the ground conditions and the shape, extent and load of the structure. Suffice it to say that holes should be located so as to detect the stratal sequence, the thickness of its individual members and its geological structure. Exploration should extend to a depth which includes all strata which are likely to be significantly affected by the structural load. The location of old mine workings is generally done by exploratory drilling, the borehole locations being influenced by a pre-assessment of the possible pattern of the old workings. For the most part, drilling to prove the existence of old workings is done by open holes. The amount of rotary coring which needs to be done will depend on the complexity of the geology at the site. The primary purpose is to locate either voids in the strata or seam horizons where the increased rate of drilling suggests the presence of loosely packed material. Even when a close pattern of exploratory drilling has been carried out it is not always possible to make a sufficiently satisfactory judgement about the nature and extent of past mining. However, once the basic pattern of the old workings has been established then the details can perhaps be filled in by using hand drills[17].

Examination of below-surface workings can also be carried out by using borehole cameras and/or closed-circuit television. In some instances it may be possible to enter old workings; however, since this could prove dangerous, it should not be undertaken except with the co-operation and assistance of the National Coal Board.

During drilling operations it would prove useful if the mechanical properties of the rock cores were also logged, such as fracture spacing and point-load strength. Incidentally, in fractured or soft rock a double-tube core barrel is required to obtain reasonable core recovery.

Sampling is an important part of any investigation. Samples should be taken from each rock type and their testing in the laboratory should take place at the same time as the investigation. In this way results can be fed back to the site operators which in turn should help the development of their programme.

Accurate recording of ground-water conditions is important. Not only should the water levels be observed in boreholes but at least one stand-pipe should be installed for long-term observation. Piezometers may be installed in boreholes and *in-situ* permeability tests carried out. In some instances the ground-water may contain substances in great enough quantity to be injurious to concrete, the sulphate content and pH value being of particular interest. A chemical analysis of the ground-water is then required to assess the need for special precautions.

Standard and dynamic penetration tests are of limited value in foundation investigation in Coal Measures areas. Field loading tests are usually the best method of assessing the strength and deformation characteristics of the rocks concerned. Loading tests can either be carried out on bearing plates or piles. Usually the maximum loading in plate-bearing tests is approximately twice the design load so that they rarely reach the ultimate bearing capacity of the ground, at which settlement continues without increasing load. As a consequence it is generally only necessary to demonstrate that a foundation is capable of carrying a given load rather than determining the point at which it will fail. By contrast, pile-loading tests are carried to failure. More than one pile must be tested before the ultimate bearing capacity of the ground is thereby assessed. For practical purposes the ultimate bearing capacity from the latter type of test may be taken as that load which causes the head of the pile to settle 10% of the pile diameter. According to Price, Malkin and Knill[18], random pile testing does not lend itself to Coal Measures strata due to the rapid variations in lithology. They maintain that it is necessary to test either the weakest member of the sequence or that rock unit which has been chosen as the foundation level.

## Foundations in areas of old mine workings

Where a site which is proposed for development is underlain by shallow old mine workings there are a number of ways in which the problem can be dealt with. The first and most obvious method is to locate the proposed structure on sound ground away from the old workings or over workings proved to be stable.

After a recent site investigation for a hotel at Wideopen, Newcastle-upon-Tyne, it was found that part of the site was underlain by old pillar and stall workings and that coal was going to be extracted from beneath within the next few years. It was therefore recommended that the hotel complex should be relocated to avoid the area of potential subsidence and that the design of the building should be altered.

It is not generally sufficient to locate immediately outside the area undermined as the area of influence should be considered. In such cases the angle of influence or draw is usually taken as 25°; in other words the area of influence is defined by projecting an angle of 25° to the vertical from the periphery and depth of the workings to the surface. Such location is, of course, not always possible.

Rafts have been used as foundations in areas of shallow mine workings. For example, the 12 storey block at Sheffield Polytechnic was provided with a reinforced raft foundation. This precaution was taken even though the old workings involved were overlain by the Silkstone Rock, a massive sandstone. This together with the estimated percentage extraction (43%) allowed the engineers to judge that the ground would remain stable. However, rafts tend to be costly.

Reinforced bored-pile foundations have also been resorted to, one of the most recent examples is in the construction of the new library for the above-mentioned polytechnic. In such instances the piles bear on a competent stratum beneath the workings. They should also be sleeved so that concrete is not lost into voids, and to avoid the development of negative skin friction if overlying strata collapse. However, some authorities have suggested that piling through old mine workings seems inadvisable because, firstly, their emplacement may precipitate collapse, and, secondly, subsequent collapse at seam level could possibly lead to piles being either buckled or sheared.

If old mine workings are at very shallow depth then it might be feasible, by means of bulk excavation, to found on the strata beneath. This is an economic solution, particularly at depths of up to 7 m or on sloping sites, and is well suited to areas which were worked by means of bell pits. For example, Taylor[9] quoted an instance in Leeds where founding below bell pits in the Beeston Bed Coal meant that potentially 21 740 t of coal could be open-casted, so providing a handsome return. Such excavations may be carried out rapidly if the overburden consists of clays, shales or fragmented and weathered rocks.

Where old mine workings are believed to pose an unacceptable hazard to development and it either is impossible or impracticable to use adequate measures in design, or to found below their level, then the ground itself must be treated. Such treatment involves filling the voids in order to prevent void migration and pillar collapse. It is not essential to fill voids with material of roughly equivalent strength to the host rocks, and generally flushing via boreholes with crushed mine waste, fly ash or sand provides a satisfactory solution. This method cannot guarantee that every void will be completely filled, but pressure grouting might not give better results either.

Grouting via boreholes from ground level has frequently been used as a method of treatment of old ground workings. However, pressure grouting near the surface can lead to ground heave and in some cases to the extrusion of grout. Grouting the surface rocks can, of course, solve this problem, but it is a costly solution. The grouts used in these operations commonly consist of cement, fly ash and sand mixes, economy and bulk being their important features. If the workings are still more or less continuous then there is a risk that grout will penetrate the bounds of the zone requiring treatment. In such instances dams can be built by placing pea gravel down large-diameter boreholes around the periphery of the site (Fig. 7.6[17]). Pea gravel, because of its shape, can easily adapt itself to the configuration of a void. When the gravel mound has been formed it is grouted[17–18]. The area within this barrier is then grouted, the grout holes usually being laid out on a grid pattern. If the old workings contain water then a gap should be left in the dam through which the water can drain as the grout is emplaced. This minimises the risk of trapped water preventing the voids being filled. Pea gravel may also be used as a bulk filler where the amount of grout-take proves excessive.

The extent of the grouted area must take account of the area of influence. This can be determined by using an angle of 25° to the vertical between the outer limits of the structure and the base of the workings. Although 35° is usually cited as the angle of draw in UK coalfields, an angle of 15° was quoted by Vandale[19] as being sufficient to define an area of support to property, this being calculated outside a safety area 5 m wide around the foundation (Fig. 7.7[20]). Also on the outer fringe of the area of influence, subsidence effects are not significant. Incidentally it was

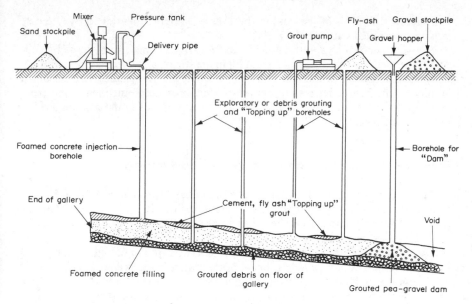

Fig. 7.6. Schematic layout of plant and boreholes for filling and grouting old mine workings (after Scott[17])

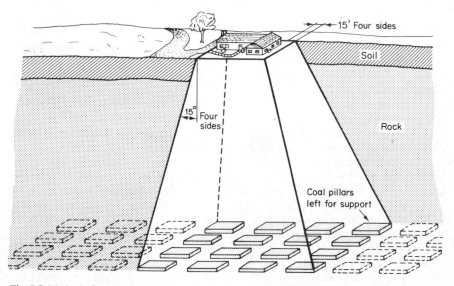

Fig. 7.7. Method of supporting surface structures by leaving pillars of coal in place (after Gray and Meyers[20])

considered that 50% of the coal in the area of support mentioned by Vandale could be removed without ill effects.

The success of the grout-take needs to be verified. This can be done by core drilling and noting the amount of grout fill in the sticks, and by injecting grout under pressure into the drill holes. The volume of the grout injected in excess of the volume of the hole, after a short period of time, provides some idea of the grout take. Knill[21] suggested that seismic refraction techniques could also be used to assess grout take.

### Subsidence caused by factors other than coal mining

Although the extraction of coal is the major cause of subsidence in the UK, subsidence can and is brought about by the removal of other substances from the ground. These substances may be either fluids or solids and their removal may be by artificial or natural means.

The most important metal ore mined in the UK is iron. The sedimentary ores of the Jurassic system, as well as being open-casted, have been mined in several areas, notably in Northamptonshire, Lincolnshire and the Cleveland Hills. These mines were and are worked by pillar and stall methods and there has been no significant subsidence associated with them. By contrast the hematite ores of Cumberland were worked by total extraction methods and these have given rise to subsidence, e.g. that due to extraction of ore from the Hodbarrow Mine, Millom, by 1922 was responsible for the formation of four large depressions, each about 400 m wide and 15 m deep.

Many other metals have been worked in the UK, notably lead and zinc in the Pennine orefield and the Lake District, and copper and tin in Cornwall. Many of these are vein deposits in competent rock and do not give rise to subsidence problems when mined. Old, unrecorded shafts do, of course, still represent a problem, e.g. an old mine shaft recently opened on Masson Hill, Derbyshire, causing a boy to fall in. Gangue minerals such as fluorspar, barytes and calcite have been and are still worked in the Pennine orefield. Although most metal-mining districts are in rural areas, these same areas now provide recreational space for urban dwellers and accidents like the one just mentioned will no doubt happen again.

Limestone is a carbonate rock which is subject to solutioning, which in turn leads to the formation of sinkholes and ultimately to subterranean caverns linked together by an integrated system of underground passages. However, karstic features are only produced in thick sequences of limestone. Solution features are also developed in dolomite. Chalk, although subject to solution, because of its relative softness, tends not to allow the formation of subterranean solution features. Although of a very infrequent occurrence, rapid subsidence can take place when these cavities in limestone collapse after prolonged solutioning. Differential settlement under loading has occurred in limestone which at ground level appeared competent, but immediately beneath the surface consisted of long, narrow pinnacles of rock separated by solution channels occupied by limestone rubble in a clay matrix.

Limestone is occasionally mined but because of its competence it does not give rise to subsidence of any significance, e.g. the Hopton Wood Limestone is worked at Middleton-by-Wirksworth, Derbyshire. The pillar and stall workings are on two levels, the individual pillars being approximately 148 m² by about 5·2 m in height and the extraction ratio is almost 50%. There is some 137 m of limestone overburden and the workings are interrupted by three small faults. The amount of subsidence is negligible.

Shallow mine workings occur in the Chalk, particularly of East Anglia and Kent. Some of these were made by Palaeolithic man in his quest for flint. They are usually similar to bell pits, they may be about 3–6 m in height and have small tunnels, following the flints, running from the main chamber. A notable subsidence in the Chalk occurred in Bury St. Edmunds in July, 1966. The subsidence took the form of crown holes and happened in Jacqueline Close with the result that the houses were eventually declared unsafe and therefore abandoned (Fig. 7.8). As far as these workings were concerned the pavement was usually

Fig. 7.8. Shaft opening into workings in the Chalk, Bury St. Edmunds (courtesy *East Anglian Daily Times*)

between 15 and 18 m below the surface and the galleries 2–3·5 m high. Although the ground was potentially unstable, in that crown holes were likely to occur, the process was accelerated by site development which gave rise to a change in the sub-surface drainage regime. It appears that soakaway water led to extra solutioning and consequently the rapid decay of the roofs above galleries.

Gypsum is more readily soluble than limestone and therefore caverns can develop in thick beds of gypsum much more rapidly than they can in limestone. Indeed they have been known to form in the USA within a matter of a few years where beds of gypsum have been located below dams. Extensive surface cracking and subsidence has been attributed to the collapse of cavernous gypsum in states like Oklahoma and New Mexico. The problem is accentuated by the fact that gypsum is weaker than limestone and therefore collapses more readily. The solution of gypsum gives rise to sulphate-bearing waters and these may attack concrete.

Gypsum, which occurs in the Permian and Triassic systems, was and is mined in various parts of the UK, e.g. in the Lake District, Durham, Nottinghamshire and Staffordshire. The pillar and stall method of extraction is used. Most of the beds which have been worked did not exceed 5 m in thickness and the extraction ratio was not usually more than 75%. Such mines are generally not extensive, at most extending over 0·4 km² or so and they may be at shallow depth. They have not given rise to any significant subsidence problems.

Salt is even more soluble than gypsum and the evidence of slumping, brecciation and collapse structures in rocks which overlie the salt-bearing strata testify to the fact that salt has gone into solution in past geological times. But it is generally believed that in areas underlain by saliferous beds, measurable surface subsidence is unlikely to occur except where salt is being extracted. Perhaps this is because equilibrium has been attained between the supply of unsaturated ground-water and the salt available for solution. Exceptionally, cases have been recorded of rapid subsidence, e.g. the 'Meade salt sink' in Kansas, USA, was explained by Johnson[22] as due to solution of deep salt beds. This area of water, about 60 m in diameter, occurred as a result of subsidence in March, 1879.

The occurrence of salt springs in Cheshire has been quoted as evidence of natural solution and it is thought that the Cheshire meres were formed as a result of subsidence, probably in post glacial times. Such subsidences take place very slowly and over large areas. Localised solution is thought to develop collecting channels along the upper surface of salt beds. The incompetence of the overlying Keuper Marl inhibits the formation of large voids, roof collapse no doubt taking place at more or less the same time as salt removal. This action eventually gives rise to linear subsidence depressions or brine runs at ground level.

The classic examples of subsidences due to salt working have occurred in Cheshire where salt has been won for over 300 years. There the salt occurs in two principal beds, the Upper and Lower Keuper Saliferous Beds. The upper one was worked, mainly by pillar and stall methods, in the seventeenth, eighteenth and nineteenth centuries. Few of these mines had a life of more than 40 years, their abandonment being brought about by flooding and collapse; the upper bed is in wet rock head. The lower bed was also (and still is) mined, but it has been worked mainly by some form of brine pumping since the nineteenth century.

There are now three ways in which salt is extracted in Cheshire: by mining using the pillar and stall method, by natural or wild brine pumping and by controlled pumping. The Meadowbank Mine at Winsford is now the only salt mine in the UK. Working is confined to the bottom 5·5 m in the thick 'bottom' rock in the Lower Keuper Saliferous Beds at a depth of about 140 m. The pillar and stall methods give 65–75% extraction (incidentally in the old mines around Northwich the extraction ratio was often as high as 90%). What is more this mine is in dry rock head and the possibility of subsidence is so remote that it can be discounted. The pumping of natural brine runs at wet rock head has, and does, lead to subsidence. It inhibits major developments since the subsidence it gives rise to, although gradual, is unpredictable. Few companies are now involved in this practice and any large-scale expansion will be resisted by the planning authorities. The latter are trying to have these companies change to the controlled system and hope that the wild brine pumping operations will soon disappear. The controlled system operated by I.C.I. produces solution cavities of predetermined size and shape in the salt deposits at dry rock head. Around Holford, where the Lower Keuper Saliferous Beds are approximately 260 m thick and at the shallowest depth are some 130 m below the surface, the individual cavities are each said to be capable of accommodating St. Paul's cathedral. The extraction ratio is approximately 20% and the method accounts for 88% of the brine production in Cheshire. The disused chambers now act as containers for the disposal of waste products.

In the eighteenth and nineteenth centuries the collapses in salt mines produced flooded rock-pit holes whilst wild brine pumping gave rise to gradual sinking over wide areas and was responsible, for example, for the formation of the Witton and Winsford Flashes. But the catastrophic subsidences of the late nineteenth and early twentieth centuries were the result of pumping bastard brine from flooded mines (Fig. 7.9[23]). The last disastrous subsidence in Cheshire occurred in 1928

Fig. 7.9. Subsidence due to pumping of bastard brine, Northwich (courtesy Calvert[23])

with the collapse of the Adelaide mine. Now controlled brine pumping means that subsidence is no longer a serious problem except that gradual subsidence still occurs around Lymm, Marston, Middlewich and Sandbach because of natural brine pumping. Salt has also been extracted in Lancashire, Staffordshire, Worcestershire and Teesside.

An interesting example of past mining activities occurs in the Upper Greensand near Merstham, Surrey. There the rock was worked on an apparently extensive scale, by a crude pillar and stall method, mainly for hearthstone. The extraction ratio varied between 65 and 75%. The workings occur around and beneath the M23 and M25 interchange and therefore required extensive grouting.

The removal of fluids from sediments reduces their pore pressures and causes consolidation to occur. This in turn leads to subsidence. Peat is the most compressible of soils, it being highly porous so that its water content may range up to 2 000%. Its specific gravity is low, usually about 1·0 and it has little strength. Drainage of peat leads invariably to subsidence (Fig. 7.10), the Fenlands

Fig. 7.10. Subsidence damage caused to Benwick church, Huntingdonshire, due to settlement in peat as a result of its drainage

providing a classic example. There peat has been drained for over 400 years and in some areas the thickness of the peat has been halved as a result.

It is estimated that drainage of the Dutch polderlands caused 30–35% consolidation in clays and 20% in silts over a period of about 100 years. Consolidation in sands was negligible.

Abstraction of water from the Chalk over the past 150 years has caused subsidence in some areas of London in excess of 0·3 m. In 1820 the artesian head in the Chalk was approximately +9·1 m OD but by 1936 this had declined in some places to −90 m OD. The decline in artesian head has been accompanied by underdrainage in the London Clay. Between 1865 and 1931 subsidence averaged between 60 and 180 mm throughout much of London (Fig. 7.11[24]). Abstraction

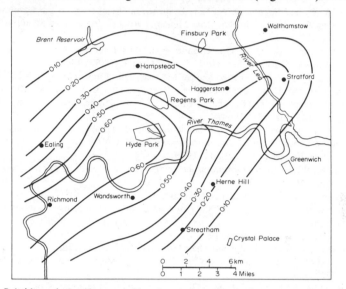

Fig. 7.11. Subsidence in London caused by abstraction of water from the Chalk; contours are in tenths of a foot (after Wilson and Grace[24])

of water from a sand, gravel aquifer had by 1959 been responsible for subsidences amounting to 4 m over most of the older parts of Mexico City and in some parts as much as 7·5 m had been recorded.

A spectacular and costly subsidence occurred at Wilmington oilfield in the harbour area of Los Angeles and Long Beach, California, USA. This was first noticed in 1940 and by 1962 the subsidence had increased to about 8 m at its centre, the greatest subsidence due to fluid withdrawal known to have occurred in the world, and included an area of about 64 km² that had subsided 0·6 m or more. The problem of subsidence was acute since much of the area affected was only 1·5–3·0 m above sea level and was highly industrialised. In 1947 subsidence occurred at the rate of 0·3 m/year; this increased to 0·7 m/year in 1951 when peak production was reached. After this production declined, so did the rate of subsidence. Remedial action was taken in 1958 by repressurising the oil zones with water. This had brought subsidence to a halt in much of the field by 1962.

## Acknowledgement

The author wishes to acknowledge the help of Dr. R. K. Taylor of the Dept. of Geological Sciences, University of Durham, for his useful comments on the draft of this chapter.

REFERENCES

1. Jaeger, C., *Rock Mechanics and Engineering,* C.U.P. (1972)
2. Badger, C. W., Cummings, A. D. and Whitmore, R. L., 'The Disintegration of Shale', *J. I. Fuel,* **29,** 417–423 (1956)
3. Taylor, R. K. and Spears, D. A., 'The Breakdown of British Coal Measures Rocks', *Int. J. Rock Mech. Min. Sci.,* **7,** 481–501 (1970)
4. Taylor, R. K. and Spears, D. A., 'The Influence of Weathering on the Composition and Engineering Properties of In Situ Coal Measures Rocks', *Int. J. Rock Mech. Min. Sci.,* **9,** 729–756 (1972)
5. Wardell, K. and Wood, J. C., 'Ground Instability Problems Arising from Old Mine Workings', *Proc. Mid. Soc. Soil Mech. Found. Eng.,* **7,** 5–30 (1966)
6. Orchard, R. J., 'Partial Extraction and Subsidence', *Min. Engr.,* **123,** 417–427 (1964)
7. Wilson, A. H., 'An Hypothesis Concerning Pillar Stability', *Min. Eng.,* **131,** 409–417 (1972)
8. Bryan, A., Bryan, J. C. and Fouche, J., 'Some Problems of Strata Control in Pillar Workings', *Min. Engr.,* **123,** 238–266 (1964)
9. Taylor, R. K., 'Characteristics of Shallow Coal Mine Workings and Their Implications in Urban Redevelopment Areas', *Site Investigations in Areas of Mining Subsidence,* ed. by F. G. Bell, Newnes–Butterworths, London (1975)
10. Tincelin, E., *Pression et Déformations de Terrain dans les Mines de Fer de Lorraine,* Jouve Editeurs, 284, Paris (1958)
11. Report on Mining Subsidence, Inst. Civ. Eng., London (1959)
12. Burton, A. N. and Maton, P. I., 'Geophysical Methods in Site Investigations in Areas of Mining Subsidence', *Site Investigations in Areas of Mining Subsidence,* ed. by F. G. Bell, Newnes–Butterworths, London (1975)
13. Dean, J. W., 'Old Mine Shafts and Their Hazards', *Min. Engr.,* **126,** 368–377 (1967)
14. McKechnie, T. G. and Rodin, S., 'Colliery Spoil Tips—After Aberfan', *Proc. Inst. Civ. Eng.,* Paper 7522 (1972)
15. Spears, D. A. and Taylor, R. K., 'The Geotechnical Characteristics of a Spoil Heap at Yorkshire Main Colliery', *Quart. J. Eng. Geol.,* **5,** 243–263 (1972)
16. Taylor, R. K., 'Compositional and Geotechnical Characteristics of a Hundred Year Old Colliery Spoil Heap', *Trans. Inst. Min. Met.,* **82,** A1–A14 (1973)
17. Scott, A. C., 'Locating and Filling Old Mine Workings', *Civ. Eng. Pub. Works Rev.,* **52,** 1007–1011 (1957)
18. Price, D. G., Malkin, A. B. and Knill, J. L., 'Foundations of Multi-Storey Blocks with Special Reference to Old Mine Workings', *Quart. J. Eng. Geol.,* **1,** 271–322 (1969)
19. Vandale, A. E., 'Subsidence, a Real or Imaginary Problem', *Min. Eng.* (Amer.), **19,** 86–88 (1967)
20. Gray, R. E. and Meyers, J. F., 'Mine Subsidence and Support Methods in the Pittsburg Area', *Am. Soc. Civ. Eng.,* Soil Mech. and Found. Div., **96,** 1267–1287 (1970)
21. Knill, J. L., 'The Application of Seismic Methods in the Prediction of Grout Take in Rocks', Paper 8, *Site Investigations in Soils and Rocks,* British Geotechnical Society, 93–100, London (1970)
22. Johnson, W. D., 'The High Plains and Their Utilization', *U.S. Geol. Surv. 21st Ann. Rept.,* pt. 4, 601–741 (1901)
23. Calvert, A. F., *Salt in Cheshire* (1915)
24. Wilson, G. and Grace, H., 'The Settlement of London due to Underdrainage of the London Clay', *J. Inst. Civ. Eng.,* **19,** 100–127 (1942)

BIBLIOGRAPHY

*Subsidence Engineer's Handbook,* N.C.B., London (1966)

# Chapter 8

# Clay Grouting and Alluvial Grouting

Pressure grouting was invented by Charles Bérigny in 1802 and introduced into the UK by W. R. Kinipple[1]. Clay slurries and hydraulic lime were the constituents of these first grouts. Later, in 1876, Thomas Hawksley used a Portland cement grout.

With the development of high-pressure pumps, cement grouts came to predominate, and they were frequently associated with the sinking of mine shafts. Clay and other additives were used occasionally to facilitate the injection, but clay grouting later came into prominence with the growth and construction of large rock-fill dams on deep alluvial and morainic soils. Local clays modified by peptisers were being used in north Africa in the 1930s and 1940s, and with the series of large earth- and rock-filled dams constructed in Europe in the 1950s and 1960s these techniques reached their peak. By this time, bentonites, either natural sodium bentonites or montmorillonitic clays treated to increase the sodium content, had come into use, and the property of such materials to form stable and impermeable gels with the ability to penetrate medium-to-fine sands had been utilised. Although there is now a tendency to consider other forms of seepage control such as slurry trenches or upstream blankets with relief wells, grouted 'cut-offs' are often used in many parts of the world, and examples of local clays enriched in various ways have been recently reported[2]. In certain ground conditions, e.g. boulder clays and in earthquake-prone areas, grouted cut-offs have attractions.

In the last decade there has also been a distinct trend towards the use of single-fluid chemical-solution grouts in tunnelling, and more recently a renewed interest in silicate gel systems. Nevertheless, clay and clay cement together with other particulate systems such as P.F.A. nowadays play a very important role in grouting (especially in the filling of large voids with a low cost material) and in grouting systems which may well include the use of the more expensive single-fluid chemical grouts at later stages.

## Alluvial deposits

In strict geomorphological terms, *alluvial* applies only to sediments associated with rivers. It is used, however, in grouting for all uncemented and porous soils. Nevertheless, when dealing with natural deposits, their structure and properties will depend upon their geological history and it is important in the choice of

141

grouts and the grouting systems to fully understand the ground conditions prior to treatment.

There are three stages in the formation of a sediment: a breakdown of the source rock, transportation of the debris and deposition of the debris. Water-borne sediments usually show some sorting or stratification, particularly in broader river valleys. In broad river valleys and estuaries successive channels may have cut through the older flood-plain deposits and resorted them, perhaps leaving buried channels.

Recent alluvium, especially that found in the mouths of estuaries and wide valleys, is often of a very fine nature containing much silt and clay. It is not usual-ly groutable.

Fine-sand deposits may show a quite marked structure which is not apparent-ly obvious. This can be reflected by the difference in the coefficients of permeability in the horizontal and vertical sense. Occasionally gravels are en-countered which have no fine infilling; these may be called *open-work* gravels, and they have extremely high permeabilities.

Within a simple alluvial sequence one should not expect to find extensive con-tinuity of a particular stratum, and although it may be recognised between boreholes it must nevertheless not be assumed to be a simple layer. Gravel, par-ticularly open-work gravels, are often present in highly localised lenses. General-ly, river-borne alluvials show more continuity than fan-washed deposits, which are often associated with the higher and younger phases of river development.

The bulk permeability of an alluvial system may be quite different from that of its constituents because of their lack of continuity and limited communication between beds. A particular problem exists where buried channels are present in that they can constitute a connecting conduit upstream, downstream and possibly between alluvial materials.

Typically, the permeabilities in river alluvial deposits (including silts and clays) may range from 100 to $10^{-3}$ mm/s. The bulk permeabilities of alluvial systems may often be within the range $10–10^{-2}$ mm/s.

Whilst there is some recognisable sorting and order in water-borne deposits this is not so in those which have been borne by ice. Glacial tills may contain all materials in chaotic distribution, but they often are associated with local fluvio-glacial deposits because of local retreat of an ice sheet and the deposition of materials from the peripheral melt waters. Some indication of the complexity of the system can be seen in the section from the Whiteinch tunnel (Fig. 8.1).

In such variable material it can be seen that given general hydraulic gradients the pore-water velocities may be quite variable, but nevertheless on the whole they are within the range $10–10^{-2}$ mm/h. Locally, high pore-water velocities may be encountered near fast flowing streams with high drawdown, but very high pore-water velocities that could affect grouting methods are usually associated with excavations, e.g. in tunnels where there may be local percolation through a tunnel face notwithstanding the efforts to reduce the overall permeability. They may also occur in excavations with sheet piling where clutches may have sprung. Gradients there may be high and one has to take this into account in designing a grout system to resist local erosion.

From this general discussion it may be seen that a systematic grouting exer-cise cannot be mounted without a knowledge of the local geology and the water conditions. The investigation procedures which may have to be adopted on large-scale projects are quite elaborate, ranging from conventional site investiga-

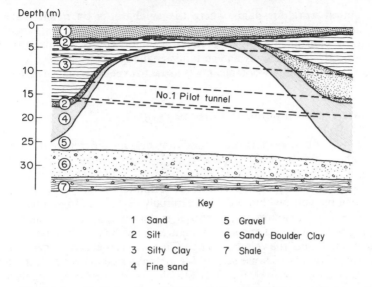

Fig. 8.1. Longitudinal section of Whiteinch tunnel under the river Clyde

tion boreholes to large-scale pumping test exercises, with perhaps water-current measurements in boreholes using special instruments together with tracer methods to establish water velocities in different layers. Recent developments in using differential thermal scanning and electrical streaming potentials indicate that sub-surface water flows are relevant to regional and local studies prior to geotechnical activity.

## Objectives

Grouting is carried out either on a prearranged basis to form part of the overall construction to be effected, or as urgent remedial action when some constructional method or expedient has failed. Grouting is now sufficiently recognised as a serious geotechnical process to be planned for in the early stages of a project. It must, however, be competitive and therefore has to stand up to comparison with other solutions to geotechnical problems such as simple pumping from sumps, ground-water lowering by well-points or deep wells, sheet piling or diaphragm-wall construction.

Grouts and grouting systems have been classified according to the function which they may be expected to perform. They may be classified as systems for improving the strength of the ground, for rendering the ground less permeable to either air or water, or to a combination of both these effects. A rather rare use is to change the elastic parameters of ground beneath a vibrating foundation.

Grouting may be regarded as a temporary measure or a permanent part of some construction. In tunnelling, for example, the grouts are usually not expected to last indefinitely. Tunnelling includes small-diameter sewers, and thrust boring as well as such large undertakings as the Clyde, Dartford and Blackwall tunnels. Often it is adequate that in such instances grouts perform their function for a period of months rather than years.

In cut-off work for dams where the emphasis is on maintaining an impermeable barrier over a long period of time, one requires assurance that the grout or its constituents will not break down in the course of time, possibly contaminating the water supply and certainly enabling greater seepage losses to take place. In underpinning work, again it is usual to expect permanence in the grout.

## Stability and permanence of grouts

The behaviour of a grout in the ground may be quite different to its performance in the laboratory. In particular, many single-fluid chemical grouts are subject to syneresis, i.e. the explusion of water from the gel. If this property is present to an extreme extent then it could result in the formation of new water passages even though all the voids within a soil have initially been filled. In practice the degree of syneresis is a function of the ratio of surface area to volume since a certain bonding between the gel and a solid surface can withstand the internal shrinkage stresses and reduce the volume change. This means that certain gels which show syneresis, of say, 5–10% are acceptable in fine to medium sands, but may not be acceptable in open gravel (Fig. 8.2). Stability over a period of time may be very difficult to demonstrate experimentally especially for complex chemical com-

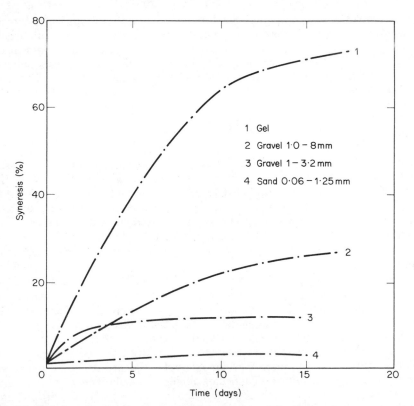

Fig. 8.2. Variation of syneresis as a function of grain size; 60% silicate–ethyl acetate gel (after Caron[14])

positions. Much work has been done on the stability of silicate based gels; it has been shown that certain compositions are much better in this respect than others[3]. The complex chemistry of the silicate gelling requires that in certain silicate organic systems great care should be maintained over the correct proportions and the right type of silicate used, otherwise quickly reversible silicate gels may result.

The stability of some of the bentonite gel compositions is extremely high. Laboratory tests have shown no change in volume over periods of up to four years when the specimen has been protected from loss of moisture.

The stability of a number of the clay-cement compositions and clay-gel compositions has been brought into question in the past and concern has been expressed over the risk that the seepage of waters carrying calcium ions would lead to shrinkage in clays, the properties of which depend upon them having sodium as the exchangeable base. However, experience at several large dams, e.g. Serre-Ponçon, has shown the fear to be groundless.

## Specifications of grout properties

Two kinds of specification can be envisaged for a grout, or more correctly, for grouted ground. Firstly, the permeability which must be achieved, and secondly the strength which is desired. In the former case it is realistic to expect improvements in permeability from the order of 10 mm/s to $10^{-3}$ mm/s in an efficiently grouted cut-off. This level of achievement has been obtained on numerous occasions.

Greater difficulties arise when a specification for strength is called for, and this is no more so than in tunnelling practice. An upper-limit strength approaching soft rock is technically achievable. Experience in tunnelling has shown that the Joosten process, a two-shot hard-silicate system which will be referred to later, gives strength more than adequate for both hand and shield operation in Thames gravel. In fact, in the very densest gravel the strength can be a positive discouragement to rapid progress. The limiting strengths which are prudent to adopt in field tunnelling have yet to be established with confidence. One can examine the problem using a classic Terzaghi arching analysis, and require either an improvement in the angle of internal friction or an improvement in the value of cohesion[4]. If one was considering an unsupported crown for a tunnel it may theoretically be desirable to specify a tensile strength, since for conditions of significant deviatoric stress, that is the limiting factor, but variable soil conditions in practice render such a specification hazardous.

Thus formal analytical procedures have not been used in establishing the design parameters for grouted tunnels, although one can conceive of an approach based on elastic–plastic theory for soft rocks. Design methods for tunnel linings are being improved with the aid of finite element analysis. Such procedures require ground strength and deformation parameters and, with minor modifications, could take into account the properties of the grouted ground. This has been carried out in rock grouting[5], but not as yet in alluvial grouting. Usually one relies upon experience in estimating the thickness either of a strengthened hood of treated ground, or a strengthened block through which the tunnel would be driven (Fig. 8.3), but in the absence of specified parameters it is extremely difficult to produce a rational and cost-optimised system.

## Methods of grouting

Grout may be introduced into the ground with a view to (*a*) filling all the voids, (*b*) the creation of multiple fissures, or (*c*) forming a number of discrete but expanding inclusions. Permeation grouting was, until the 1950s, the generally accepted aim, and grouts were therefore chosen to have small enough particle

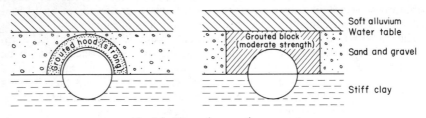

Fig. 8.3. Alternative grouting concepts

size to pass freely into the soil interstices, and to have a sufficiently low viscosity and an adequate length of time before a set to permeate an economically viable volume of ground. In Fig. 8.4 the viscosity–time relationships of a range of grouts are shown.

### *Permeation*

Permeation of fine-grained soils, e.g. silts by solution grouts such as resins, can be a lengthy process requiring extended gel times of sometimes up to 20 h and

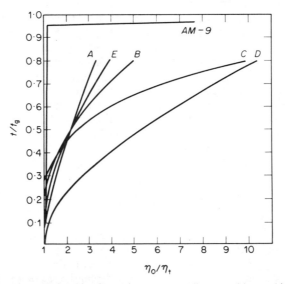

Fig. 8.4. Viscosity–time relationships for various grouts. All compositions gel in 60–100 min. *A* Durcisseur, *B* silicate–organic (Caron[14]). *C MO5, D* calcium lignosulphate, *E* silicate–aluminate, $t_g$ time to gel and $\eta_0$ initial viscosity

multiple injection with small dosing pumps. Care has always to be exercised in order to keep the injection pressures below the values which would cause ground rupture. Permeation is never complete in practice.

Permeation grouting of alluvial soils often requires successive treatments starting off usually with the cheapest grouts filling the coarsest voids. This process was greatly facilitated by the invention of the *tube-à-manchette* (T.A.M.), and similar tube systems have later been used[6]. The T.A.M. has been well described; it consists of a tube with rubber sleeves covering the holes through which the grout will subsequently be injected. This tube is then grouted into the ground with a grout on the outside called a *sleeve* grout. This is a low cost grout and it seals off one injection point from another. It is usually composed of a low-grade bentonite and a cement. Injection is then carried out through a perforated tube between two packers, the tube being located at a position opposite one of the rubber sleeves covering the holes in the outer tube. The injection grout pressure opens up the rubber and fractures the sleeve grout. This method is now widely used throughout the world and there are a number of variations on the system basically aimed at the same end, some using inflatable double packers[7]. With this grouting method it is possible to retreat successively with different materials at the same horizon.

Prior to the introduction of the T.A.M., the injection lance with the 'lost' point or with side ports for infiltration grouting was the principle mode of access for the grout. The traditional grouting arrangement for the classical Joosten process is shown in Fig. 4.2. Usually this grouting system uses a driven lance, sodium silicate being injected on the inward phase and calcium chloride injected as the lance is withdrawn. Some variations upon this are used from time to time involving sequential alternate injections of silicate and chloride to deal with variable ground, but this often brings with it difficulties in cleaning and keeping the system clear. Another injection device from West Germany of interest, which is used in that country to stabilise embankments, is a composite lance driven into the ground by pneumatic hammer (Fig. 8.5). An enlarged driving point and trailing collar act together as a double packer, the distance between them providing a relatively large space for grout injection into the ground. The enlargement of the leading section also has the effect that the wall resistance to driving is limited to the length of this section. This makes deep penetrations possible and furthermore enables the rate of driving to be used as a standard penetration test to assess the relative soil density and provide information for the spacing of subsequent pipes.

## Claquage

The techniques of 'claquage' or rupture grouting have grown largely from the experience of the almost inevitable local occurrence of ground rupture when grouting varied types of ground. It was first used to compress silty soils. The aim is to produce a network of grouted fissures in an otherwise very low permeability sediment. This criss-cross of veins of grouts greatly reduces the permeability and also compresses and improves the mechanical properties as a consequence of this general compaction. Great care must be exercised to ensure that damaging ground heave at the surface does not occur. The theoretical limit for the pressures required to rupture the ground with grout have been described by Morgenstern and Vaughan[8].

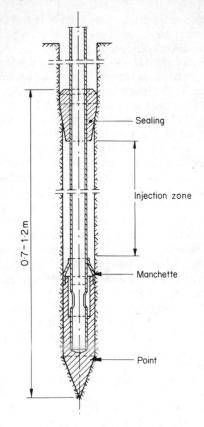

Fig. 8.5. Composite grout lance

## Compaction

A more recent technique of grouting (which is almost a reversion to the unfortunate consequences of trying to grout with cement in fine sand) is the method based upon expanding a non-penetrating fluid grout within a compressible ground without causing 'claquage' and maintaining a controlled ground heave. This method has been described by Graf[9].

## Short-gel-time injections

Karol[10] has described a grouting technique with injection continuing after initial gelling *in situ*; Moller[6] described a recent case. The problem was to solidify the filter media, a graded gravel of particles from 4·8 mm to No. 7 British Standard sieve size, over the required length without losing the grout through channels into the surrounding fissured chalk. As a first step, a viscous bentonite–cement–silicate grout was injected outside the well through lances driven from ground level to depths of 18 m to help towards blocking any major water passages to the overlying gravels.

The main sealing operation then followed. The well had previously been backfilled with a 4·8 mm and under sharp washed sand, an injection lance being placed in the well to the required lower depth of sealing during the filling. A resin grout was injected into the backfilled sand at 0·3 m stages of lance extraction, to travel outwards into the filter media. The grout mix was designed so that at each stage the initial injection had gelled before the final injection was completed. A pronounced build-up of pressure occurred towards the end of each stage to suggest that blocking of preferred channels and rupturing through the gelled grout was taking place as required. The well was subsequently bored out to full depth again, flushed clean, and reinstalled with a pump for further use. This technique can only be used with a few chemical-solution grouts and is useful in variable alluvium.

## Mixing and batching

In Fig. 8.6 the variations in mixing, batching and pumping are outlined. Installations can vary from a simple double-drum high-speed mixer (colloidal type) which can be used effectively for both powder compositions and for single-fluid chemical grout, to elaborate pump houses with stock suspensions of, for example, bentonite and with automatic dosing systems[11]. Examples of such large-scale pump houses are at Blackwater dam Dundee (Fig. 8.7), Mattmark and Fessenheim. Usually in a large grouting exercise involving tunnel protection, or dam cut-off, a variety of grout compositions is needed and the pumping station may often be very far removed from the injection point.

It has generally been found advantageous to hydrate bentonite. This makes the resultant product, a cement bentonite mix or a bentonite chemical-gel system, much more uniform and predictable in its behaviour.

Chemical dosing is now usually carried out either by volume dispensers programmed to give a sequential operation or by the use of dosing pumps or flow-rate-controlling valves. These latter valves have been used with some

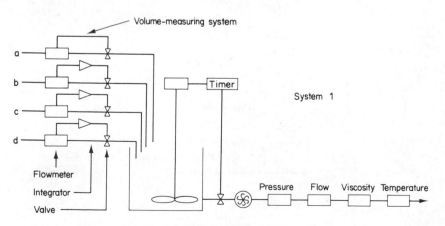

Fig. 8.6. Grout batching systems

150

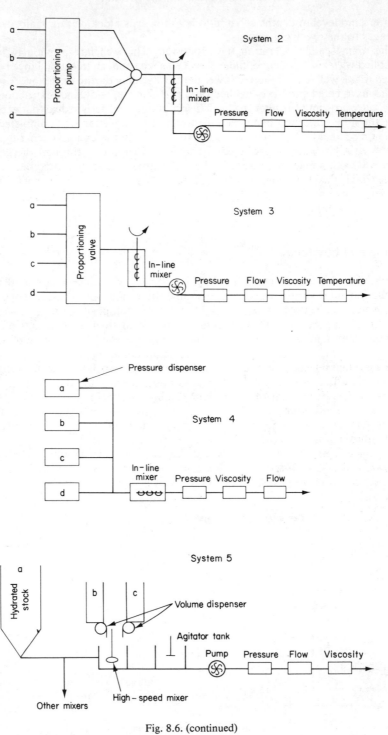

Fig. 8.6. (continued)

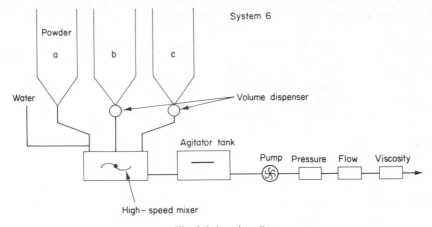

Fig. 8.6. (continued)

success in the USA in resin-solution systems. Recently some attention has been paid to the advantages of using dosing pumps which have a wide range of flow and which can deliver at high enough pressures to be able to dispense with the use of a separate pump. Colloid mills show promise for preparing bentonite slurries.

In designing a mixing system one must take into account the space available, the risks of premature gelling and the possible chemical reactions between solutions, containers and plant. Galvanised tanks are *not* suitable for acid catalysts. On large projects a central grouting plant is an expensive item and must be carefully planned, but with smaller jobs, of which there are many, there are advantages in having compact purpose-assembled grouting 'packs' which can be designed for use with a wide range of grouts.

Fig. 8.7. Grout pumping station, pumping and batching units

## Choice of grouts

A grout or combination of grouts must be chosen on economic grounds, given that the technical requirements can be fulfilled. Moller and Dempsey[6] have itemised the factors to be considered for chemical grouts.

Technically to establish an appropriate grouting system the first determinant is the pore size of the ground to be treated, which is approximately related to particle grading. The limits for suspension grouts are generally regarded as a 10:1 size factor between the $D_{15}$ of the grout and the $D_{15}$ size of the granular system to be injected. This may be compared with the Terzaghi infiltration criteria which is again based on the $D_{15}$ and $D_{85}$ sizes. These are known to be conservative and it has been shown by several workers that filters perform effectively with ratios much higher than the ratios of Terzaghi, and this would appear to be the basis for most grouting specifications. Generally particulate grouts are limited to soils with pore dimensions greater than 0·2 mm. Although a certain amount has been done to show the considerable difference in the injectability of properly dispersed bentonites as against flocculated suspensions, little work has been done on the limits of injection due to the physical size of the elementary particles in the case of large-molecule systems.

The limits of injectability were set down by Glossop and Skempton[12] and Glossop and Ischy[13], and subsequently Caron[14] has produced a further range. These have been combined in Table 8.1. There is always an uncertain boundary to the limits of injectability of single-fluid Newtonian solutions since theoretically

**Table 8.1**  LIMITS OF GROUTING ABILITY OF SOME MIXES (AFTER CARON)

| Type of soils | Coarse sands and gravels | Medium to fine sands | Silty or clayey sands, silts |
|---|---|---|---|
| **soil characteristics** Grain diameter | $d_{10} > 0.5$ mm | $0.02 < d_{10} < 0.5$ mm | $d_{10} < 0.02$ mm |
| Specific surface | $S < 100$ cm$^{-1}$ | $100$ cm$^{-1} < S < 1\,000$ cm$^{-1}$ | $S > 1\,000$ cm$^{-1}$ |
| Permeability | $K > 10^{-3}$ m/s | $10^{-3} > K > 10^{-5}$ m/s | $K < 10^{-5}$ m/s |
| Type of mix | Bingham suspensions | Colloid solutions (gels) | Pure solutions (resins) |
| Consolidation grouting | Cement ($K > 10^{-2}$ m/s) Aerated mix | Hard silica gels: double shot: Joosten (for $K > 10^{-4}$ m/s) single shot: Carongel Glyoxol Siroc | Aminoplastic Phenoplastic |
| Impermeability grouting | Aerated mix Bentonite gel Clay gel Clay/cement | Bentonite gel Lignochromate Light carongel Soft silicagel Vulcanisable oils Others (Terranier) | Acrylamids Aminoplastic Phenoplastic |

they could diffuse into materials of extremely low permeability given time and given the delay in setting time which would be required. Some of the more advanced single-fluid systems do have the ability to be formulated with an extremely wide range of setting times, ranging from a few seconds to many hours, but cost is the determining factor since it is theoretically possible even to grout a clay. Again the limits of injectability within economic bounds are affected by the pressures which may be tolerated. If one cannot grout at high pressures, e.g. in the proximity of a tunnel or the surface, then it may be necessary to use a more expensive single-fluid low-viscosity grout under circumstances where, with greater cover, one could use a cheaper more viscous solution or even a dispersed particulate system.

The unit cost of a grout formulation is often not the most important factor in the cost of the overall exercise, but for purposes of comparison Table 8.2 has

**Table 8.2** MATERIAL COSTS OF TYPICAL FORMULATIONS

| Formulation | Cost £/m³ |
|---|---|
| Cement–bentonite | 6 |
| Bentonite gel | 8 |
| Chrome–lignins | 15 |
| Joosten | 15 |
| Silicate–aluminate | 14 |
| Silicate–ester | 28 |
| Polyphenolic (*MQ5*) | 35 |
| Resorcin–formaldehyde | 80 |
| Acrylamide | 140 |

*Note.* This table should only be used as a guide.

been drawn up and gives the relative prices of some commonly available grouting systems currently in use (*cf.* Cambefort[15]). Compositions which are currently in use are listed with a very simple classification in Table 8.3.

Classifications serve to indicate the function of a grout, but choice for a particular application must also take account of the availability, scale of the operation, level of skills available, and time to optimise a procedure. Package systems *MQ5* have attractions here. For large operations it may be worthwhile to carry out extensive trials to optimise. This is especially the case in clay grouting.

## Control and evaluation

This key aspect of a grouting operation may be considered under three headings:

1. Specification and control of raw materials.
2. Control and monitoring of the grouting operation.
3. Evaluation of the end product.

Items 2 and 3 are linked. The records of grout take and pressure versus time are often the best indicators of successful operations.

**Table 8.3** GROUTS USED IN ALLUVIAL GROUTING

| *Suspensoids* | *Two-shot solutions* | *Single-shot solutions* |
|---|---|---|
| Cement | Sodium silicate– | Chrome–lignin, Sumisol*, |
| Cement–sand | calcium chloride | T.D.M.† |
| Cement–clay | Hydrochloric acid– | Sodium silicate–sodium |
| Cement–bentonite | urea formaldehyde | bicarbonate |
| Cement–bentonite, P.F.A. | monomer | Sodium silicate–sodium |
| Waste mine slurries | | aluminate |
| Bentonite–gel (with sodium | | Sodium silicate–ethyl acetate† |
| silicate and acid phosphate) | | Sodium silicate–mixed esters |
| | | (Durcisseur)* |
| | | Sodium silicate–formamide (base) |
| | | (Siroc)* |
| | | Sodium silicate–oxalate salt |
| | | (Cemex)† |
| | | Resorcinol–formaldehyde (acid |
| | | or alkali catalysis)† |
| | | Polyphenolic–formaldehyde, |
| | | alkali catalyst ($MQ4$*, $MQ5$*, |
| | | Terranier†) |
| | | Acrylamide, $AM9$*, Progil |
| | | $R.1295$* |

*Proprietary grouts on sale.
†Patent protected.

## Specification for grouting materials

Proprietary grouts arrive with the makers' assurance that their properties will be adequately uniform. It is prudent nevertheless to have standard procedures to monitor successive batches. For water-based gel systems tests should be carried out with 'site' water at 'site' temperatures using site mixers until a relation between a laboratory scale and field batch is assured. One should test for gel time (using a standardised indicator of gelling), viscosity–time curve, synersis and shrinkage, water tolerance and gel strength (with a vane or penetrometer). Often manufacturers quote strengths in a standard sand. This procedure should be matched and particular care taken to reproduce curing conditions. Once the product has had this clearance then a simple setting/gel time value may be a sufficient index for routine monitoring.

Where formulating grout from raw materials, e.g. with bentonite gels, then a systematic screening of batches is essential. Such a screening would require:

1. Apparent viscosity at a minute hydration with 6% w/w suspension should give a value 11 cP $\pm$ 1.
2. Wet sieving on BS No. 200 sieve should not leave more than 5% residue.
3. Moisture content should be 10% $\pm$ 2%.

These should not be taken as a universal model.

Steps which can be followed in the search for a suitable local clay are summarised as follows.

*Examination of a clay for grouting*

1. Determine water content.
2. Determine liquid limit, 60 preferred.
3. Relate concentration to viscosity aiming at the weight to give 38–40 s Marsh (often 340–440 g/l).

*Examination of a bentonite*

1. Determine liquid limit.
2. Determine 'yield' typically as the concentration to give 15 cP in the hydrated state, or the quantity to give 40 s Marsh.
3. Retained wet sieve on 200 BS sieve.
4. Moisture content as delivered.

*Study of mixes*

1. Start with clay plus water, add cement plus sand.
2. Use Marsh cone with grouts and Prepaket cone with mortars. With bentonites often the Fanm viscometer is used.
3. Estimate bleed on 1 litre.
4. Injectibility and set test with Vicat needle for cement–clay and laboratory vane for softer gels.
5. Pumpability—estimate head losses for non-Newtonian consistency.
6. Measure cylinder strength for stronger cement–clay mixes, or use small laboratory vane.

*Study of additives*

1. Sodium carbonate ⎫ Test with the aim of maintaining 38–40 s Marsh and
2. Sodium silicate ⎬ stable suspension with increased range of solids con-
3. Phosphates ⎭ tent

*Optimisation of bentonite gels (bentonite, phosphate, sodium silicate)*

1. Determine the quantity of bentonite to get 35 s Marsh.
2. Adding deflocculent fluidifies the mix; adding of silicate thickens it to 40–60 s Marsh.
3. Some 20–30 mixtures are made, and gel time and shear strength (vane) measured.
4. Optimise on cost for adequate gel time and satisfactory 'bleed'. Cost of grout $Q$ is given by:

$$Q = xP + yS + C$$

where $x$ = % deflocculent of unit price $P$,
 $y$ = % silicate of unit price $S$ and
 $C$ = price of clay and other fixed expenses.
Minimum price for given strength is given by

$$\frac{dQ}{dx} = P + S\frac{dy}{dx} = 0$$

Therefore optimum compositions are on lines with gradient $P/S$ tangential to curves of equal strength.

## Monitoring of grouting progress

Quantities of grout should be closely measured. Often this is done enthusiastically because the contractor is paid according to how much grout he puts in! Furthermore, at each stage there should be a record of grouting pressures. It then needs systematic office procedures to build up a picture of the acceptance at each stage of each grout, until an acceptable refusal pressure has been achieved. It is at this juncture that one must take into account the porosities expected and the

Fig. 8.8. Modern dosing pump grouting unit (courtesy Bram and Luebbe (G.B.) Ltd.)

rheological nature of the materials injected, cross checking, for example, with 'Bingham' grouts that the anticipated Quantity-Pressure ($Q/P$) relationship is being achieved.

On many small operations the technical level available on site will not permit elaborate checking, but it must be appreciated that only extensive experience on the part of the operatives is a reasonable substitute. On big projects monitoring is essential and quite elaborate recording instrumentation must be provided.

Ground heave and uplift should be closely watched and cross-correlated to 'take' and pressures. Ground fractures can be recognised on a $Q/P$ record.

During the course of a contract, systematic borings with permeability and penetration measurements should be made to check that the grout is indeed in position. Some progress has been made by electrical resistivity surveying[16] and seismic velocity measurement in order to detect grouted ground.

### Evaluation of performance

Some evaluation of adequacy of treatment is required in many undertakings. In cut-off work this may be established by comparing piezometric head on either side of the membrane when impounding starts. Boreholes and inspection shafts may be called for and observations may need to be made regularly over a long period.

In tunnelling the progress of the works reveals all, but advance borings are a prudent measure especially in difficult ground with 'borderline' conditions, and chemical analysis on disturbed 'returns' can indicate the spread of grout.

The proper evaluation of grouting effectiveness is a field in which there is still room for development.

### Acknowledgement

The author wishes to acknowledge the permission of the Directors of Soil Mechanics Ltd to publish this chapter.

REFERENCES

1. Kinipple, W. R., *Engineering*, **50,** Oct.–Nov. (1890)
2. Ponimalkin, P. U. and Kheifets, V. B., 'Construction of the Grout Curtain for the Downstream Cofferdam at the Toktogulsk Hydroelectric Plant Dam, *Gidrotecknischeskoe Stroitelstvo*, No. 12, 79, Dec. (1969)
3. Cambefort, H. and Caron, C. 'Le Délavage des Gels de Silicate de Soude', *4th Int. Cong. Soil Mech. and Found. Eng.*, London (1957)
4. Skipp, B. O. and Renner, L., 'The Improvement of the Mechanical Properties of Sand', *Symposium on Grouts and Drilling Muds in Engineering Practice*, Butterworths, London (1963)
5. Litvinskii, G. G. and Druzhko, E. B., 'Geotechnical Parameters of Strengthening of Broken Rock Around a Working', *Fiziko-Technicheskie Razrabotki Poleznykh Iskopaemykh*, No. 6, 3–7, Nov.–Dec. (1970)
6. Moller, K. and Dempsey, J., Ground Engineering Conference, I.C.E. (1970)
7. Kutzner, C. and Rupper, C., 'Chemische Bodenverfestigungbeim V.—Bahnbau in Köln Strasse Brucke Tunnel', Aug. (1970)

8. Morgenstern, N. and Vaughan, P., 'Some Observations on Allowable Grouting Pressures', *Grouts and Drilling Muds in Engineering Practice,* Butterworths, London (1963)

9. Graf, E. C., 'Compaction Grouting Technique, Observations', *J. Soil Mech. and Found. Eng.,* SM5, Am. Soc. Civ. Eng., 1151–1156 (1969)

10. Karol, R. H., 'Chemical Grouting Technology', *J. Soil Mech. and Found Eng.,* SM1, No. 94, Am. Soc. Civ. Eng., 175–204 (1968)

11. Perrot, E. E., 'British Practice for Grouting Granular Soils', *J. Soil Mech. and Found. Eng.,* No. 92, Am. Soc. Civ. Eng., 57–59 (1965)

12. Glossop, R. and Skempton, A. W., 'Particle Size in Silts and Sands', *J. I. Civ. Eng.,* **25,** 182, Dec. (1945)

13. Glossop, R. and Ischy, E., 'Introduction to Alluvial Grouting', *Proc. Inst. Civ. Eng.,* **21,** 449–474, March (1962)

14. Caron, C., 'Étude Physico-Chimique des Gels de Silice', *Annals de l'Institut du Batiment et des Travaux Public,* No. 207–208, March–April (1965)

15. Cambefort, H., *Injection des Sols,* Vol. I, Eyrolles, Paris (1964)

16. Bogoslovskii, V. A., 'Use of the Resistance Method in Constructing Grout Curtains', *Gidrotechnicheskoe Stroitelstvo,* No. 8, 10–12, Aug. (1969)

BIBLIOGRAPHY

Barbadette, F. and Sarbarly, F., 'Étude et Utilisations Récent des Coulis d'Injection Argile–Cément', *3rd Int. Cong. Soil Mech. and Found. Eng.,* Zurich (1953)

Bethauser, A., 'Stabilisierung und Abdichtung von Erdbauten durch Injektionen', *Die Tiefbau,* **11** No. 4., April (1969)

Geddes, W. G. M. and Rocke, G. S., 'The Backwater Dam', *Proc. Inst. Civ. Engs.,* 51, 433–464 (1972)

Janin, J. J. and Le Scielour, G. F., 'Chemical Grouting for Paris Rapid Transit Tunnels', *J. Const. Div. A.S.C.E.,* **96,** 61–74 (1970)

Leonard, M. W. L. and Dempsey, J., 'Clays for Grouting', *Symposium on Grouts and Drilling Muds in Engineering Practice,* Butterworths, London (1963)

## Chapter 9

# Ground Freezing

Ground freezing is simply the cooling of the sub-surface so that pore water is converted into ice, imparting strength and impermeability to the ground formations. It is a physical process, and the term should not be extended to include treatment where temperature fall is not basic, e.g. consolidation by chemical reactions.

### Historical

The application of freezing to geotechnology followed the development of mechanical refrigeration in the 1800s, and was first reported in south Wales where a mine shaft was sunk through water-bearing strata in 1862. An ether engine supplied by Siebe Gorman & Co. Ltd. cooled brine which was circulated through tubes in the ground in a system which has not changed in principle since its inception. It is interesting to note that all the early examples appear to be related to mining. F. H. Poetch was granted a patent in Germany in 1883 after using the same principle for the development of a lignite mine at Schneidlingen; five years later, an iron-ore mine shaft was sunk by the freezing method in Michigan, USA. In such cases, water-saturated superficial deposits above the rock-head were frozen in order to gain access to minerals below, but later mining projects have extended freezing from the surface downwards into water-bearing rocks at depths of up to 900 m, and unstable sediments have been successfully treated at depths of 600 m. As Ostrowski[1] has pointed out, in his description of freezing to great depth in Canada, such depths should not be taken as the ultimate limit for the process. Whilst it may be true to say that challenges from the mining industry have been largely responsible for growth and development in the technique of ground freezing, the civil engineer has not neglected to take advantage of the facility in appropriate circumstances. In fact, in the last twenty years or so, increasing attention has been given to the particular requirements of the construction industry. A stimulus was provided when north American and Russian engineers began to examine systematically the properties of naturally frozen ground met with during construction activities in the Arctic environment; this has led to fundamental studies of considerable interest to the ground freezing practitioner, e.g. Sanger and Kaplar[2] on the plastic deformation of soils in permafrost areas. Finally, the availability in recent years of liquid nitrogen in bulk has provided an alternative source of cold energy which has special appeal in certain civil engineering problems.

## The engineering scope of ground freezing

The main field of application is in the planned stabilisation of ground (containing moisture, or below the water table) prior to sub-surface construction work. It is usually a temporary expedient; the ground is allowed to return to normal temperatures once the structure has been built. It is employed for shafts and tunnels and in foundation and storage excavations. Less frequently, it has stabilised incipient ground slides and has served as underpinning for buildings. On a smaller scale, weak soils have been frozen in order to recover cored samples, and local leakage points through sheet-steel piling have been sealed by freezing. Freezing has been instrumental in stabilising a long-abandoned flooded mine shaft in a dangerous condition, in order that it could be safely plugged at the rock-head. Other proposals have included mat freezings to provide a temporary road over marshland, and a lake-bottom freezing to facilitate exploitation of ore reserves below. Paradoxically, artificial ground freezing is sometimes carried out on a relatively permanent basis to maintain the 'status quo' below heated buildings founded on permafrost. All these possibilities pose an interesting variety of problems in a very specialised field of engineering.

## Description of the process

Heat is removed from the ground via probes placed into boreholes, or alternatively drilled or thrust into the required positions. The probe itself consists of an external pipe, closed at the lower end, and containing an open-ended inner tube of slightly shorter length. Cooling fluid is normally introduced through this inner tube; the radial dimensions and composition of the assembly are determined by the nature of the cooling fluid employed. Outer pipes may vary between 50 mm and 150 mm in diameter, and inners range from 20 mm to 75 mm. Steel, copper or plastic materials are employed.

In the classic system the coolant is a brine (Fig. 9.1a). Generally this is a solution of calcium chloride in water, of specific gravity 1·24–1·28; other brines made up of the chlorides of sodium, magnesium or lithium have also been used. The crystallisation point of the chosen brine should be at least 5°C lower than the ultimate temperatures at which ground freezing will proceed. As the brine rises in the annular space between the freeze probe members, heat is extracted from the environment and a warmer brine is discharged from the head of each probe into a collection main, from where it is piped back to the refrigeration plant. Here it is pumped through a chiller—normally a shell and tube heat-exchanger—and is recooled and then delivered via a distribution main to the inner tubes of the probes. The coolant is therefore confined in a closed, recirculatory flow path. Industrial refrigeration plant is required to cool the brine. For ease of installation, this is brought to site packaged into units, either skid or trailer mounted. The choice of equipment and refrigerant is a wide one: rotary or reciprocating compressors, using either Freon or ammonia as refrigerants, are in common use. Compound compression is often required to produce the necessary temperature depression. Abstracted heat is dissipated into a nearby watercourse if available, if not then into the atmosphere by forced-draught cooling towers or evaporative condensers. Such a system, with two-stage compressors, can ultimately lower the brine temperature to −40°C if required, but a greater mechanical efficiency is gained if design temperatures are limited to about −30°C.

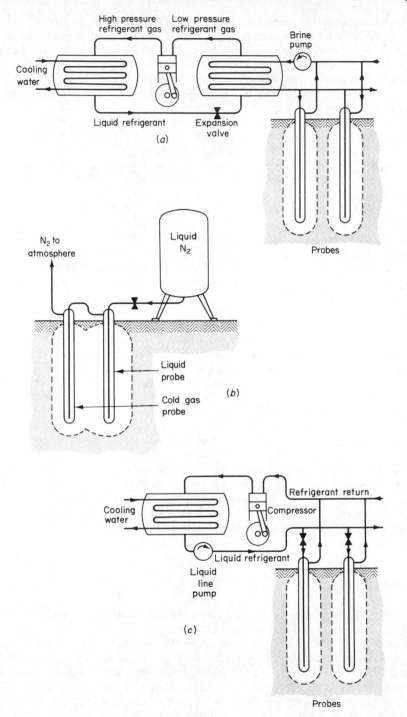

Fig. 9.1. (*a*) Circulatory brine cooling, (*b*) expandable refrigerant and (*c*) circulatory refrigerant

In the non-recirculatory system (Fig. 9.1*b*), a refrigerant is passed directly into the freeze-probe assembly from a storage vesself and is allowed to evaporate at the primary point where cooling is required. In the process it attracts heat energy equivalent to its latent heat of vaporisation from the soil. The resulting gas is exhausted to atmosphere. Liquid nitrogen, brought to site in bulk and stored in vacuum-insulated vessels, reaches a temperature of −196°C when allowed to evaporate at atmospheric pressure.

Occupying an intermediate position between the two systems just described, a system is possible whereby primary refrigerant cools the ground directly, but is recovered, reliquefied and recirculated on site in one single or two interlocked flow paths (Fig. 9.1*c*). Dispensing with a secondary coolant or brine, a much smaller volume flow of refrigerant is used with greater efficiency, heat energy being abstracted by change of state in the freeze tubes themselves, as in the case of expendable refrigerants such as liquid nitrogen. Although the latter could theoretically be used in this manner, reliquification plants are large, expensive and unsuitable for temporary installation on construction sites. Carbon dioxide is a practicable refrigerant, but yields temperatures only down to −55°C and is not in general use. Shuster[3] makes reference to these intermediate systems in greater detail. They may well have a bright future in this field with the benefit of advancing technology, but remain of theoretical interest at present.

The technical merits and disadvantages of the recirculatory brine system compared with the use of expendable refrigerant should become more apparent in a later part of this chapter, but one or two practical implications may be helpful at this stage. Nitrogen, evaporating in a probe, will freeze soil to a given radius roughly five times faster than would a brine-filled probe operating at −35°C. As will be seen, this factor may be increased still further since the eventual low temperature regime with nitrogen will produce a stronger membrane, and therefore one whose design thickness may be reduced. A nitrogen freeze will therefore look very attractive where the consequences or costs of delay are substantial. Ice walls are built in a matter of days, or even hours if the probes have been closely spaced, whereas in a brine-cooled system the building period is measured in weeks. On the other hand, the high cost of the consumable normally limits the size and scope of the freezing operation. Nitrogen is, however, finding increasing application in smaller, compact projects. Here, the cumulative cost of the refrigerant is offset by the small establishment charges; there is no mechanical installation which can assume a disproportionate cost in a brine freezing of modest extent.

## ARRANGEMENT OF FREEZING PROBES

Freezing will transform weak and water-laden materials into a condition where they become both self supporting and impervious. Consequently, most field applications of the process are concerned with the temporary support of an excavation and the exclusion of ground-water from it. Normally, freezing probes are laid out in linear fashion, so that an adequate boundary wall of frozen ground will enclose the future excavation. While the frozen barrier is forming, growth is at first radial from each freezing tube. The first stage is completed when these separate cylinders unite. The second stage lowers the average temperature and extends the thickness of the ice wall to design values. This is often planned to occur at about the same time that the future excavation line attains a sub-freezing temperature. The third stage is a maintenance of the freeze, during which physical removal of ground and associated permanent construction is carried out. Finally, the frozen barrier having served its purpose, thawing takes place and the freezing elements are removed and the holes backfilled, or else they are suitably abandoned *in situ.*

The simplest configuration of freeze probes results where a surface excavation through unstable ground is planned to pass into or approach an impervious substratum. In this case, the enclosing ice barrier will be seated in, and sealed by, the basal bed. Each vertical probe will extend at least 2–3 m into the 'tight' formation, and the horizontal spacing will vary between 0·8 and 2·0 m according to requirements.

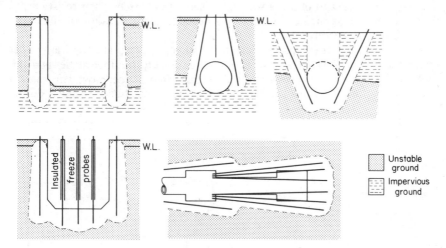

Fig. 9.2. Typical freeze probe patterns

Where there is no convenient basal formation to provide a cut-off below the water table, interior freezing elements are placed in such a manner that the floor of the future excavation becomes frozen. Their spacing can be significantly wider than that of the perimeter tubes, since they are protected laterally from the warming effect of the environment. In some cases, measures are taken to insulate their effect in the ground to be excavated. Cold brine circulation can often be discontinued before maintenance freezing of the perimeter holes is at an end.

There are many variations from the two idealised examples just given; some of these are illustrated diagrammatically in Fig. 9.2. For tunnelling operations, the same principles may be used, but with horizontal freezing probes in water-bearing ground it is often necessary to place them through the cover of gland packings and valves, and to advance the tunnel in stages.

In all cases, accuracy of alignment is important. In deep vertical freezings special techniques are required to prevent or correct undue deviation of the freezing tubes, and surveys are made so that the magnitude and location of the greatest gap between neighbouring probes is known[4]. For inclined and horizontal freezings a limiting factor may be imposed by the progressive directional inaccuracy in placing long freeze probes. Theoretical design will suggest a certain spacing of freezing elements, but a realistic working tolerance must be allowed. This factor is an example where the experience of specialist contractors is often indispensable.

## The effect of freezing on soils

The behaviour of soils during freezing and their structural properties in the frozen state are complex subjects which have been studied theoretically and experimentally by several researchers. Only a brief review is possible here. The reader is referred to References 5–9 for a more thorough treatment.

Ice creeps under a steady load, and the same is true of saturated sands and silts in the frozen state, and of clays whether frozen or unfrozen. Their resistance to failure when used as engineering materials depends on the duration of loading as well as on the temperature.

When strain is plotted against time, three stages of creep are apparent under uniform load (Fig. 9.3). At first, strain increases quickly, but then settles at a uniform minimal rate of increase in its second stage. In practice, most deformation occurs in the latter stage. A third, plastic stage is eventually reached during

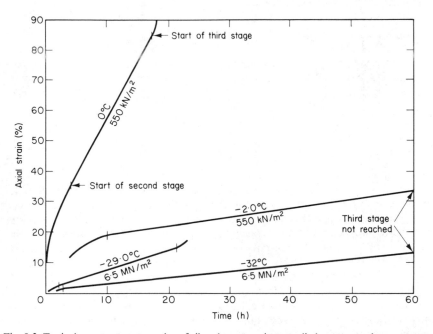

Fig. 9.3. Typical creep-curves samples of silty clays at various applied stresses and temperatures (after Sanger and Kaplar[2], and Shuster[3])

which complete loss of resistance occurs. This feature is well demonstrated in a typical clay at temperatures near the freezing point of water. Testing an organic silty clay, Sanger and Kaplar[2] have shown that at 550 kN/m², this failure point occurs after 17 h when the sample was maintained at 0°C, but no failure point had been reached at 60 h when tested at −2°C.

Soils rich in silt-clay fractions may exhibit this behaviour to a significant extent at the temperatures currently used in ground freezing, and in this case it would be prudent to estimate the long-term creep strength[3] and the stage-two deformation[6] if excavations are open for a long period of time. One reason for this phenomenon in fine-grained sediments is to be found in the intimate bond existing between the water and the clay particles. This results in a significant proportion of the total soil moisture remaining unfrozen at temperatures as cold as −25°C. Apparently, the more clay material in the soil, the greater the quantity of unfrozen moisture. Andersland and Akili[8] refer to this in their treatise on creep rates of a frozen clay soil. However, there is no evidence, either theoretical or practical, to support the generalisations sometimes made that clays cannot be effectively frozen for purposes of ground support. Lovell[9] measures the unconfined compressive strength of frozen clays, and whilst this does not characterise the time-dependent factor, it is valid as an indication of the dramatic increase in structural strength with decreasing temperature. In fact, it appears to increase exponentially with the relative proportion of moisture frozen. Using silty clay as an example, the amount of moisture frozen at −18°C is only 1·25 times that frozen at −5°C, but the increase in compressive strength is more than four-fold.

By contrast, the water content of granular soils is almost wholly converted into ice at 0°C. Frozen sands and other soils with relatively large pore spaces exhibit a reasonably high compressive strength only a few degrees below freezing, and there is justification for using this parameter as a design index of their performance in the field, providing that a suitable factor of safety is incorporated. The order of increase in compressive strength with decreasing temperature is shown in Fig. 9.4.

The structural advantages in using an expendable refrigerant are considerable, even allowing for the fact that the volume of refrigerant required to depress every part of the frozen barrier to temperatures below −60°C would be formidable.

## Mode of heat extraction

As heat is abstracted via elements in the ground, cooling is proceeding in three separate regimes: frozen ground already formed is being cooled further, water at the interface is being converted into ice, and ground beyond the interface is being cooled below its natural temperature. A full analysis of this process, involving sophisticated mathematical treatment, is also dependent on data difficult to gather for any specific location. For example, thermal conductivity will vary vertically with each change in water content and lithology. It also changes horizontally from the frozen to the unfrozen condition. At the interface itself, energy is absorbed without depressing the temperature. However, reasonably accurate forecasts can be derived by an experienced engineer, and these are invariably checked by temperature and energy measurements as the process is developing in the field. A typical temperature profile through one of a circular arrangement of freeze probes is illustrated in Fig. 9.5. In plan view, isotherms can sometimes be drawn from field measurements by drilling holes for temperature measurement into a 'safe' section of the ice wall. In a deep mine shaft freezing, such as that shown for the Duval Corporation's mine in Saskatchewan, it is possible to observe the effect of freeze-hole drilling deviation on the temperature pattern (Fig. 9.6).

Ground freezing is basically an exercise in heat transfer and in the absence of moving ground-water transfer in the ground is by conduction. Thus, as already suggested, the property which governs the rate at which freezing proceeds is the thermal conductivity of the frozen materials. It is interesting to note that these

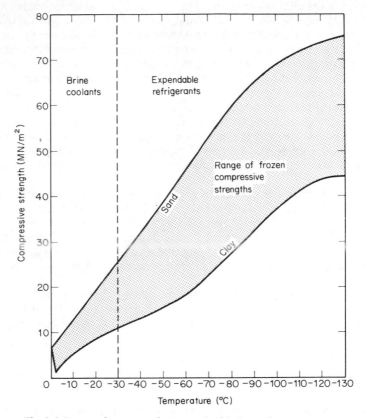

Fig. 9.4. Increase in compressive strength with decreasing temperature

values fall within quite narrow limits for all types of frozen soil. This is the reason why ground freezing is such a versatile technique, dealing effectively with a great variety of soils and rocks in one strata section. By contrast, alternative penetrative processes rely on permeability, and are, in varying degrees, sensitive to changes. Permeability, however, may fluctuate over several orders of magnitude, and any one injection procedure will not readily accommodate such gross variations. Whilst it is essential for the proper assessment of any ground-control method to obtain accurate information from prior site investigation, freezing is less affected by minor errors or omissions in the description of soil types than is grouting. Having said this, it must be emphasised that a limitation on freezing is imposed by unidirectional flow of ground-water. For a brine-freezing project, a velocity exceeding about 2 m/d will seriously affect and distort

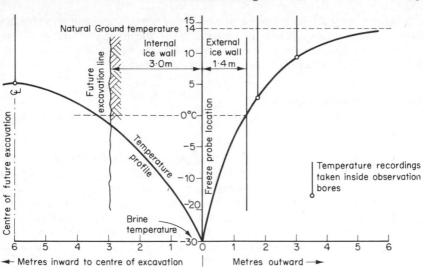

Fig. 9.5. Typical radial section through frozen barrier

the growth of the ice wall. The tolerance is much wider with liquid-nitrogen freezing. A study of the hydro-geological environment will usually indicate whether or not special investigation is required. For the same reasons, underground water abstraction by pumping in the locality should be carefully

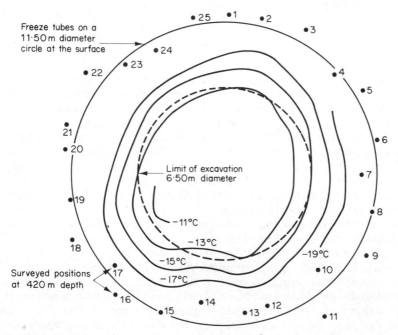

Fig. 9.6. Structure of the internal part of a fully developed ice wall, 420 m deep, No. 2 shaft, Duval Corporation

checked. Another related situation occurs where heat is carried into the freezing zone by water mains, drains or sewers. When the locations are accurately known, remedial action is possible, but unsuspected utilities such as are described by Ellis and McConnell[10] have proved troublesome.

## Abnormal circumstances

### Saline water conditions

Where dissolved salts are present in the ground-water, chemical analysis and freezing-point tests on samples are taken into account in the design. Sea-water presents no special problem in this respect since its freezing point is only about 3°C below that of fresh water. However, when a volume of saline water in granular soils has been confined by a perimeter array of probes, further inward advance of the frozen wall will cause a progressive increase in the salinity of the unfrozen residue. In narrow excavations, salinity of the water in the unfrozen core is commonly several times that of the original ground-water.

Tidal variation in ground-water levels near the coast will involve oscillatory ground-water movement, and a close spacing of freezing tubes will be required to develop an ice wall in a given time.

Ground freezings have been satisfactorily carried out even in the presence of a salt-saturated solution, which will not begin to freeze until a temperature of −21°C is reached. In Louisiana, the combination of incompetent sands and silts overlying the salt-domes structures produces such conditions. There, freezing is a normal technique for shaft sinking.

### Frost heave

There is a volume change of 9% on conversion of water to ice. In granular soils, water is expelled from the pores to accommodate ice formation and no *in-situ* volume change results. This mechanism, incidentally, is used to advantage as confirmation that an enclosing ice wall is complete. When this occurs the level of the contained water table begins to rise. As permeability is reduced by finer particles, *in-situ* expansion will occur if the advance of the frost line exceeds the migrating velocity. Confining pressure will reduce the vertical ground heave[11], and in practice the rise in surface level due to this aspect of freezing is insignificant (up to about 75 mm). After thawing, the ground level slowly trends back towards the original. Where precise levelling has been carried out it is found that complete recovery is rarely attained.

An abnormal situation might occur where capillary attraction of water to the freezing interface takes place. This is more generally observed where a surface layer of soil is subject to climatic freezing. Jukumis[12,13] has conducted a series of experiments to illustrate the upward migration and freezing of moisture. The latter can, in some instances, result in an appreciable and continuous rise in ground level—the classic case of frost heave. Special conditions must be met, i.e. free water in excess of that contained originally in the soil voids must be available to be moved to the surface of freezing. For this movement to take place the classification of the soil must fall within narrow limits with respect to texture and permeability[14].

The conditions created by artificial freezing, near-vertical freezing planes cutting across the water table, with greater temperature gradient, are radically different from those typical of climatic frost heave and in the author's experience of many ground freezings only two examples have exhibited progressive ground heave of more than a few centimetres. However, where silts or fine sandy silts predominate in close proximity to the ground water table, Shuster[3] has proposed a procedure designed to evaluate the potential for frost expansion prior to site operations. According to this author, the likelihood of frost heave occurring is reduced if freezing is rapid. He nevertheless suggested that monitoring the ground movements in the immediate neighbourhood of the freezing installation was worthwhile.

## Organic remains

Organic clays, and especially peat and lignite deposits, are stabilised by freezing. Those having a fibrous texture however, are prone to permanent alteration after a freezing cycle, and properties of interest to the designer of the permanent works (such as bearing capacity) may undergo change. The possibility should be recognised in the design stage of a project.

## The placement of concrete against frozen ground

In order to capitalise on the self-supporting nature of excavations in frozen ground and the dry working conditions, concrete is normally placed directly against the frozen boundary. Numerous tests have confirmed that this is a perfectly legitimate practice. As with frost heave, the physical conditions are not comparable with those leading to frost damage from cold weather, where heat loss by radiation is involved. At the junction of the two masses, heat conduction will cause the frozen ground to rise well above freezing point for a considerable period. Well-designed concrete, based on the use of cement giving a reasonable initial strength with uniform release of heat of hydration will, in sufficient mass, result in a concrete of normal long-term strength. Cored samples from linings set against frozen ground indicate that, as a rule of thumb, thicknesses exceeding 0·45 m will be completely unaffected. Below this, designers will sometimes allow for a skin of about 70 mm of affected concrete.

## Conclusions

Ground freezing as a civil engineering process has been a successful tool for a long time, and is now able to draw on a substantial body of technical study to augment the practical experience gained by the specialist contractor. The procedures are relatively expensive and require proper programming, with the result that any restriction in their use stems more frequently from economic rather than technical considerations. But, with the increased cost of delays in a highly mechanised industry, freezing, because of its positive and predictable effect, can offer a valuable insurance against the interruptions (often incapable of evaluation) imposed by other methods during the construction phase. It should be pointed out that in the freezing of pits or vertical shafts, prior tests are made to ensure that once started construction will proceed without recourse to pumping or unforeseen temporary support systems.

In this sort of application, ground freezing becomes increasingly competitive in cost with increasing depth. It becomes an attractive technique where nearby foundations and buildings dictate caution in the use of pumping or pile-driving plant, as it can be operated without causing vibrations or loss of ground. As a salvage operation, it will continue to play its part, often where other techniques have proved ineffective. Here the use of liquid nitrogen opens up the possibility of prompt remedial action. Whilst ground freezing will probably remain one of the more exotic geotechnical processes, an increased understanding of ground-freezing techniques together with advancing refrigeration technology will ensure the future of this, the most versatile of all ground-control procedures.

REFERENCES

1. Ostrowski, W. J. S., 'Design Aspects of Ground Consolidation by the Freezing Method for Shaft Sinking in Saskatchewan', *Canadian Mining and Metallurgical Bulletin*, Oct. (1967)
2. Sanger, F. J. and Kaplar, C. W., 'Plastic Deformation of Frozen Soils', International Permafrost Conference, Purdue University (1963)
3. Shuster, J. A., 'Controlled Freezing for Temporary Ground Support', Proceedings of North American Rapid Excavation and Tunnelling Conference, Chicago (1972)
4. Adamson, J. N. and Storey, J. H., 'Turbo-drilling as Applied to Potash Developments in the Saskatchewan Field', Proceedings, 9th Commonwealth Mining and Metallurgical Congress, Vol. 1 (1969)
5. Khakimov, Kh. R., *Artificial Freezing of Soils—Theory and Practice*, translated from the Russian by A. Barouch, Israel Programme for Scientific Translations, US Dept. of the Interior, Washington, D.C. (1966)
6. Sanger, F. J., 'Ground Freezing in Construction', *Journal of the American Society of Civil Engineers*, **94**, SM1 (1968)
7. Vialov, S. S., *Methods of Determining Creep, Long Term Strength and Compressibility Characteristics of Frozen Soils* (Russian), Technical Translation No. 1364, National Research Council of Canada (1966)
8. Andersland, O. B. and Akili, W., 'Stress Effect on Creep Rates in a Frozen Clay Soil', *Geotechnique*, **17**, 27–39 (1967)
9. Lovell, C. W., 'Temperature Effects on Phase Composition and Strength of a Partially Frozen Soil', Highway Research Board Bulletin No. 168, Washington, D.C. (1957)
10. Ellis, D. R. and McConnell, J., 'The Use of the Freezing Process in the Construction of a Pumping Station and Storm-water Overflow at Fleetwood, Lancashire', Proceedings, Institute of Civil Engineers, No. 6302 (1959)
11. Hoekstra, P., 'Water Movement and Freezing Pressures', *Soil Science Society of America*, **33** No. 4 (1969)
12. Jukumis, A. R., 'The Effect of Freezing on a Capillary Meniscus', Highway Research Board Bulletin No. 168, Washington, D.C. (1957)
13. Jukumis, A. R., 'The Soil Freezing Experiment', Highway Research Board Bulletin No. 135, Washington, D.C. (1956)
14. Jackson, K. A. and Chalmers, B., 'Freezing of Liquids in Porous Media with Special Reference to Frost Heave in Soils', *Journal of Applied Physics*, **29** No. 8 (1958)

BIBLIOGRAPHY

Braun, W. A., 'Cryogenic Underground Tanks for L.N.G.', *Ground Engineering*, Sept. (1968)
Collins, S. P. and Deacon, W. G., 'Shaft Sinking by Ground Freezing: Ely Ouse, Essex Scheme', *Proc. Inst. Civ. Eng.* (1972)

Maishman, D. 'Shaft Sinking Using the Freezing Process—Application at Kellingley Colliery', Iron and Coal Trades Review (1959)

Mussche, H. E. and Waddington, J. C., 'Applications of the Freezing Process to Civil Engineering Works', *The Institute of Civil Engineers,* Works Construction Paper No. 5 (1946)

Potevin, G., 'La Congélation des Terrains dans les Travaux Publics', *Revue de l'Industrie Minérale,* **54** No. 4 (1972)

# Chapter 10

# Stabilisation of Soil by Cement

In the UK the planned road building programme for the next 10–20 years could make excessive demands on the country's resources of traditional road-building materials. These materials will also be required for other civil engineering and building works. Many soils and industrial wastes, which in their natural state would not be suitable for road bases or sub-bases because of lack of stability can, by the addition of cement, be stabilised. Stabilisation with cement can add considerable shear strength to a wide range of low-cost materials, this strength being retained under the combined actions of traffic and weathering.

In the UK the cement requirements for satisfactory stabilisation are selected on the basis of 7-day compressive strength, other simple tests being used to check the material's physical and chemical suitability. Construction may be by premix or mix-in-place methods, and although mix-in-place construction gives the highest productivity, it has been less popular in the UK than the premix method, probably because of the very specialised nature of the plant. Work abroad has shown that deep stabilisation is practical with *in-situ* mixing.

Although cement-stabilised materials are most widely used in road and airfield pavement, many other applications have been found in which a material which lacks sufficient stability in its natural state can be modified and made usable by the addition of cement.

## Introduction

The structural layers of a road or airfield pavement are required to serve two main functions: firstly, to distribute traffic loads to an extent that the sub-grade is not deformed beyond acceptable limits within the working life of the pavement, and secondly, to protect the underlying soil or sub-grade from damage by water or frost. There are two recognised forms of pavement structure, which function in entirely different ways. These are known as *flexible* and *rigid* pavements.

Traditionally the main part of a flexible pavement was a layer of material which had no tensile strength, load distribution arising through the material's internal friction or natural shear strength, in the manner illustrated in Fig. 10.1. Pavement structures formed in this way do not prevent moisture percolating to the sub-grade, nor do they provide sufficient abrasion resistance to prevent surface damage by traffic. Bituminous surfacings are used on flexible pavements to provide both a wearing surface resistant to damage by vehicles and a waterproof

172

layer to minimise water penetration into the sub-grade. The materials used in flexible pavements have traditionally been selected graded stone compacted by rolling and sometimes vibration. Due to difficulties in obtaining suitable stone, and problems arising from the very high imposed loads on major roads and air-fields, this form of construction is becoming less popular, preference being given to stabilising the base layers with bituminous or cement binder.

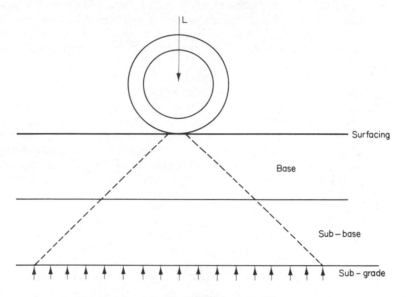

Fig. 10.1. Load distribution through a flexible pavement

Rigid pavements, of which concrete is the only practical example, have considerable tensile strength and distribute traffic loads by acting as a stiff plate, as illustrated in Fig. 10.2. To minimise high local stresses a concrete slab requires uniform support; it is also sometimes necessary to provide a 'working platform' on which to build the concrete. For these reasons a sub-base is often laid beneath a concrete pavement.

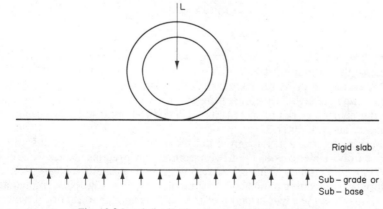

Fig. 10.2 Load distribution through a rigid pavement

Although the final functions of the sub-base layer in the two forms of pavement are different, contractors are finding that improvement of the natural stability of the sub-base materials is desirable to permit the paving plant, building the upper layers, to operate with greater efficiency and to minimise delays due to inclement weather.

Although cement-stabilised materials have tensile strength, they are normally defined as 'flexible'. Although the tensile strength would improve the load-spreading characteristics of cement-stabilised materials compared with unbound materials, it is doubtful if advantage could be taken of this strength in the long term because of the development of shrinkage cracks, which may be increased by traffic.

The first 1 000 miles (1 600 km) of motorway were completed in the UK in 1972, and it is intended to double this distance by the early 1980s, the ultimate target being 3 000–4 000 miles (4 800–6 400 km)[1]. This road-building programme could consume large quantities of high-grade aggregates leading to a national shortage, a problem which has already arisen in many other countries. Engineers anxious to conserve aggregates and reduce costs are now finding greater application for stabilisation processes to modify soils and other materials which lack adequate natural stability to allow their use in pavement construction. Stabilising soils already on site not only conserves good quality aggregates, but saves costs by reducing the amounts of materials which have to be removed and imported to the site. In some areas, use can be made of industrial wastes such as colliery shale, pulverised fuel ash, screen washings from gravel pits, etc. in which case road construction can reduce environmental problems.

Soil cement has been accepted as a sound and economic material for road and airfield pavement construction for many years in a large number of countries abroad[2]. The wealth of easily won traditional aggregates has retarded progress in the use of stabilised materials in the UK to date, but good aggregates are becoming scarcer. Greater use is being made of aggregates from the sea, but their costs are likely to be high if used far inland; coastal erosion problems may also arise if these are obtained from areas near the shore. When all these factors are considered, greater use of cement-stabilised materials in the UK may be anticipated.

## The function of cement in stabilised materials

Cement-stabilised materials should not be considered as poor quality concrete. The purpose of the cement is to improve the stability of an otherwise unsuitable material so that it may be used as a flexible material in the sub-bases of rigid or flexible pavements, or as the base of flexible pavements. A very wide range of materials may be stabilised ranging from silt-clays to gravels, and the way in which the cement works in increasing and maintaining the shear strengths of these materials, will differ.

The grains in cohesive soils are much finer than the cement grains and it is therefore impossible to coat them with cement. In practice, cohesive soils are broken into small lumps which are coated with cement and then pressed together by compaction, forming a mass of the type illustrated in Fig. 10.3. Immediately after compaction the shear strength of the mass is similar to that of the natural soil, but as the cement hydrates the strength will increase. The hydrated-cement coatings form a skeletal structure of considerable strength, the actual strength depending on the 'lump' size and amount of cement used. With clay soils a secondary change will occur due to the free lime from the cement, which will disperse into the clay within the lumps, making it less cohesive and less prone to volume change with moisture change. Silts are frost susceptible, but coating lumps with cement limits moisture movement within the soil, which in turn greatly reduces frost susceptibility except in parts of the stabilised material exposed directly to the elements[3].

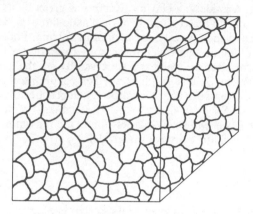

Fig. 10.3. Diagrammatic representation of a clay–cement mix

Non-cohesive materials have a grain size larger than cement grains and therefore they may be coated with cement paste. The hydrated cement paste will bond the soil grains at points of contact, as illustrated in Fig. 10.4, leading to an increase of shear strength in the whole mass. The actual increase in strength depends (*a*) on the number of points of contact between soil grains (which in turn depends on the overall material grading), (*b*) on an increase in the amount of cement used and (*c*) on compaction to bring grains into the most intimate contact.

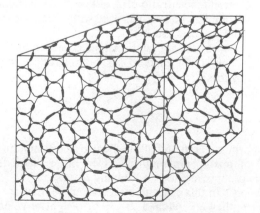

Fig. 10.4. Diagrammatic representation of a sand–cement mix

In the case of mixtures of cohesive and non-cohesive materials, those that are predominantly cohesive can be considered as cohesive, the granular fractions acting as 'filler' suspended within the stabilised matrix. Non-cohesive materials are improved by the addition of a small proportion of silt and clay, if this leads to an improvement in the overall grading.

Nearly any soil or waste material can be stabilised with cement, although some may be ruled out on economic grounds, and others contain chemicals deleterious to cement. Heavy clays, for example, require excessive power for adequate mixing. A guide to a clay's suitability is given by its Atterberg limits; soils with liquid limits greater than 45% or plastic limits greater than 20% are normally considered too cohesive for economic mixing. Podzolic soils contain small quantities of humic acid which retards the hydration of ordinary Portland cement. These can often be stabilised successfully by the addition of calcium chloride to the cement. Soluble sulphates, which occur in some shales, clays and industrial wastes, give rise to concern, although in practice they have not caused serious problems. As a safeguard, the Department of the Environment's *Specification for Road and Bridgeworks*[4] limits the maximum soluble sulphate content to 1% (0·25% for cohesive materials).

## Mix design criteria

Some form of material selection and mix design is essential to decide if a particular material can be stabilised and to determine the minimum amount of cement needed. It is also necessary to know the optimum moisture content and maximum anticipated density for site control purposes.

The original methods of mix design developed by the Portland Cement Association in the USA relied on the testing of samples for durability against freezing and thawing, and wetting and drying, combined with abrasion tests[5]. In the UK, compressive strength criteria have been adopted for mix design purposes[4]. Although durability, as assessed by the American tests, improves with increase in compressive strength, there is no simple correlation between strength and durability. For most work in the UK cement-stabilised materials are designed to have a minimum 7-day compressive strength of 2·8 N/mm² based on cylinders with a height : diameter ratio of 2, although soil cement, with a strength of the order of 1·8 N/mm² at 7 days, was used with success in the bases of minor roads and airfields during the 1950s[6,7].

Knowledge of moisture–density relationships is needed to take the maximum benefits from the compaction method, as both strength and durability are adversely affected by loss of density.

## Construction

To achieve a uniform material and allow the use of a minimum cement content, good standards of mixing are required. Two basic methods of mixing are employed, i.e. the pre-mix method and mixing *in situ*.

*The pre-mix method*   In this case, all materials to be used are transported to a central point, where they are batched, either by weight or volume, into a mixer. The mixers employed are of the forced-action type, operating on a continuous or

batch process. Forced-action mixing is essential to obtain a commercially acceptable output of materials which are predominantly fine grained or contain a
significant quantity of silt and clay. In normal practice, the combined silt and
clay content of materials fed into this type of mixer is limited to 10%. A small
continuous mixer with a volume-batching process producing cement-stabilised
material for a motorway hard shoulder is shown in Fig. 10.5.

Fig. 10.5. Continuous mixer producing cement stabilised material (courtesy Soil Stabilisation Ltd.)

After mixing, material is transported to the laying site, normally by open lorry,
and is covered *en route* to minimise moisture change. Material may be spread by
hand, grader, stone spreader, concrete spreader or bituminous paver. To obtain
the highest standards of surface regularity, contractors have used rail-mounted
concrete paving equipment, or bituminous pavers fitted with equipment for
automatic control of both line and level. Compaction is usually by roller, the
choice of best type of roller being a function of the type of material being compacted; vibrating rollers are ideal on granular materials and dead-weight rollers
on cohesive materials. Rubber-tyred rollers appear to operate efficiently on a wide
range of materials, and judging from experience in the Netherlands, where they
have been used to compact sand-cements made from very unstable single-sized
sands[2], they can compact in single layers to depths of 400 mm.
*Mixing in situ*    In this case mobile mixers mix the materials on the paving site in
place. If the natural soil already on site is used, savings accrue from a reduction

in the volume of earthworks required. A further benefit is that much less of the formation is exposed to the weather or construction traffic. However, in some cases it is more economic to treat imported materials which are spread, compacted and trimmed to level, prior to cement spreading and mixing. The machines used for mixing vary from agricultural rotary tillers, such as that shown in Fig. 10.6, to large purpose-built units of the type shown in Fig. 10.7. A

Fig. 10.6. Agricultural rotary tiller

major difference between these machines is their engine capacity which affects both the rate and depth of processing. The smaller machines are limited to processing depths of 150–200 mm, while under some circumstances, the larger machines can process depths in excess of 400 mm. Standards of mixing are improved, especially in cohesive materials, if the rotary tillers are used to pulverise

Fig. 10.7. Rex mix-in-place machine (courtesy P. C. Zanen N.V.)

the soil into small lumps prior to adding cement. It is also often convenient and desirable to add water at this stage, either through a spray bar, mounted to discharge inside the mixing chamber of the rotary tiller, or by means of a tanker fitted with a spray bar. On small jobs bagged cement may be spread manually, but this is not economic on medium- to large-size jobs, where mechanical spreaders are used. Figure 10.8 shows a bulk-cement spreader. After mixing-in

Fig. 10.8. Cement spreader (courtesy Hoes)

the cement and any additional water needed to reach the optimum moisture content, compaction and grading to final level is carried out. Finally, the processed layer is covered with a waterproof membrane, commonly bitumen emulsion, to prevent drying-out and ensure cement hydration.

Mix-in-place construction has several advantages over pre-mix work: outputs are higher per man hour and costs are consequently lower. It also appears somewhat easier to mix cohesive materials *in situ* than with present premix machines[3]. However, standards of surface regularity achieved with *in situ* construction are below those possible with the sophisticated pavers available for placing premixed materials. But this position may change with the use of some of the most modern plant from the USA. Plant produced by Construction Machinery Inc. (now known as CMI Corporation) for example, is capable of processing material *in situ* and is controlled automatically for level from a pre-set line, kerb or existing paving. This machine is shown in Fig. 10.9.

Fig. 10.9. Autograder producing mix-in-place stabilised material (courtesy CMI Corporation)

Mix-in-place construction has been more popular abroad than in the UK, where the greater plant utilisation which arises with pre-mix plant, which can be used for mixing and laying a variety of materials other than stabilised soil, is a major factor when deciding to adopt one form of construction over another. Abroad, where there has been a much greater need to treat soils, because of the shortage of traditional road-building materials contractors have preferred mix-in-place construction.

## Other applications

Although the main application for cement-stabilised materials has been in road and airfield pavements, other applications have also proved useful. For instance, railway ballast lying on silt or clay becomes unstable as the soil is 'pumped' through the ballast by passing trains. This leads to maintenance problems. Stabilising the soil beneath the ballast has, in Austria and Switzerland, shown itself an effective method of overcoming this difficulty[8]. In many parts of the USA soil cement has been used for lining irrigation canals[9].

In the Netherlands, sand cement made into blocks $0.3$ m $\times$ $0.3$ m $\times$ $0.4$ m, has been used as a water-flow-resistant material for damming inlets and forming polders[10]. The blocks are made by stabilising an $0.4$ m deep layer of sand with mix-in-place plant and slicing the freshly compacted, stabilised sand with blades attached to the rear of a crawler tractor. When hardened, the blocks are taken up from the construction area, loaded onto barges and taken to the dam construction site.

The back filling of materials behind bridge abutments can present difficulties, as space restrictions make it difficult to achieve standards of compaction comparable with the associated embankments, which in turn may lead to differential settlement problems. Several solutions to the problem have been tried, one of which has been to stabilise the material behind the abutment. In this case the cement is employed to make up some of the deficiencies in compaction.

## Conclusions

The term *unstable ground* is relative, as evidenced by the variety of problems discussed in this text. Very few natural soils or industrial wastes are sufficiently stable to be used as part of a modern road or airfield pavement. However, many materials can, by the addition of cement, be converted into sound sub-bases and road bases. This allows high-grade aggregates to be conserved for the final road running surfaces and other structural purposes.

Although cement functions in different ways in stabilising different materials, present knowledge and test procedures ensure that only materials which can be stabilised economically and permanently to resist stresses arising from weather and traffic are treated.

Although engineers in the UK have not, unlike many of their overseas colleagues, made great use of cement-stabilised soils and waste materials, indications are that economic and environmental factors are encouraging changes in attitudes.

REFERENCES

1. Page, G., opening address on conference entitled *Motorways in Britain—Today and Tomorrow,* April 26–28, Inst. Civ. Eng., 1 (1971)
2. Lilley, A. A., 'Current Overseas Practice', *J. Inst. Highway Engs.,* **19** No. 3, 4–11, March (1972)
3. Lilley, A. A., *Cement-stabilised Materials for Bases and Sub-bases of Road and Airfield Pavements,* Thesis, The City University, London, 196, June (1970)
4. *Specification for Road and Bridge Works,* Dept. of the Environment, H.M.S.O., 195 (1969)
5. Catton, M. D., 'Soil-cement Technology—a Resumé, *J. Portland Cement Assoc. Res. Dev. Labs.,* **4** No. 1, 13–21, Res. Dept. Bulletin No. 136 (1962)
6. Wright, M. J., *The Performance of Roads with Soil-cement Bases,* London Cement and Concrete Assoc., Tech. Rep. TRA 418, 23, June (1969)
7. Hill, T. B. and Williams, K. H. G., 'Stabilised Soil Pavements of Southend-on-Sea Municipal Airport', *Proc. Inst. Civ. Eng.,* **6,** 595–611, April (1957)
8. Sommer, H., *Bodenstabilisierung mit Zement und Magerbeton in Europäischen Strassenbau. (Soil Stabilisation with Cement and Lean Concrete in European Road Construction.)* Beton-Verlag GmbH, Dusseldorf, 149 (1970)
9. *Soil-cement for Paving Slopes and Lining Ditches,* Portland Cement Association, Chicago, SCB 14, 6 (1953)
10. van der Sluis, F. A., *Enige Bijzondere Toepassingen van Zand-cement,* Studiedag 'Zand-Cement', Rotterdam, 23–29, Oct. 30 (1968)

## Rapid Methods of Soil Stabilisation

The military requirement for surface stabilisation differs from the civil requirement in two important aspects. The first is that it is usually essential for the stabilised medium to acquire its full strength as quickly as possible after the application of the stabiliser. The desired time is of the order of minutes, or, at most, a few hours, rather than a day or more which is generally acceptable in civil practice. The second is that the stabilised surface is usually intended to be a finished running surface and may be required to sustain the loads applied by modern high-performance aircraft, in the case of temporary airfield pavements. These loads can be of the order of 10 t single wheel load with tyre pressures in the range $1 \cdot 7 – 2 \cdot 4$ MN/m$^2$. On the other hand, the operational life of such a pavement is very short compared to the life expectancy of a civil pavement. When these special requirements have to be met, it is obvious that something other than ordinary Portland cement must be used as the stabilising agent, and a number of other materials are under study to determine their suitability. The investigations are on two levels; a paper study of likely materials is first made and then laboratory and field investigations are made of those materials which appear to satisfy the requirement in the majority of respects. A summary of the range of material which has been investigated so far is given in Table 10.1.

Detailed laboratory and field studies have been made on the following three materials:

1. Portland cement/high-alumina cement mixes.
2. Polyacrylate resin.
3. Elemental sulphur.

All of the work done so far has been by a mix-in-place technique, either by applying liquid stabiliser to the surface and raking in, or by placing a selected aggregate with a high voids ratio and flood grouting under gravity. At this point it should be stated that this contributor agrees with A. A. Lilley's preference for mix-in-place over pre-mix methods, not only for the reasons which he gives, but also because it is difficult to use rapid hardening materials in any other way. Instability in the material may lead to 'flash' sets in the mixing equipment rendering it completely unusable. By using mix-in-place methods this risk can be greatly reduced.

**Table 10.1**  COMPARISON OF VARIOUS STABILISING AGENTS

| General class of material | Stabiliser* | Min. curing time | Compressive strength† (N/mm²) | Cost index‡ |
|---|---|---|---|---|
| Inorganic cements | Ordinary Portland cement | 12 h–24 h | 1·72–6·89 | 1 |
| | Rapid-hardening Portland cement | 6 h–24 h | 1·72–6·89 | 1·1 |
| | High-alumina cement | 4 h–24 h | 1·72–41·37 | 4 |
| | Dehydrated gypsum | 30 min–1 h | 3·44 | 3 |
| | Portland cement–gypsum | 30 min–24 h | 10·34–17·24 | 6 |
| | Portland cement–high-alumina cement | 15 min–1 h | 4·14–17·24 | 6 |
| | Portland cement–gypsum–high-alumina cement | 15 min–1 h | 10·34 | 13 |
| Cement–resin mixes§ | Polymer cements | 3 h–24 h | 6·89–20·68 | 25 |
| Organic resins§ | Epoxy resins | 12 h–24 h | 13·78‖ | 75 |
| | Acrylic resins | 12 h–24 h | 13·78‖ | 75 |
| | Polyacrylate resin + hardener | 30 min–6 h | 3·44–48·26 | 80 |
| | Polyurethane resin + hardener | 30 min–6 h | Not known | 25¶ |
| | Solvinated resins | Not known | Not known | 50 |
| Miscellaneous inorganic materials | Sulphur | 20 min–30 min | 13·78–31·02 | 1·1 |
| | 'Joosten' process—silicate grouting | Not considered, time/strength factors too low | | |
| | Tar–bitumen | Not considered because of slow curing time | | 2 |

* Properties can be affected over a wide range by varying the proportion of components in mixtures.
† Compressive strength ranges are given to take account of differences brought about by differing aggregates.
‡ Cost figures are based generally on average costs in 1971.
§ Organic compounds are marketed under proprietary names and compositions are not disclosed; the general type of resin is therefore used in this table to distinguish between them.
‖ With epoxy and acrylic resins the strength varies very greatly with the proportion of resin in the mix. The figures quoted are those corresponding to 4% of resin.
¶ The figures quoted are those from a German source, the contributor has no direct knowledge of this resin.

A number of commercially available mixes of cement have been investigated, together with mixes designed in the contributor's own laboratory. In laboratory tests these meet the requirement in terms of strength and setting time. Special techniques have to be used, however, to mix and dispense such materials in quantity. The only effective method which eliminates the risk of flash set is to convey the dry aggregate and cement pneumatically and add water at a nozzle, in which mixing takes place. The grout can then be placed by a cement-gun technique. Using a neat cement grout, penetrations of up to 100 mm into a base consisting of crushed stone (20–40 mm) have been achieved. In the field, however, it is impossible to control finished surface level to a sufficiently high degree of tolerance, since the surface cannot be graded in the normal way because of the rapid set.

Slower-curing colloidally mixed grout has also been studied, but is subject to the same disadvantages. Penetration in this case is greater, 300 mm as opposed to 100 mm, but with a minimum curing time of 3 h. These techniques are most effective when used with large single-size aggregate, but if a level surface is required, the difficulty of grading such aggregates prevents the optimum condition from being reached.

The cement materials give the highest strength of all those studied up to the time of writing. A mix of four parts of Alag (crushed aluminium-silicate clinker) and one part of high-alumina cement sets in 20 min with a compressive strength of 75 N/mm² after curing for 24 h. The density of the material is 2 620 kg/m³. The high density and the instability of this mix are such that, apart from very special applications, it is of more academic than practical interest.

A number of resins were considered. Of these a commercial two-part polyacrylate resin of German origin was selected for further study. This is easily mixed using simple equipment and sets over a wide range of ambient temperature in times of 20–30 min. With a 50% air-voids aggregate the compressive strength is 48 N/mm² after curing for 1 h in the laboratory. Field strengths are lower and dependent on uniform penetration being achieved. Small areas of up to 2 m² can be treated satisfactorily, but as the area increases it becomes increasingly difficult to ensure uniform treatment. In addition, with larger areas, shrinkage

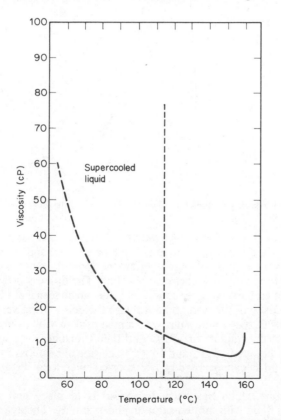

Fig. 10.10 Viscosity of molten sulphur at 50–160°C (after Fanelli)

becomes a major problem during curing. For these reasons, in addition to the very high cost, work on resins is not being proceeded with further at this time.

Sulphur, which is widely available at low cost as a by-product of the petrochemical industry, has been used in the past in place of cement in the manufacture of concrete[1]. With the exception of a report that it was used by the

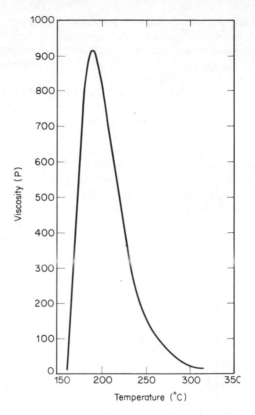

Fig. 10.11 Viscosity of molten sulphur at 150–300°C (after Bacon and Fanelli)

Japanese during World War II in pavement repair[2] there is no record of its previous use as a grout. Its attraction is that hardening, and consequent gain in strength, is solely a phase-change phenomenon and does not depend either on solvent evaporation or on a chemical reaction. The process is therefore largely independent of ambient weather conditions. As can be seen from Figs. 10.10 and 10.11, the viscosity of the normal liquid varies widely[3], being very low between 115°C and 158°C, then rising sharply to a high peak at 188°C. For this reason it is usual to heat the sulphur to 150°C and then transport for pouring when the temperature is between 130°C and 140°C. The rate of heat loss from molten sulphur is low and it can be readily transported over long distances in lagged tankers.

The technique which has been developed is to place and grade selected aggregate and flood with molten sulphur under gravity. The aggregate grading, pore size, specific surface and temperature at the time of pouring all affect the time of flow, and therefore the depth to which the sulphur penetrates, since penetration ceases when the sulphur solidifies. The variation of penetration with grain size of nominally single-sized aggregates is given in Fig. 10.12 for an ambient temperature of 10°C. It should be noted that for sizes greater than 25 mm the sulphur flows freely through very large voids and the penetration increases very rapidly. As an illustration of the effect of aggregate temperature, it was

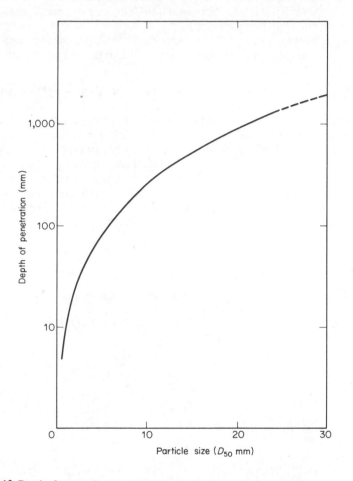

Fig. 10.12. Depth of penetration of sulphur into single size aggregates; sulphur temperature 130°C, aggregate temperature 30°C

found that a penetration of 5 mm in medium Leighton Buzzard sand ($D_{50} = 0.8$ mm) at ambient temperature was increased to 225 mm when the aggregate was preheated to 120°C. Similar effects were noted for other aggregates.

The compressive strength of a sulphur concrete formed in this way is between 13.8 N/mm² and 20.7 N/mm², and is attained immediately on setting, normally 20–30 min after pouring. Tests made at 1 h, 1 day and 1 week indicate that the increase in strength over a period of time is low—of the order of 2–3%.

The durability of the material appears to be high, provided that it is not subjected to abrasion. Buildings erected a number of years ago at the South-west Research Institute[4] are still in use. Trial pavement sections constructed at M.V.E.E. showed some resistance to abrasion, but it is considered that an untreated pavement will require maintenance of the running surface at regular intervals. There are indications that the durability of the surface can be increased by incorporating chopped fibre reinforcement in the top skin or by covering the surface with a thin skin (3–5 mm) of a rapid hardening cement mix. Both of these procedures are currently being studied.

There are still gaps in our knowledge in the field of sulphur concrete and work is in hand or is planned to close these, some of these aspects being summarised as follows:

1. The use of foaming agents will reduce the total weight of sulphur required, these are being investigated.
2. Very little work has been done on grouting aggregates at high-moisture contents. At moderate moisture contents it has been observed that the water is boiled off as steam and a vesicular structure results. As the moisture content increases the effective heat capacity of the aggregate will increase and it can be assumed that penetration will decrease.
3. The effects of long-term ageing in sulphur concrete are unknown.
4. It is known that the properties of sulphur can be modified by additives; the total effect of such additives on sulphur concrete has still to be studied.

REFERENCES

1. Dale, J. M. and Ludwig, A. C., Sulphur Aggregate Concrete, *The Civ. Eng.* (1967)
2. Ahlvin, R. G., *unpublished personal communication* (1972)
3. Turner, W. M., (Ed.), *Sulphur Data Book,* McGraw-Hill, New York (1954)
4. 'Sulphur Building Revisited', *J. Sulphur Inst.,* **8** (1972)

## The Use of *Terram*\* Fabric to Provide High-quality Access Roads

One of the most common problems confronting the civil engineer is the construction of access, haul or permanent roads over very soft or loose soil strata with low bearing strength. Each of these types of road comprises one or more layers of granular material (base or sub-base) the depth and quality of which is dependent on the road in question. In all instances, however, there is a tendency for sub-base material to penetrate the sub-grade, especially if the latter has a low bearing strength. This can result in a reduction in the strength of the sub-grade and the loss of large amounts of valuable sub-base material as is schematically illustrated in Fig. 10.13*a*. This problem can be solved with the use of *Terram* melded fabric.

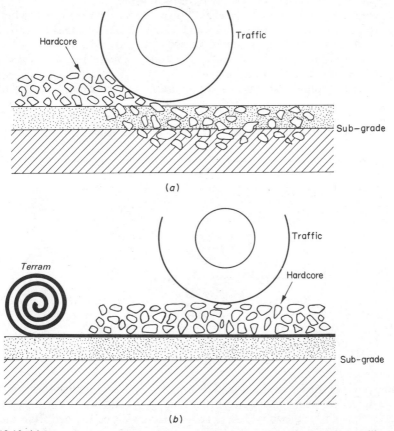

Fig. 10.13. (*a*) Loss of sub-base material due to a reduction in sub-grade strength, and (*b*) use of *Terram* melded fabric to solve the problem

The fabric is placed on the sub-grade, as shown in Fig. 10.13*b*, and is overlain with aggregate material. Ground preparation is minimal; the high extensibility (50%) of the fabric ensures that it can conform to all but the largest ground contours. *Terram* effectively eliminates loss of hardcore material by preventing

\* *Terram* is the registered trademark of ICI Ltd.

penetration of the latter into low load-bearing sub-grades. It also prevents sub-base deterioration by reducing pumping, whereby fines become suspended in water and are carried into the sub-base under the action of wheel loading. The fabric has the ideal filament construction to allow passage of water, thus relieving pore pressure, while filtering out fine soil particles.

The tensile strength of the fabric also benefits access-road performance. Generally, wheel loading will produce rutting to an extent which is dependent on the vehicle weight and speed, and condition of the sub-grade. Under load a deflection occurs in the road and the sub-base/sub-grade interface is therefore in tension. Unless constrained, the sub-base is able to move due to the tensile forces and a rut develops. The introduction of fabric at the interface constrains the sub-base and reduces the ease of rutting of the road. The fabric also redistributes wheel loads and reduces the possibility of local settlement.

A comprehensive series of trials has shown that the civil engineer can derive a number of benefits, both practical and economical, by utilising *Terram* in access roads, e.g. (*a*) access can be gained onto very soft ground that would otherwise have been very difficult, and (*b*) once constructed, the access road requires little or no further maintenance.

The initial depth of sub-base varies according to the bearing capacity of the sub-grade, upon which the former is inversely dependent.

The filtration characteristics of *Terram* can be utilised in drainage applications. Figure 10.14 shows two types of drain where the fabric has been

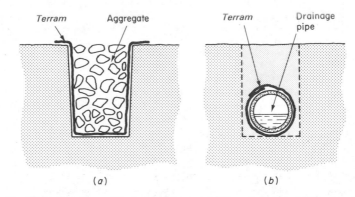

Fig. 10.14. Two types of drain using *Terram*. (*a*) French drain and (*b*) land drain

employed, i.e. the French and land drains. In each case *Terram* performs the same functions; unimpeded water flow into the pipe is allowed while soil particles are filtered out by the fabric. As a result, water can be drained from the soil without the pipe or channel silting up.

BIBLIOGRAPHY

McGown, A. and Ozelton, M. W., 'Employment of Fabric Membrane in Flexible Pavement Construction Over Soils of Low Bearing Strength., *Civ. Eng. and Pub. Works Rev.*, Dec. (1972)

Chapter 11

# Vibroflotation: Rationale for Design and Practice

Vibroflotation is used to improve poor ground below foundations of structures. Typically, foundation settlement is reduced by more than half and the shearing strength of the treated soils is increased substantially. Variants of vibroflotation can be applied to a wide range of soils; thus unsuspected soil variations discovered during treatment can generally be accommodated without trouble and loss of time. This, together with the relative economy of the process, appeals to foundation engineers.

This chapter describes vibroflotation—its evolution, practice and rationale, so that its scope will be better appreciated. Its use is already commonplace, indicating the confidence of engineers and architects.

### Evolution of vibroflotation

Vibroflotation was conceived in the early 1930s. It was known that vibrations of appropriate form could eliminate intergranular friction of cohesionless soils so that those that were initially loose could flow by gravity into a dense state. A poker vibrator was developed which hung vertically in order to penetrate depths of soil beyond the range of surface vibration. The poker, known as a *Vibroflot*, could also operate efficiently below ground-water thus compacting soils that were inaccessible to surface plant without drainage. The volume of compacted soils was less than that of their initial loose state, and consequently similar material was imported in order to make up levels. It was found that this could be done by compacting the fill directly into the bores formed by the Vibroflot or by subsequent rolling on the surface. This basic compaction technique is still used in suitable sands.

However, it was soon discovered that with a simple vibrator the range of compactable soils was limited. It was economically impracticable to extend this range by complex machines with variable vibration parameters which could be matched precisely to ground conditions to give the best effect. Certain fine sands remained quick and could not be compacted in the bore, whilst uniform cobbles proved impenetrable. These difficulties were easily overcome, the former by importing coarser and heavier backfill and the latter by increasing the power and improving the shape of machines. Nevertheless, the range of treatable soils was generally restricted to clean sands and fine gravels.

189

In north America and in northern Europe there are wide tracts of relatively uniform sands in populous areas in which this compaction process has established itself with proven reliability over more than 25 years. It has been used most frequently for housing and light industrial buildings, but also for a wide variety of engineering structures, some of them substantial multi-storey blocks or with foundations carrying concentrated loadings of up to 550 kN/m$^2$.

In other parts of Europe and the UK where past glacial activity has left soils with wide particle size ranges, attempts at vibratory compaction were often frustrated by cohesion or low permeability due to the finer constituents. However, it was found that columns of coarse imported backfill formed at each compaction centre were effective in stiffening granular soils containing fines, either distributed or in laminae. Even though they did not compact much, settlements were reduced. Thus the stone column method evolved and by 1962 it was being used in the UK for strengthening genuine clays for both housing and industrial structures. Strengthening cohesive soils now constitutes the major application of the process in the UK.

Such empirical developments in many small steps follow the natural course of development of many civil engineering techniques and are common to most piling and foundation systems. They ensure the practical success and reliability of the method. A rationale leading to an equally reliable design approach follows step by step. The stone-column method is no exception and has proven value over more than a decade.

Whilst studies continue to improve the understanding of the composite column–soil system, knowledge of appropriate situations, field technique and design methods is now well established; prediction of foundation behaviour has reached a stage where quality of site investigation or inadequate general theory of soil mechanics tends to restrict greater accuracy.

## Machine characteristics

An essential feature of a Vibroflot is its laterally vibrating element at its bottom end. This contains in the lower part an eccentrically mounted weight rotating on an axial shaft driven by a motor mounted immediately above and directly linked to the shaft. Above the vibrating element containing the motor and eccentric is a vibration isolator separating the vibrator from the follower casing from which the active part is suspended. Thus vibrations in an essentially horizontal plane are applied to the ground near the lowest point of the machine which is also the active part buried in the ground. The direct drive from the motor ensures minimum energy loss.

In recent years various forms of vibrator have been produced and incorrectly termed 'Vibroflots'. These include casing drivers which, from a motor mounted at the top above ground, generate an essentially axial (vertical) vibration in the whole of a continuous tube. These types of machine are generally efficient penetrators of frictional soils but do not compact very efficiently in the radial direction; hence compaction centres must be relatively closely spaced. Other developments have had the motor placed below the eccentric, both being mounted in a vibrating tip below an isolator.

Original Vibroflot developments were powered by electric motors. Most recent machines, however, are driven hydraulically by oil because this is capable of generating greater power from a motor of relatively small volume; thus dimensions of the machine which affect its penetrability in the soil can be kept small. Power input to Vibroflots ranges from 75 to 150 kW, the larger powered machines generally being of most recent development.

Typically, the vibrating tip has a diameter of 300–400 mm and a length of about 2–3 m. The follower tubes on which the machine is suspended may be added in sections so that any reasonable desired depth of treatment can be achieved. Normally, treatment depths over 8 m are not required but depths exceeding 20 m have been achieved when necessary.

Figure 11.1 illustrates a Vibroflot suspended from a crawler crane on which the hydraulic pump and prime mover are mounted together as a counter weight for the crane. The Vibroflot and the crane can then easily move together as a single unit.

Current machine developments are aimed at matching machine characteristics more closely with the soil to be treated by providing alternative frequency, amplitude and power levels within a single machine. Whilst high

Fig. 11.1. Vibroflot suspended from a crawler crane (courtesy NCK)

*Vibroflotation*

power is required for penetrability and large compaction radius, induced vibration energy levels must be appropriate to the soils requiring treatment; in certain circumstances over excitement prevents compaction.

Currently, separate machines with differing fixed characteristics are used for treatment of soils with widely differing properties. Although there is some overlapping of the ranges of soil types appropriate to these machines, the development of a facility to vary characteristics on site will clearly improve operating efficiency, providing it can be produced economically.

## BASIC OPERATING TECHNIQUE

A Vibroflot may be used for both compaction of cohesionless soils and for forming stone columns in clays. The basic techniques for both treatments are virtually the same with only minor variations according to soil type.

The Vibroflot is usually suspended from a standard crawler crane. When lowered into the ground it penetrates by its own weight and energy. It is usually assisted by jets of water or air from the lower conical point, but these fluids are not essential to penetration; their prime function is to support the borehole during treatment.

Water is used wherever the borehole formed by the Vibroflot is likely to be unstable and always where ground-water flowing into the bore will be encountered. The water circulation forms a hole leaving an annular space about 50–100 mm wide surrounding the machine. Water is encouraged to overflow the borehole at the surface so that excess hydrostatic pressure and outward seepage forces support the uncased hole. On reaching the designed depth of treatment an imported coarse-gravel-sized fill is shovelled into the annular space as the machine is slowly withdrawn. Compaction of responsive loose cohesionless soils occurs during penetration and the Vibroflot is extracted slowly surging it up and down. If sand-sized backfill or *in-situ* sand is used the volume of water flow must be regulated in the bore to provide a negligible upward velocity in the water stream so that the fine-grained backfill can fall to be compacted in place. This requires considerable operating skill.

This compaction technique for cohesionless soils is also used for the wet treatment of clayey soils. The result is to form compacted columns of coarse backfill at each treatment centre with natural clay between. Typically the columns so formed are 900 mm in diameter, but the maximum diameter achieved depends on the clay properties. Since the granular backfill replaces the original clay this process is sometimes known as *vibro-replacement*.

A dry technique of forming stone columns in clays is also widely used, especially for buildings in city-centre sites where disposal of waste water and suspended soil solids can sometimes be troublesome. The dry method is employed only where the borehole remains stable and where there is no risk of ground-water running into the bore. It is most effective in partially saturated firm clays.

The Vibroflot penetrates by shearing and displacing the soil around it. This process can therefore be termed *vibro-displacement*. The machine fits tightly into the borehole so there is no annular space into which backfill may be tipped. To place backfill the machine must be removed from the hole. In soft soils the resultant suction created as the machine is withdrawn tends to collapse the bore. To counter this, compressed air is circulated through the conical tip. A small compressor is adequate; $0.03$ m$^3$ at $100–200$ kN/m$^2$ is sufficient.

Compressed air should not be used wherever standing water appears in the bore. The combination results in a soft clay slurry in the hole which is detrimental to construction of a sound column. Furthermore, in weak materials with shear strengths less than about $20$ kN/m$^2$, there is a risk that poorly regulated air flow will fissure the surrounding soil and escape to the surface several metres from the bore. This is very damaging to soil properties, especially in sensitive or laminated deposits with weak fabric.

There are therefore clear distinctions between wet (replacement) and dry (displacement) techniques, with correspondingly clear-cut situations where each should be used.

## Effects of vibro-replacement and vibro-displacement on cohesive soil

Vibro-replacement is commonly used in soft, normally consolidated compressible clays, thin peat layers, saturated silts and all laminated alluvial or esturaine soils. Stone columns have been formed successfully in soils with undrained cohesive strengths of as low as $7$ kN/m$^2$.

The hypothesis for wet treatment in these soils suggests that the Vibroflot penetrates mainly by water jetting in combination with displacement which erodes a hole larger than the machine. Verticality is assured since the Vibroflot hangs as a pendulum in the water-filled bore. When backfill is placed with water still flowing up the annular space, vibration transmitted through the backfill to the soil may cause local collapse of surrounding clays, especially if they are sensitive. Collapsed lumps are removed by the flowing water and the diameter of the base of the bore expands as more backfill is placed. Attenuation of vibration energy through the backfill results in a balance wherein radial expansion of backfill volume is halted because there is insufficient energy to cause significant disturbance to the soil retaining the column. When this happens further backfill allows column building upwards at more or less constant diameter, but with compensating bulges where softer layers are encountered. Thus a column is constructed which is considerably larger than the diameter of the machine and which is essentially free from silt and clay due to the washing action of the water.

Vibro-replacement does not have a significant destructive effect on the soil structure. Figure 11.2 shows a column through soft hydraulic fill comprising soft clayey silts. In contrast, vibro-displacement is not suitable for these soils.

Shearing action during displacement of the soil in order to allow penetration of the machine in the dry technique destroys the adjacent soils structure, frequently reducing them to an almost fluid condition. Thus it is impossible to introduce backfill with the certainty that the gravel particles are in mutual contact, which is an essential prerequisite for column stability. Shearing displacement also tends to block free-draining layers intersected by the column in laminated soils and so inhibits their consolidation.

Vibro-displacement is therefore restricted to the strengthening of insensitive soils with sufficient cohesion to maintain a stable bore—usually over $20$ kN/m$^2$ undrained strength. These soils are neither very weak nor very compressible, but require treatment primarily to boost the bearing capacity to give an increased safety factor. They are generally confined either to glacial deposits of clayey sands, or to sandy or silty clays.

In these soils, displacement methods induce some measurable increase of strength of original clay between columns; this is barely detectable with replacement. Dynamic penetrometer tests made in firm clays between columns about one week after vibro-displacement tend to show improved resistance, relative to similar pretreatment tests and post-treatment tests made immediately after stone-column construction.

Fig. 11.2. Column through a soft hydraulic fill comprising soft clayey silts

The improvement noted is up to one and a half times for a typical column spacing of 1·5 m. It is probably due to the gain in strength resulting from the dissipation of pore pressure generated by shear distortions during displacement. Further studies of this phenomenon with more sophisticated and sensitive testing methods are being pursued. At the moment it cannot be relied upon for bearing capacity.

Vibro-replacement and vibro-displacement are thus distinct separate techniques. However, intermediate circumstances can often be encountered in practice wherein some displacement occurs during wet treatment.

Replacement processes can be employed throughout the range of soils suitable for stone columns. They are not subject to the risks and inconsistencies of dry treatment, in that less operator skill is required and larger columns are formed. Security is therefore greater.

## Design considerations

In common with all foundation problems it is necessary to establish at the outset the maximum intensity and distribution of the contact stresses anticipated. Usually the structural engineer will have decided desirable foundation sizes and depths, but final decisions should not be taken until foundation treatment has been resolved and appropriate structural design adjustments made, in order to take maximum advantage from the chosen system. Structural factors usually dictate the range of possible unit pressures and tolerable total settlements. The latter vary considerably according to the type of structure and are frequently not given adequate consideration. All foundations must provide support with minimum differential settlement; the exploitation of tolerance to differentials can often permit the use of low-cost foundation techniques, with great economy.

The primary aim of vibroflotation is therefore to provide the most economic foundation that will contain differential settlements within structural tolerances, but it is also to improve bearing capacity where necessary. This objective can be achieved for a very wide range of structures and foundation soils. It is possible to cater for items ranging from relatively rigid multi-storey framed blocks on frictional soils or moderately firm clays, to embankments and oil tanks on soft organic alluvial soils. Clearly, treatments for this range are not mutually interchangeable, and specific designs must be determined for each case.

Design of vibroflotation treatments resolves into decisions on the depth and spacing of compaction centres. Depth of treatment is generally decided by a consideration of the interrelation of soil stresses induced by the foundation, and the magnitude of the resulting settlement. Spacing is determined mainly by the degree of improvement of the soil properties required to limit settlements and to achieve safe bearing capacity.

## DEPTH OF TREATMENT

Unlike conventional piling, vibroflotation seeks to improve existing superficial soils. This permits the use of conventional spread footings at shallow depths.

Where foundations are of comparatively small area and isolated, they may not induce significant stresses within the soil at depths of more than twice their width following pseudo-elastic stress-distribution patterns. Thus there is generally no need to treat greater depths beyond the limits of a hypothetical stress bulb defined by significance of induced settlements. Treatment may 'float' within a homogeneous stratum and need not necessarily penetrate stronger underlying materials. Thus even for narrow footings, treatment depths rarely exceed three times the footing width. For wider foundations the necessary depth may be less than half the width of a raft, because the compressibility of frictional soils is reduced with increasing overburden pressure; consequently it is rarely necessary to compact these to depths greater than about 8 m. However, control of settlement arising in compressible clays may require stone columns extending to a firmer clay or to sand; in such cases the columns are akin to end-bearing piles.

Most frequently, strong and incompressible strata are encountered within the depth of the pressure bulb and treatment need not extend by more than a metre into them. Such situations occur where silty hydraulic fills cover beach deposits or overlie desiccated clay crusts of original ground surface. Similar natural circumstances are found where post-glacial alluvium derived from underlying boulder clays has been deposited over a stiff moraine. Large tracts of sand exist in northern Europe preconsolidated by ice overburden, but in the vicinity of recent rivers the upper layers have been disturbed and redeposited substantially unaltered, except for low density and low residual stress. Lateral boundaries between old compact zones and recent loose zones cannot be defined with certainty, but depth horizons are usually clear from field testing. Coastal dune sands also show ill-defined variation between preloaded and fresh zones. These examples indicate how the recent geomorphological history of a site can influence the depth of treatment required.

When vibrating machinery or earthquakes are envisaged, other more complex factors will determine the depth of treatment. In these cases vibroflotation is used to subject the soil to greater dynamic stress than that anticipated from post-treatment vibrations, to reduce the risk of further settlement or liquefaction.

## SPACING OF COMPACTIONS

Compaction spacing determines the properties of the ground within the treated depth. The design problem is to provide adequate incompressibility and strength for maximum compatible spacing, and hence least cost. Methods used to decide spacing depend on whether the soils compact in response to vibration or whether stone-column philosophy must be adopted.

The preceding discussion has touched on compaction response of the soil to vibration. This is very complex but depends principally on cohesion and permeability of loose soils. Cohesion prevents compaction except by vibro-displacement methods. Low permeability of a cohesionless saturated soil hinders expulsion of pore water during the short time of vibration. Soils whose permeability is less than about 10 $\mu$m/s cannot be relied upon to compact using *in-situ* material as backfill; an imported coarse backfill should be used for finer soils. In any event it is prudent to use gravel-sized backfill in all cases unless economically impracticable as compaction then requires less skill and is accomplished more quickly; the resulting stone column also caters for thin cohesive laminae or unexpected clay lenses which often occur in alluvial sands. Spacing of treatment centres for compactable soils is not influenced by the choice of backfill.

In compactable sands or gravels the radius of effective compaction from the treatment centre depends on the specific characteristics of the type of Vibroflot employed. With current machines it ranges from about 1·5 to 2·5 m according to power. With a given Vibroflot, some sands are more responsive than others according to grading and angularity of particles and degree of saturation. The radius is greater in saturated soils in which effective intergranular stresses are smaller than in dry soils; this is the principal reason for using wet compaction in sands and gravels.

Typically, treatment centres are spaced 2–4 m apart to provide overlapping compacted zones covering any desired plan area. These spacings produce respective relative densities of the order of 90% and 60% with an apparent compressibility $[E/1 - v^2)]$ under strip and pad footings in the range 35–75 MN/m$^2$, according to spacing.

On sites where very large quantities of sand compaction are contemplated it is prudent to make preliminary trials to determine the most economic compaction spacings for desired load : settlement ratios, but for the majority of projects the typical soil response to proprietary Vibroflot characteristics is sufficiently well known to decide spacing without trial.

Monitoring trial or contract results in frictional soils is relatively simple. The whole range of standard soil tests by static or dynamic penetrometer or pressure meter may be used to check them. Differential compaction revealed between tests near compaction centres and at centroids of common compaction patterns is insignificant in comparison to pre-compaction results; it is so small that statistical analysis of large numbers of tests is needed to establish its value. Perhaps contrary to expectation where *in-situ* sand backfill is employed, the resulting density at the treatment centre may sometimes be less than that achieved a short distance away. However, for practical purposes a uniform high density is achieved in compactable sandy soils to a degree which is controllable by varying compaction spacing.

Where a 'stone-column' approach is dictated by finer soil a more sophisticated concept must be adopted. This is because the stone column and natural clays intervening are clearly defined elements in the resulting composite material, each element having widely differing properties.

The complexity of the stress–deflection relationships for a soil strengthened by stone columns is such that no fully developed theory exists to describe the relationship in the whole field at all stages of loading. It is necessary at least to be able to estimate the maximum working load correlated with settlement; ultimate bearing capacity is of lesser interest. Various semi-empiric methods have been suggested. One of these regards the stone columns in the soil as analogous to steel reinforcement in concrete. Reinforced-concrete design principles can be used, however it is necessary to assume values for the elastic moduli of the soil and column. These are not easily determined for soils and some average value must be adopted within the anticipated strain range. Furthermore, with respect to the column, the modulus of granular material is unique at each point of the column according to ambient stress. Under small foundations the load stress is not constant but diminishes rapidly with depth, leading to an added complication in this form of analysis. There are thus difficult problems of establishing appropriate material constants and of defining analogous reinforced concrete theories. The latter objection does not apply under wide-loaded areas for which approximately constant bearing stress can be assumed.

An alternative method of greater simplicity has given satisfactory results over a number of years. This is based on consideration of the column as an axially loaded frictional material supported by the passive resistance of the surrounding natural soil. It is summarised in Figs. 11.3 to 11.5, and it predicts the maximum stone-column load capacity and links this with limits of settlement. The sum of column capacities should not be confused with ultimate foundation bearing capacity, which may be 25–100% more, and can be estimated conventionally from rotational shear considerations. A sufficiently comprehensive site investigation is necessary to plot the profile of maximum passive resistance to determine its least value. The stress–strain characteristic and maximum and minimum friction angle for compacted column material must also be known or assumed. The required properties of soil and column can all be simply determined from standard soil tests, with reasonable certainty.

It is assumed that excess pore pressure generated by load in the column and soil is negligible. This is not unreasonable bearing in mind the relatively large column diameter and close spacing, and also taking account of the maximum possible rate of loading for most practical situations. It is also assumed that the natural properties of the soil are unaltered by column formation which is practically true for wet techniques in soft clay. Vertical stress distribution in the plane of the critical depth corresponding to minimum passive restraint is taken as constant over the column plan area and over that of the soil with a discontinuity at the soil–column boundary. In practice the form of distribution is more likely to be as indicated in Fig. 11.3 for the foundation–soil contact.

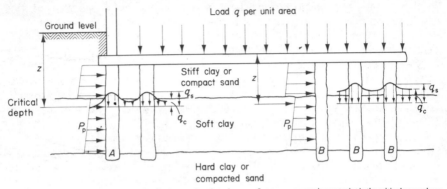

At critical depth, the average stress on the clay is $q_c$ and on the column $q_s$. Let $q_c = xq$; passive restraint in the critical zone where columns are weakest is then given by:

$$P_p = \gamma z K_{pc} + 2c\sqrt{K_{pc}} \qquad \text{and} \qquad P_p = (\gamma z + xq)K_{pc} + 2c\sqrt{K_{pc}}$$

(*A*: at *periphery* or under narrow footings)                                (*B*: under *central areas* of wide foundations)

Fig. 11.3. Stone column design—passive restraint

The maximum column-bearing capacity will be achieved when the ratio of applied stress on the column to passive restraint at the critical depth, is a maximum. Corresponding settlement depends on vertical strains in the column which in turn depends on radial strain in the soil as passive resistance develops. Passive restraint is fully developed at relatively small radial strain because of the mode of column construction in which backfill is packed into the bore. Radial shear strains in the soil associated with development of passive resistance are greatest where passive strength is least. Peak stress ratio is therefore first achieved at critical depth. Elsewhere in the column, radial strains will be smaller and the stress ratio will not have reached its peak value.

The maximum load which can be supported by the column cannot exceed the peak stress $q_s$ multiplied by the estimated column plan area, which should include a suitable margin for variation occurring in practice. A check must be made to ensure that soil below critical depth can support the load as a pile.

For structures with close restrictions on total settlement, it is assumed for the purposes of spacing columns that all the foundation load is carried by the columns and none on the natural soil. This is conservative since it is known by experiment, as will be described later, that as the columns approach maximum bearing capacity a substantial share of the total load is carried by the natural soil. The spacing is chosen so that the maximum stress ratio is not exceeded (allowing a small factor of safety). In this way, strain is restricted primarily to the zone of

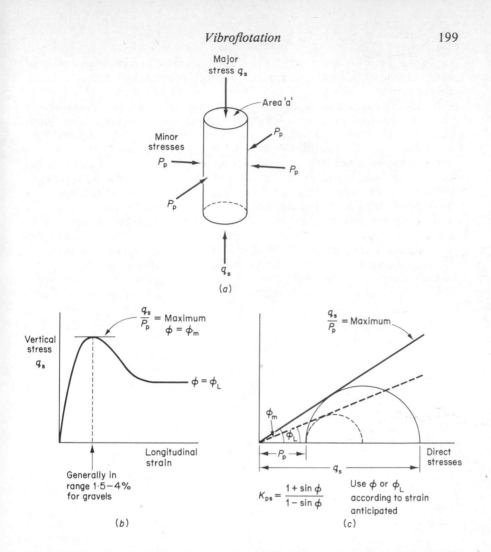

Fig. 11.4. Estimation of column bearing capacity. (*a*) Critical zone of column stressed triaxially, (*b*) longitudinal stress–strain graph for critical zone and (*c*) Mohr diagram for critical zone. The equation for column bearing capacity $q_s a$ is:

$$q_s a = K_{ps} P_p a = K_{ps} a(\gamma z K_{pc} + 2c\sqrt{K_{pc}} + xqK_{pc})$$

the column near critical depth which therefore contributes the major part of settlement. An estimate of its magnitude can be made from vertical strain to peak stress ratio and length of the critical zone, which may be taken as between 1 and 2 column diameters. For compact gravels the vertical strain corresponding to maximum stress ratio is in the range 1·5–4%. For lesser strains a large stress change produces only a small change of strain. Contributions to settlement arising outside the critical zone of the column are comparatively insignificant because peak stress ratio is nowhere approached; the stress–strain characteristic for the column material may be used to estimate them if necessary. On this basis, working-load settlements are restricted to 20–40 mm, which is the normal range for framed or brick structures. By designing columns to have a capability of sustaining the whole load being applied, the effects of simultaneous consolidation are discounted.

It may be noted that as the gravel column dilates, vertical strains will be somewhat less than twice the radial strain. Outward movement of column boundaries as peak stress ratio is approached represents $0 \cdot 25$–$0 \cdot 5\%$ of the length of the critical zone. This is sufficient to mobilise passive resistance.

For columns under strip or small pad footings which have an adjacent unloaded area, passive restraint is derived only from the combination of strength and overburden weight of the soil. In the direction of the axis of the footing its contact pressure will contribute to passive resistance, which will not, however, be the minimum in these circumstances. Where columns are placed under the central area of a wide raft or tank foundation, that proportion of applied stress acting on the soil will contribute to passive restraint and will be equal all round the column. The amounts by which stress on the column will be greater, and stress on the soil less, than the average bearing pressure on the footing are unknown. Figures 11.4 and 11.5 suggest a method of estimating the stresses in the column

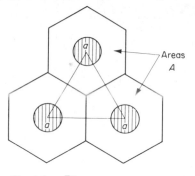

Total area of foundation $= \Sigma A$
Total load stresses on area $A = q_c$
Average stress on soil area $= (A - a)$
Average stress on column area $a = q_s$

Let $q_c = xq$
then $q_c = \dfrac{qA - q_s a}{(A - a)}$
and hence from Fig. 11.4:

$$q_c = xq = \frac{qA - K_{ps} \, a(\gamma z K_{pc} + 2c\sqrt{K_{pc}} + xqK_{pc})}{(A - a)}$$

from which $x$ is obtained. The stresses and bearing capacity can thus be determined. Since columns and soil settle together the magnitude of settlement may be estimated conventionally from the average stresses $q_c$ on the soil between columns

Fig. 11.5. Estimation of column bearing capacity and settlements

and soil at critical depth after having first chosen a trial column spacing. The stress $q_c$ on the soil should not overstress the soil in shear. The calculation must be repeated for different trial spacings if the first chosen is inappropriate.

For structures such as oil tanks and embankments which can tolerate large total settlements, it is uneconomic to space columns so closely that peak stress ratio within them is not overtaken. These structures are often built on very soft estuarine soils which would require columns almost in mutual contact to gain close control of total settlement. In practice, spacings of 2 m or more are used to reduce foundation cost. The total peak bearing capacity of all columns is insufficient in this case to support the whole applied loading. Hence settlement occurs which induces strains in the column greater than those corresponding to peak stress ratio. With increasing strain the properties of the columns reduce to residual characteristics. Even in this condition the columns are relatively stiff compared with the natural soil and are capable of sustaining a proportion of the total load, thereby reducing stress on the soil. They function strictly as vertical reinforcement in this condition. To estimate vertical stresses in the column and clay at critical depth the residual friction angle for the column material is used in the calculation.

As the columns are subject to large vertical strain and have insufficient capacity to support the total load, consolidation settlements assume significance. Consolidation settlements can be estimated using conventional methods with the calculated vertical stress on the clay representing unit load. Thus settlements are reduced by stone columns in the ratio of stress on soil to average bearing pressure on the foundation. This method can only be used where radial expansion of the columns is sufficient to mobilise full passive restraint, i.e. near peak stress ratio or beyond, as otherwise there is no means of estimating the degree of passive resistance in the soil or frictional strength of the column mobilised.

In soft soils there may also be an element of settlement from shear strains in the clay, although reduced by the columns. They must also be estimated conventionally. Typically, the total column area represents about 20% of the foundation area. Local stiffness of the foundation ensures that columns and soil settle together.

This semi-empiric design method ensures that column spacing is determined rationally on the basis of soil properties which are relatively easily obtained from site investigation providing the investigation is sufficiently comprehensive. The method does not purport to describe states of stress or strain in the treated soil, but only to establish some limiting points important for safe design. It gives an indication of the likely limiting settlement relevant to the working load, but does not give ultimate bearing capacity of the foundation. The latter must be estimated by conventional soil mechanics using rotational slip analysis with proper allowance for the effects of stone columns. In practice ultimate strength is of little relevance so long as a factor of safety is allowed on total maximum column capacity, but it should be calculated for designs which envisage columns working beyond their peak stress ratio in order to determine the factor of safety at working load.

This design approach may be used for columns formed by vibro-displacement, but takes no account of possible improved soil properties resulting from compaction during column construction. A method proposed by Dr. A. Senthivel* which attempts to allow for this is currently being studied. This is based on limiting parameters from laboratory shear tests on the natural soil necessary to establish the appropriate stress path and final shear strength. From this it is possible to determine the required column spacing to achieve the desired bearing properties. Further proving work necessary to establish its practicality and reliability as a working method is needed. This will take the form of specific field tests and the study of structure performance in appropriate practical cases.

---

* Private communication.

## Foundation load–settlement characteristics

Several instances of results of loading tests on compacted sands, ash fills and demolition debris are given in References 1 and 2, one of which is reproduced in Fig. 11.6. The load versus settlement graphs display properties similar to those expected for tests on natural, dense, granular materials with distinct settlement reductions relative to untreated ground. It is of more interest to examine load settlement curves for footings on clays strengthened by stone columns. Plots for tests on natural clays generally show smooth and gentle curvature virtually from the beginning of loading through to ultimate load. Strengthened clays, however, have a much flatter characteristic representing lesser settlement for loads up to that corresponding to ultimate total column capacity (i.e. peak stress ratio in the critical zone), beyond which settlement rapidly increases to ultimate load.

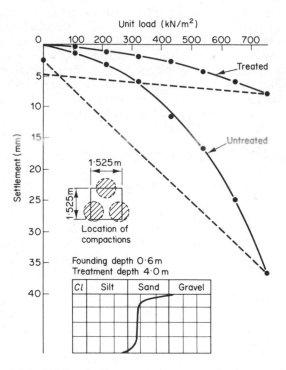

Fig. 11.6. Port Talbot: loading test results on treated and untreated sand

Figures 11.7 and 11.8 illustrate this trend. They show test results for a site south-east of Glasgow where stiff boulder clays underlie softer re-sorted and finer clays at depths of about 3 m. Figure 11.7 relates to tests made with a circular plate. The calculated ultimate bearing capacity for natural clay was 177 kN as subsequently confirmed by the test result. An identical test made on a stone column in substantially similar ground 3 m distant indicated an ultimate load of between 210 and 240 kN, whereas the calculated peak and residual column loads were respectively 140 kN and 104 kN. Whilst the ultimate plate load has not been increased very significantly, the amount of settlement experienced up to peak column load has been halved.

Figure 11.8 shows a result on the same site for a strip footing supported by five columns. In this case, calculated ultimate bearing capacity of the natural clay was 790 kN and the peak column load approximately 166 kN, giving 830 kN total. This compares with the ultimate capacity of the footing on treated ground of 1·4 MN. Again, a relatively sharp increase in settlement begins when total peak column load has been surpassed. Thus the point at which settlement began

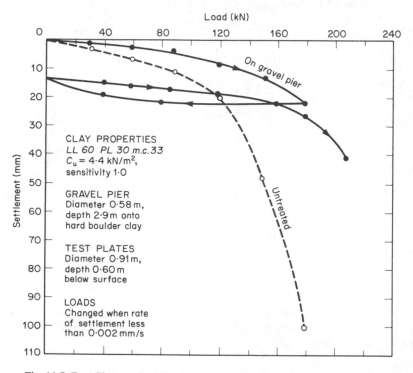

Fig. 11.7. East Glasgow: load bearing tests on clay strengthened by gravel pier

to be critical was correctly predicted from total peak column load. The working load for the completed structures was 160 kN/m² equivalent to a total of 565 kN on the test footing. The factor of safety on ultimate capacity was 2·5, and on total peak column capacity 1·47. Had the footing been placed on untreated ground a factor of 3·0 on ultimate bearing capacity would have restricted the working load to 284 kN; a factor of safety of 2·5 would probably have resulted in too much settlement at working load. Indeed, factors of safety of 3·0 calculated on ultimate bearing capacity are only used in foundation engineering because it is necessary to keep settlement at the working load within reasonable limits. The improved characteristic of clays reinforced by stone columns makes this high factor unnecessary, subject to proper evaluation of the factor needed to cater for potential variations of soil strength within the site concerned. It is thus

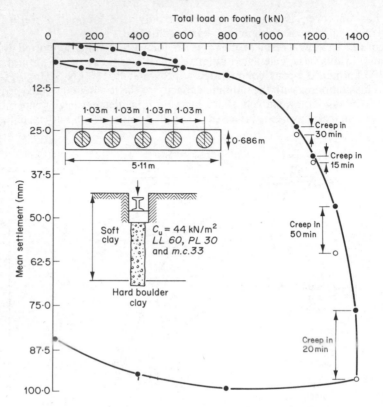

Fig. 11.8. East Glasgow: load test on simulated footing

possible to work with considerably reduced load factors on peak column capacity whilst retaining a reasonable safety factor, on an ultimate bearing value of 2·0 or more as in piling designs.

## Contact pressure distribution at base footing

Figure 11.9 illustrates the results of a test made to determine how pressure on the base of a rigid footing varies over the column and the soil. Earth pressure cells were built in to a precast concrete foundation so that cells were located over the columns and over the soil. In this case the soil was an industrial waste consisting of finely ground spherical silica particles entirely within the silt range of sizes arising from the glass-making industry.

The result shows how the ratio of stresses on column and soil diminishes with increasing average footing load. This indicates that the columns carry virtually all the load initially when the average footing load is small, with the soil taking an increasing share as the load increases. Thus at high stress levels the contact pressure is comparatively uniform. This has economic significance with respect to the provision of reinforcement in footings. Relatively small bending moments are experienced by the footing and only nominal reinforcement is required.

It is of interest to note that in this case the critical zone was close to the base of the footing, so that measured contact pressures were substantially those of the critical zone. The calculated ratio of vertical stresses on column and soil at the maximum test bearing pressure of 193 kN/m$^2$ was 2·2, compared with a measured ratio of 2; corresponding settlement of the footing was 15 mm which should have induced sufficient radial strain in the column to mobilise the maximum passive restraint.

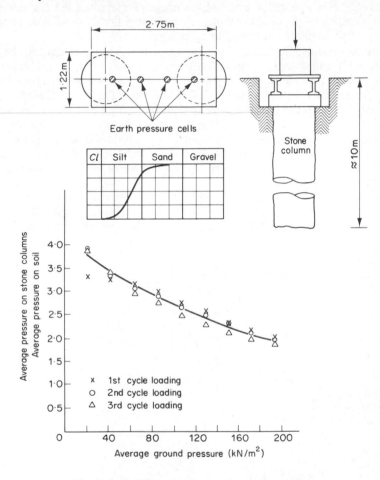

Fig. 11.9. St. Helens: loading test for contact pressure

This comparatively uniform contact pressure is a consequence of the relative compressibility of the stone column compared with a rigid conventional pile and suspended ground-beam system. A further consequence is that if one of a line of stone columns supporting a strip footing settles more than expected, the lateral distribution of changed contact pressure is wide so that the footing 'dishes' with only gentle curvature, similar to strip footings on natural soils. Most buildings can accept limited settlements of this kind.

## Practical considerations

In practice, soils rarely have uniform characteristics across a site except in the broadest classification terms. Not only do constituent proportions of individual strata vary, but often the main classifications of sands, clays, silts, etc. are interleaved in irregular fashion. Knowledge of the formation and history of the superficial deposits can suggest the probable form of variation, but not the scale. Site investigation can define limits of the range of variation, but can never be specific except at individual boreholes. Site investigations for building projects are very often so limited as barely to categorise the site.

To be successful in these circumstances any geotechnical process must be able to cope with anticipated variations without alteration of projected structural design. This is a prime reason why stone columns are almost invariably used whether or not compaction is intended. The unexpected presence of a lens of soft silt in alluvial sands can be embarrassing if its thickness is substantial. However, influence on settlement can be rendered almost negligible by stone columns, providing the lens thickness is not greater than column diameter. The column forms a very stiff structure through the compressible material as illustrated in Fig. 11.10a. Thicker lenses should be detected by site investigation and catered for in design (Fig. 11.10b).

Except when working in ideal sands, stone columns usually prove most economical because they demand less operator skill and can be constructed quickly. Coarse backfill particles, being heavy, readily sink into the bore against

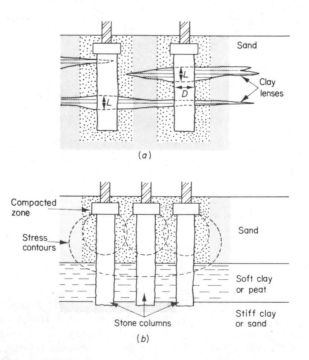

Fig. 11.10. Treatment of mixed clays and sands. (a) Stone columns stiffening clay lenses and (b) compacted sand raft over soft clay

upflowing water, whereas fine sand will not sink unless very careful control of upward-water velocities is exercised, often in conditions where varying soil permeability imposes continual changes. This demands constant skilled attention, and risks of poor or slow work are increased. When working wet, backfill size range is kept within 20–70 mm to facilitate its fall through the annular space between the Vibroflot and sides of the borehole where coarser particles might choke the hole. With dry treatment this restriction on backfill grading is unnecessary because the machine is removed from the bore to allow backfill to be tipped. Whilst a well-graded backfill has greater mechanical strength than uniform stone, the practical difference is insignificant, especially when working wet, because the coarser particles from the natural soil in the bore fill the voids between coarse imported particles as the finer material is washed out. On examination, this filling normally consists of coarse silt and fine sand which becomes coarser and cleaner towards the central core of the column. The chosen backfill must be mechanically and chemically stable to resist disintegration from any cause during construction, and in subsequent working life.

In most locations a sufficient supply of coarse backfill is available. Each Vibroflot unit can consume 300–500 t/day. It is important both for economy and quality of work that the supply should keep the Vibroflot working continuously. Delays during the cycle of column construction can have an adverse effect on soil fabric in the vicinity of the bore, so that additional jetting and stone is required to restore stability. Saturated silts are especially prone to this problem.

Spacing of compaction centres is such that each one represents an effective probe beneath the foundation areas so that significantly large zones of poor soil are discovered in the process. Since the time to construct a column is generally of the order of 10–30 min, the process usually permits sufficient strengthening of these zones by the simple expedient of additional columns, without serious delay to the project. It cannot, however, be considered as a substitute for site investigation. Vibroflot probes can also quickly define outlines of buried obstructions which can then be removed by other means. Normally, however, it is a simple matter to place alternative probes around a small obstruction which can remain in place.

Efficient operation demands a sound working surface. Adequate bearing must be provided for the crane which may have a pull up to five times the weight of the Vibroflot when sand compacts around the machine. On sandy sites there is always sufficient stability for tracked plant, providing ground-water level is more than 500 mm below the site surface. Where clays are exposed, however, it is necessary to provide and price in the contract for surfacing in working areas to support the tracked equipment, especially for winter working.

The vibro-replacement (wet) process requires provision and maintenance of temporary surface drainage. This should also be provided for in contract specifications. With experienced and good site management, the use of water does not cause deterioration of site surface; the converse is also true, however. After winter working or wet treatment of a clay site, surface trimming is always essential. It is necessary to remove soil affected by tracked equipment to expose undisturbed foundation soil.

Vibro-replacement requires about 35 m³/h of water supply and produces an effluent of water and suspended soil solids. These consist primarily of silt and clay since the coarser elements of the natural soil tend to remain in the column.

For current projects a 'package' of sedimentation tanks and flocculating chemicals is provided to clarify the effluent to the order of 30–50 parts per million of solids. This quality is usually acceptable to drainage authorities who take account of the temporary nature of construction works.

In soil engineering it is prudent to verify design assumptions in preliminary stages of execution and achievement on completion. This is comparatively easy in natural sands which do not contain gravel or coarser particles; dynamic penetration tests can be simply and cheaply carried out without boreholes. Where gravelly soils are encountered, or those whose properties or constituents vary rapidly, e.g. demolition waste or some boulder clays, these tests become less reliable. It also follows that they are not very useful for testing stone columns comprised of coarse backfill. The use of the Vibroflot as a probe is therefore an important adjunct to control testing during construction. Observations should be recorded of rate of penetration and energy absorbed by the Vibroflot. Both are controlled by the soil properties, and for a given machine cannot be forced. A relatively strong soil will result in low penetration speed and high-energy demand, whereas soft soils will be penetrated quickly and cannot absorb high energy, even during compaction. The importance of these observations is therefore to throw up variations in machine reaction from the site norm. When correlated with other tests and site investigation results, potentially dangerous circumstances can be spotted and dealt with.

Peculiar to building projects on firm clays, where depth of treatment is of the order of 3 m, are simple plate-load tests carried out on individual columns. In these circumstances such tests can be a useful guide to column quality, but otherwise they may not give a reliable indication of foundation performance. On large projects where stone-column technique is employed, the most reliable test is to simulate footing loading at full scale. However, this tends to be expensive (prohibitively so for small projects) and often is a more severe test than the building foundations which it represents. This is because the test footing is unrestrained by structural connections and loading is applied very rapidly compared with building loads.

## Conclusion

Vibroflotation is a geotechnical process for strengthening weak superficial soils to allow the use of shallow conventional building foundations.

The steady evolution of vibroflotation from vibratory compaction of loose sands to strengthening weak clays by reinforcing them with columns of gravel, has ensured its practical reliability. Although essentially the process uses water for temporary stabilisation of treatment boreholes, a dry technique has been evolved for firm clays which has distinct differences from the basic system; these arise from displacement of existing soil instead of its partial replacement by the gravel columns.

A rational design procedure has been derived from consideration of triaxial loading of the columns to estimate limiting settlements within the working load range. Otherwise, ultimate bearing strength and consolidation settlements must be estimated by standard soil mechanics methods. Thus conventional shallow-spread footings may be employed with permissible working loads approximately doubled relative to footings on untreated soil.

Observation of Vibroflot behaviour during column construction can yield useful information to supplement the site investigation, thus ensuring that beneath the structure foundations significant zones of ground differing from the site norm are located. The simplicity and speed of treatment enables any anomalies to be dealt with quickly without serious delay to the project.

## Acknowledgement

Permission to publish this paper is gratefully acknowledged to Cementation Ground Engineering Limited.

REFERENCES

1. Greenwood, D. A., 'Mechanical Improvement of Soils Below Ground Surface', Symp. on Ground Engineering, *Proc. I.C.E.,* 11–21, June (1970)
2. Doscher, H. D., 'Vibroflotation', *J. Ind. Nat. Soc. Soil Mechs.,* 7 No. 3, 365–385, July (1968)

# Index

211